SCHOOL AND CLASSROOM ORGANIZATION

SCHOOL
AND CLASSROOM
ORGANIZATION

Edited by
Robert E. Slavin
Johns Hopkins University

LAWRENCE ERLBAUM ASSOCIATES, PUBLISHERS
1989   Hillsdale, New Jersey   Hove and London

Lawrence Erlbaum Associates, Inc., Publishers
365 Broadway
Hillsdale, New Jersey 07642

Library of Congress Cataloging-in-Publication Data
School and classroom organization / edited by Robert E. Slavin.
    p.   cm.
Includes bibliographies and indexes.
ISBN 0–89859–998–9
    1. Classroom management.   2. School management and
organization.   3. Academic achievement.
I. Slavin, Robert E.
LB3013.S36 1989
371.1′024—dc19   88–24435
                                            CIP

Printed in the United States of America
10 9 8 7 6 5 4 3 2 1

Contents

Preface

Over the past decade, there has been a substantial increase in knowledge about teacher behaviors associated with gains in student achievement. Research on such issues as effective instructional behaviors and classroom management has identified the practices of outstanding effective teachers. However, effective instruction is more than the sum of teacher behaviors. The *organization* of the classroom and of the school provide the context within which teaching takes place, and this context may be pivotal in determining the effectiveness of the school's instructional program.

This volume presents critical reviews of research on school and classroom organization. All of the reviews focus on the achievement effects of alternative school and classroom organizational practices; each attempts to answer the question, ''What do we know now about how to organize classrooms and schools to accelerate student achievement?'' The reviews examine such school organization issues as ability grouping, departmentalization, special and remedial programs, evaluation processes, and class size. At the classroom level, questions about lesson organization and effective use of time are addressed, and research is reviewed on two widely used alternative classroom organization models, mastery learning and cooperative learning.

Each of the chapters centers on evaluations of the achievement effects of alternative school and classroom organizational practices as they are applied in practice, not as they are used in the laboratory or in brief experiments. The emphasis of the book is on practices that are under the direct control of school districts, principals, and/or teachers, and the impact that these practices have on student achievement under real-life conditions. The conclusions drawn in the various chapters do not prescribe particular practices, because there are many factors that must be taken into account in making decisions about how to organize schools, including effects of school and classroom practices on outcomes other than achievement. However, decisions about school and classroom organization must be made in light of the best available evidence concerning the achievement effects of one or another practical alternative, and that is what this book attempts to provide.

ACKNOWLEDGMENTS

This volume was compiled under funding from the Office of Educational Research and Improvement, U.S. Department of Education (Grant No. OERI-G-86-0006). However, the opinions expressed are those of the authors and do not necessarily reflect OERI positions or policy.

List of Contributors

William Bickel
Learning Research and Development Center
University of Pittsburgh

Jere Brophy
Institute for Research on Teaching
Michigan State University

Thomas Good
Center for Research in Social Behavior
University of Missouri at Columbia

Nancy Karweit
Center for Research on Elementary and Middle Schools
The Johns Hopkins University

Gaea Leinhardt
Learning Research and Development Center
University of Pittsburgh

Gary Natriello
Teachers College
Columbia University

Jeannie Oakes
Rand Corporation

Robert Slavin
Center for Research on Elementary and Middle Schools
The Johns Hopkins University

For Nancy

AN INTRODUCTION TO SCHOOL AND CLASSROOM ORGANIZATION

1 A Theory of School and Classroom Organization*

Robert E. Slavin
Center for Research on Elementary and Middle Schools
Johns Hopkins University

In the past fifteen years, research on teaching has made significant strides in identifying teaching behaviors associated with high student achievement (see chapter 3; Brophy & Good, 1986; Rosenshine & Stevens, 1986). For example, research on the presentation of lessons has examined the characteristics of effective teaching centering on such issues as type and level of questioning (e.g., Winne, 1979; Redfield & Rousseau, 1981), lesson organization (e.g., Belgard, Rosenshine, & Gage, 1971), transitions between ideas (e.g., Smith & Cotten, 1980), and so on.

However, effective instruction is not just good teaching. If it were, we could probably find the best lecturers, make video tapes of their lessons, and show the tapes to students. Consider why the video teacher would be ineffective. First, the video teacher would have no idea what students already knew. A particular lesson might be too advanced for a particular group of students, or it may be that some students already know the material being taught. Some students may be learning the lesson quite well, whereas others are missing key concepts and falling behind because they lack prerequisite skills for new learning. The video teacher would have no way to know who needed additional help, and would have no way to provide it in any case. There would be no way to question students to find out if they were getting the main points and then to reteach any concepts that students were failing to grasp.

Second, the video teacher would have no way to motivate students to pay attention to the lesson or to really try to learn it. If students were failing to pay attention or were misbehaving, the video teacher would have no way to do

---

*This chapter is adapted from an earlier article by Slavin (1987).

3

anything about it. Finally, the video teacher would never know at the end of the lesson whether or not students had actually learned the main concepts or skills.

The case of the video teacher illustrates the point that teachers must be concerned with many elements of instruction in addition to the lesson itself. Teachers must attend to ways of adapting instruction to students' levels of knowledge, motivating students to learn, managing student behavior, grouping students for instruction, and testing and evaluating students. These functions are carried out at two levels. At the school level, the principal and/or central administrators may establish policies concerning grouping of students (e.g., tracking), provision and allocation of special education and remedial resources, and grading, evaluation, and promotion practices. At the classroom level, teachers control the grouping of students within the class, teaching techniques, classroom management methods, informal incentives, frequency and form of quizzes and tests, and so on. These elements of school and classroom organization are at least as important for student achievement as the quality of teachers' lessons.

"School and classroom organization" refers to all of the elements of instruction over which the school administration and/or teachers have control, from teaching methods to grouping strategies to grading systems. However, the emphasis of the organizational perspective on instruction is not on micro-level teaching behaviors but rather on the school and classroom policies and practices that create the context within which teaching takes place, the aspects of instruction over which the "video teacher" has no control. The chapters in this volume deal with issues of school and classroom organization from many perspectives. This chapter presents a theory of school and classroom organization based on Carroll's (1963) "Model of School Learning", which attempts to identify the critical elements of school and classroom organization and their interrelationships.

Carroll's Model of School Learning

One of the most influential articles ever published in the field of educational psychology was a paper by John Carroll entitled "A Model of School Learning" (1963). In it, Carroll describes teaching in terms of the management of time, resources, and activities to ensure student learning. The model proposes five elements that contribute to the effectiveness of instruction:

1. *Aptitude:* Students' general abilities to learn.

2. *Ability to Understand Instruction:* Students' readiness to learn a particular lesson. This is related to students' abilities but also to students' knowledge of prerequisite skills or information needed to understand the next lesson. For example, no matter how able students are, they cannot learn to do long division if they have not learned multiplication and subtraction.

3. *Perseverance:* The amount of time students are willing to actively engage in learning. Perseverance is mostly a product of students' motivation to learn.

4. *Opportunity:* The amount of time allowed for learning. Opportunity relates to the amount of time teachers spend to teach a particular skill or concept.

5. *Quality of Instruction:* The effectiveness with which a lesson is actually delivered. Quality of instruction is high if students learn material as rapidly as their abilities and levels of prior knowledge and skills allow.

Carroll discusses these elements in terms of *time needed to learn* and *time available for learning*. The higher are student's aptitudes, the better their abilities to understand instruction, and the greater their perseverance, the less time it will take to teach them a skill or concept. The higher the quality of instruction, the less time will be needed. On the other side of the balance sheet is opportunity; there must be adequate time to teach a lesson. Carroll was particularly concerned with the problem that in classrooms containing students who are highly diverse in abilities, knowledge, skills, and motivation, some students are bound to require more time than others to learn the same material. This led him to consider a variety of means of adapting instruction to differences in learning rates between students in the same class.

Carroll's model mixes two kinds of elements: those that are directly under the control of the teacher, and those that are characteristics of students, which are difficult to change. Quality of instruction and opportunity (time) are directly under the control of the teacher or the school. Aptitude is mostly a characteristic of students over which teachers can have little control in the short run. Ability to understand instruction and perseverance are partly under the control of the teacher, but partly characteristic of students. For example, ability to understand instruction is partly a product of student ability, but is also a product of what teachers do to make sure that students have all the prerequisite skills and information they will need to successfully learn a new lesson. Perseverance results both from the motivation to learn that a student brings to school and from specific strategies a teacher or school might use to motivate students to do their best.

Slavin (1984) more recently proposed a model of effective instruction that focused on the *alterable* elements of Carroll's model, those which teachers and schools can directly change. The components of this model of alterable elements of effective instruction are as follows:

1. *Quality of Instruction.* The degree to which information or skills are presented so that students can easily learn them. Quality of instruction is largely a product of the quality of the curriculum and of the lesson presentation itself.

2. *Appropriate Levels of Instruction:* The degree to which the teacher makes sure that students are ready to learn a new lesson (that is, that they have the necessary skills and knowledge to learn it) but have not already learned the

lesson. In other words, the level of instruction is appropriate when a lesson is neither too difficult nor too easy for students.

3. *Incentive:* The degree to which the teacher makes sure that students are motivated to work on instructional tasks and to learn the material being presented.

4. *Time:* The degree to which students are given enough time to learn the material being taught.

The four elements of this QAIT (Quality, Appropriateness, Incentive, Time) model have one important characteristic: *All four* must be adequate for instruction to be effective. Again, effective instruction is not just good teaching. No matter how high the quality of instruction, students will not learn a lesson if they lack the necessary prior skills or information, if they lack the motivation, or if they lack the time they need to learn the lesson. On the other hand, if the quality of instruction is low, then it makes no difference how much students know, how motivated they are, or how much time they have. Each of the elements of the QAIT model is like a link in a chain, and the chain is only as strong as its weakest link.

Toward a Theory of Effective Classroom Organization

Most of the advances in recent research on teaching have come about as a result of correlational process–product research, in which the practices of instructionally effective teachers have been contrasted with those of less effective teachers, controlling for student inputs. In recent years, the findings of these process–product studies have been incorporated into coherent instructional programs and evaluated in field experiments. Other coherent instructional methods not based on the process–product findings, such as mastery learning, cooperative learning, and individualized instruction methods, have also been evaluated in field experiments. Each of these instructional methods is based on its own psychological or educational theories. However, it is the purpose of this paper to propose a theory to encompass all potential forms of classroom organization. Given a relatively fixed set of resources, every innovation in classroom organization solves some problems but also creates new problems which must themselves be solved. Tradeoffs are always involved. Understanding the terms of these tradeoffs is critical for an understanding of how to build effective models of classroom organization.

The QAIT model is designed primarily to clarify the tradeoffs involved in alternative forms of classroom organization. This chapter presents a perspective on what is known now about each of the QAIT elements, and more importantly explores the theoretical and practical ramifications of the *interdependence* of these elements for effective school and classroom organization.

Quality of Instruction

Quality of instruction refers to the activities we think of first when we think of teaching: lecturing, discussing, calling on students, and so on. When instruction is high in quality, the information being presented makes sense to students, is interesting to them, and is easy to remember and apply.

The most important aspect of instructional quality is the degree to which the lesson makes sense to students. For example, teachers must present information in an organized, orderly way (Belgard, Rosenshine, & Gage, 1971), note transitions to new topics (Smith & Cotten 1980), use many vivid images and examples (Anderson & Hidde, 1971), and frequently restate essential principles (Maddox & Hoole, 1975). Lessons should be related to students' background knowledge, using such devices as advance organizers (Ausubel, 1960) or simply reminding students of previously learned material at relevant points in the lesson. Enthusiasm (Abrami, Leventhal, & Perry, 1982) and humor (Kaplan & Pascoe, 1977) can also contribute to quality of instruction.

Clear specification of lesson objectives to students (Dalis, 1970) and a substantial correlation between what is taught and what is assessed (Cooley & Leinhardt, 1980) contribute to instructional quality, as does frequent formal or informal assessment to see that students are mastering what is being taught (Dunkin & Biddle, 1974; Peckham & Roe, 1977) and immediate feedback to students on the correctness of their performances (Barringer & Gholson, 1979).

Instructional pace is partly as issue of quality of instruction and partly of appropriate levels of instruction. In general, content coverage is strongly related to student achievement (Dunkin, 1978; Barr & Dreeben, 1983), so a rapid pace of instruction may contribute to instructional quality. However, there is obviously such a thing as too rapid an instructional pace (see Leighton & Slavin, 1988). Frequent assessment of student learning is critical for teachers to establish the most rapid instructional pace consistent with the preparedness and learning rate of all students.

Appropriate Levels of Instruction

Perhaps the most difficult problem of school and classroom organization is accommodating instruction to the needs of students with different levels of prior knowledge and different learning rates. If a teacher presents a lesson on long division to a heterogeneous class, some students may fail to learn it because they have not mastered such prerequisite skills as subtraction, multiplication, or simple division. At the same time, there may be some students who know how to divide before the lesson begins, or learn to do so very rapidly. If the teacher sets a pace of instruction appropriate to the needs of the students lacking prerequisite skills, then the rapid learners' time will be largely wasted. If the instructional pace is too rapid, the students lacking prerequisite skills will be left behind.

7

There are many common means of attempting to accomodate instruction to students' diverse needs, but each method has drawbacks that may make the method counterproductive. Various forms of ability grouping seek to reduce the heterogeneity of instructional groups. Special education and remedial programs are a special form of ability grouping designed to provide special resources to accelerate the achievement of students with learning problems. However, between-class ability grouping plans, such as tracking, can create low-ability classes for which teachers have low expectations and maintain a slow pace of instruction, and which many teachers dislike to teach (see chapters 6 and 7; Good & Marshall, 1984; Oakes, 1985, 1987; Rowan & Miracle, 1983; Slavin, 1987a). Similar problems make self-contained special education classes of questionable benefit to students with learning handicaps (see chapter 8; Leinhardt & Bickel, 1987; Leinhardt & Pallay, 1982; Madden & Slavin, 1983). Within-class ability grouping, such as the use of reading and mathematics groups, creates problems of managing multiple groups within the classroom, reduces direct instruction to each student, and forces teachers to assign large amounts of unsupervised seatwork to keep students engaged while the teacher is working with a reading or mathematics group.

Research on assignment of students to ability–grouped classes finds no achievement benefits for this practice at the elementary level (see chapter 6; Slavin, 1987b) or at the secondary level (see chapter 7; Oakes, 1985, 1987). However, forms of ability grouping in which elementary students remain in heterogeneous classes most of the day but are regrouped into homogeneous reading or mathematics classes can be instructionally effective if teachers actually adapt their level and pace of instruction to meet the needs of the regrouped classes. In particular, the Joplin Plan and certain nongraded plans, in which students are regrouped for reading or mathematics across grade lines and the instructional level is based on performance level rather than age, can be instructionally effective (see chapter 6; Slavin, 1987b). Also, research on within-class ability grouping finds this practice to increase student mathematics achievement, particularly when the number of groups used is small and management techniques that are designed to ensure smooth transitions and high time-on-task during seatwork are used (Slavin & Karweit, 1985).

Group-based mastery learning (Bloom, 1976; Block & Burns, 1976; Guskey and Gates, 1985) is an approach to providing levels of instruction that does not use permanent ability groups but rather regroups students after each skill is taught on the basis of their mastery of that skill. Students who attain pre-set criteria (e.g., 80%) on a formative test work on enrichment activities while non-masters receive corrective instruction. In theory, mastery learning should provide appropriate levels of instruction by ensuring that students have mastered prerequisite skills before they receive instruction in subsequent skills. However, within the confines of traditional class periods, the time needed for corrective instruction may slow the pace of instruction for the class as a whole. Studies of group-based mastery learning conducted in elementary and secondary schools over periods of at least four weeks have found few benefits of this approach in comparison to control groups given the same objectives, materials, and time as the mastery learning groups (see chapter 4; Slavin, 1987a).

The most extreme form of accommodation to individual differences short of one-to-one tutoring is individualized instruction, in which students work entirely at their own level and rate. Individualized instruction certainly solves the problem of providing appropriate levels of instruction, but it creates serious problems of classroom management, often depriving students of adequate direct instruction. Research on individualized instruction has not generally found positive effects on student achievement (Hartley, 1977; Horak, 1981; Miller, 1976). However, Team Assisted Individualization, a form of individualized instruction that also incorporates the use of cooperative learning groups has been found to consistently increase student achievement in mathematics (see chapter 5; Slavin, Leavey, & Madden, 1984; Slavin, Madden, & Leavey, 1984; Slavin & Karweit, 1985; Slavin, 1985).

Incentive

Thomas Edison once wrote that "genius is one percent inspiration and ninety-nine percent perspiration." The same could probably be said for learning. Learning is work. This is not to say that learning must be drudgery, but it is certainly the case that students must exert themselves to pay attention, to study, and to conscientiously perform the tasks assigned to them, and they must somehow be motivated to do these things. This motivation may come from the intrinsic interest value of the material being learned, or it may be created through the use of extrinsic incentives, such as praise, grades, stars, and so on.

If students want to know something, they will be more likely to exert the necessary effort to learn it. This is why there are students who can rattle off the names, batting averages, and other statistics relating to every player on the Chicago Cubs, but do not know their multiplication facts. Teachers can create intrinsic interest in material to be taught by arousing student curiosity, for example by using surprising demonstrations, by relating topics to students' personal lives, or by allowing students to discover information for themselves (Gregory, 1975; Berlyne, 1965).

However, not every subject can be made intrinsically interesting to every student at all times. Most students need some sort of extrinsic incentive to exert an adequate level of effort. For example, studies of graded versus pass–fail college courses find substantially higher achievement in classes that give grades (Gold, Reilly, Silberman, & Lehr, 1971; Hales, Bain, & Rand, 1971). At the elementary level, informal incentives, such as praise and feedback, may be more important than the formal grading system (see Brophy, 1981). One critical principle of effective use of classroom incentives is that students should be held accountable for everything they do. For example, homework that is checked has been found to contribute more to student achievement than homework that is assigned but not checked (Austin, 1978). Also, questioning strategies that communicate high expectations for students, such as waiting for them to respond (Rowe, 1974) and following up with students who do not initially give full responses (Brophy & Evertson, 1974) have been found to be associated with high achievement.

Several methods of providing formal incentives for learning have been found to be instructionally effective. Among these are strategies based on behavioral learning theories, which provide praise, tokens, or other rewards contingent on students' classroom behavior (O'Leary & O'Leary, 1972). One practical and effective method of rewarding students for appropriate, learning-oriented behavior is home-based reinforcement (Barth, 1979), provision of daily or weekly reports to parents on student behavior. Another is group contingencies (Litow & Pumroy, 1975; Hayes, 1976), in which the entire class or groups within the class are rewarded on the basis of the behavior of the entire group.

Cooperative learning methods (see chapter 5; Slavin, 1983a,b) involve students working in small learning groups to master academic material. Forms of cooperative learning that have consistently increased student achievement have provided rewards to heterogeneous groups based on the learning of their members. This incentive system motivates students to encourage and help one another to achieve. Rewarding students based on improvement over their own past performance has also been found to be an effective incentive system (see Natriello, 1987, chapter 9; Slavin, 1980).

In addition to being a product of specific strategies designed to increase student motivation, incentive is also influenced by quality of instruction and appropriate levels of instruction. Students will be more motivated to learn about a topic that is presented in an interesting way, that makes sense to them, that they feel capable of learning. Further, students' motivation to exert maximum effort will be influenced by their perception of the difference between their probability of success if they do exert themselves and their probability of success if they do not (Atkinson & Birch, 1978; Slavin, 1977, 1988). That is, if a student feels sure of success or, alternatively, of failure, regardless of his or her efforts, then incentive will be very low. This is likely to be the case if a lesson is presented at a level much too easy or too difficult for the student, respectively. Incentive is high when the level of instruction is appropriate for a student, so that the student perceives that with effort the material can be mastered, so that the payoff for effort is perceived to be great.

Time

Instruction takes time. More time spent teaching a subject does not always translate into additional learning, but if instructional quality, appropriateness of instruction, and incentives for learning are all high, then more time on instruction is likely to pay off in greater learning.

The amount of time available for learning depends largely on two factors: *Allocated time* and *engaged time*. Allocated time is the time scheduled by the teacher for a particular lesson or subject and then actually used for instructional activities. Allocated time is mostly under the direct control of the school and teacher. In contrast, engaged time, the time students actually engage in learning tasks, is not under the direct control of the school or teacher. Engaged time, or time-on-task, is largely a product of quality of instruction, student motivation, and allocated time. Thus, allocated time is an alterable element of instruction (like quality, appropriateness, and incentive), but engaged time is a mediating variable linking alterable variables with student achievement.

While allocated time must be an essential element in any model of classroom organization, research on this variable has found few consistent effects on student achievement. For example, research on hours in the school day and days in the school year has found few relationships between these time variables and student achievement (Frederick & Walberg, 1980; Karweit, 1976, 1981). The Beginning Teacher Evaluation Study found no effect of allocated time in specific subjects on student achievement in those subjects when time was measured at the class level (Marliave, Fisher, & Dishaw, 1978). On the other hand, research on engaged time generally finds positive relationships between time students are on task and their achievement, but even with this variable the results are inconsistent(see Karweit, 1981).

Studies of means of increasing student time-on-task generally go under the heading of classroom management research. Process–product studies (see, for example, Brophy, 1979) have established that teachers' use of effective management strategies is associated with high student achievement. However, several recent experimental studies focusing on increasing time-on-task have found that it is possible to increase engaged time and still have no significant effect on student achievement (see chapter 3; Slavin, 1986; Stallings & Krasavage, 1986; Wilson & Nachtigal, 1986).

A Model of Alterable Elements of Instruction and Student Achievement

As noted earlier, Carroll's (1963) model of school learning discusses five elements in terms of their effects on time needed to learn and time available for learning. The QAIT model, whose elements were described in the previous sections, can also be conceptualized in terms of intermediate effects on time-related variables. Figure 1 depicts a model of how alterable elements of instruction might affect student achievement. In Fig. 1, two types of independent variables are presented: *student inputs* and *alterable variables*. Student inputs

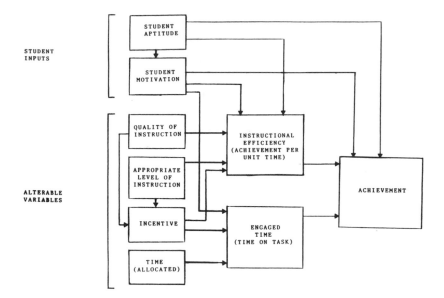

FIG. 1.1. Model relating alterable elements of instruction to student achievement.

refer to factors over which the school has little control in the short run: student ability and those aspects of motivation to learn that students bring from home (as distinct from the motivation created by classroom practices). The alterable variables are the QAIT elements discussed earlier. Of course, student inputs are not immutable, but can be affected by classroom practices. For example, student aptitude to learn a specific lesson may be strongly influenced by background knowledge resulting from earlier instruction, by specific training in thinking, problem solving, or study skills, or by general intellectual stimulation or learning skills provided by the school. Student motivation to learn is also largely a product of past experiences in school. However, in the context of any given lesson, the student inputs can be considered fixed, while the alterable variables can be directly manipulated by the school or teacher.

The effects of the alterable variables on student achievement are held to be mediated by two time-related variables: *Instructional efficiency* and *engaged time,* or time-on-task. Instructional efficiency can be conceptualized as the amount of learning per unit time. For example, students will learn more in a ten-minute lesson high in instructional efficiency than in a lesson of similar length low in instructional efficiency. Engaged time is the amount of time students are actually participating in relevant learning activities, such as paying attention to lectures and doing assignments. Instructional efficiency is simply the inverse of Carroll's "time needed to learn," and engaged time is essentially his "time available for learning." Instructional efficiency and engaged time are multiplicatively related to student achievement; obviously, if either is zero, then learning is zero.

The QAIT model can be easily related to instructional efficiency and engaged time. Instructional efficiency is a product of the quality of instruction (e.g., organization and presentation quality of the lesson), appropriate levels of instruction (students have prerequisite skills but have not already learned the lesson), and incentive (students are interested in learning the lesson). Of course, aptitude and motivation also contribute to instructional efficiency for any given student. Engaged time is primarily a product of allocated time and incentive.

The relationship between improvement in each of the four alterable elements and effects on student achievement is held to be multiplicative. Clearly, if any of the elements is at zero, learning will be zero. Above zero, the argument that the effects of the four elements are multiplicative rests in part on an assumption that effects of increasing each element are greatest at low levels and ultimately reach maximum or assymptotal levels (within a fixed amount of allocated time). For example, motivation to learn will reach a maximum in terms of affecting student achievement at some point. Effects of quality and appropriateness of instruction are similarly likely to reach a point of diminishing returns. Time-on-task not only cannot be increased beyond 100% of time allocated, but it is doubtful that increases beyond, say, 90% produce significant increases in learning. This may explain why several studies that produced substantial gains in time-on-task have produced minimal effects on student achievement (see Slavin, 1986).

The substantive implication of a multiplicative relationship among the QAIT elements is that it would be more effective to design instruction to produce moderate gains in two or more elements than maximum gains in only one. To increase a plant's growth, moderate increases in light, water, and fertilizer are likely to be more productive than large increases in only one of these elements. By the same token, substantial increases in any one element of the QAIT model, leaving all others unaffected, is likely to be less effective than more moderate, across-the-board improvements.

Another implication of the assumption that there is a point of diminishing returns in achievement effects of each of the QAIT elements is that different types of programs will work differently in different settings depending on pre-existing levels of each. For example, a program focused on increasing time-on-task is likely to be more effective in classrooms low on this variable than in those beginning at 80–90% levels. Highly motivated students may profit more from programs focusing on providing appropriate levels of instruction than from motivationally focused programs, and so on. Put another way, the relationship between each QAIT element and achievement is multiplicative, but the multiplier associated with improvements depends on where students began on each element. If, for example, quality of instruction is high but the level of instruction is inappropriate for many students, then the multiplier for increasing quality will be lower than that for increasing appropriatencss.

The contention that the relationships between the alterable variables—instructional efficiency and engaged time—and student achievement are multiplicative is pivotal to the model proposed here. In addition to implying that achievement will be zero if any of the alterable variables are zero, it also implies that while improving any one of the variables is likely to increase achievement arithmetically (up to a point of diminishing returns), improving more than one is likely to increase achievement geometrically.

Because there are many random or uncontrolled factors in student achievement, and because achievement in any particular skill is so much a function of prior knowledge, ability, and motivation, it may be that for any new program to have a measurable effect on student mean achievement, it *must* improve multiple elements of instruction and therefore have a geometric effect on learning, particularly when a measure of general learning (such as a standardized test) is used as a criterion of success for a program implemented over a substantial period of time. For example, consider how much additional vocabulary students in an experimental program would have to learn to show a measurably greater gain than control students on a standardized reading vocabulary test not specifically keyed to the material students studied. The chance elements involved in determining whether words or decoding skills taught in the experimental program actually appeared on the vocabulary test would make it unlikely that any small effect of improved instruction would be detected.

Applications of the QAIT model

The value of any theory or model lies in its usefulness in explaining or clarifying phenomena of interest. The remainder of this chapter uses the concepts of the QAIT formulation to discuss research on several innovations directed at accelerating student achievement.

Individualized Instruction

Individualized or programmed instructional methods were developed primarily to solve the problem of differences in student prior knowledge and learning rate by allowing students to work on materials at their own levels and rates. In theory, individualized instruction should bring about a substantial improvement in the provision of appropriate levels of instruction; however, reviews of research on the achievement effects of the individualized models developed in the 1960s and 1970s have uniformly concluded that these methods had few if any positive effects on student achievement (Hartley, 1977; Horak, 1981; Miller, 1976). The individualized methods were based on sound psychological theories and the materials were carefully constructed and piloted. What went wrong?

One possibility is that what individualized instruction gained in appropriate levels of instruction it then lost in quality of instruction, incentive, and time. One serious problem of individualized instruction is that it forces students to rely on printed material for the great majority of their instruction. If a teacher had enough aides or parent volunteers to check student work, manage the flow of materials, and respond to non-instructional demands, and was extraordinarily well organized, the teacher could still spend only two minutes with each of twenty-five students in a fifty-minute period. In fact, many teachers using individualized programs spend most of their class time checking student work and managing materials, not teaching at all except when students have specific problems. The quality of instruction provided by the best written material is unlikely to match that provided by a teacher. Further, the incentive value of doing the same types of worksheets day after day with little interaction with other students or with the teacher cannot be very great for many students. Finally, the necessity for a substantial amount of time for procedural activities, such as waiting for materials to be checked, reduces time available for learning, and any lack of incentive to make rapid progress may further reduce engaged time.

An individualized mathematics program designed to solve these problems of the 1960s models provides an interesting point of contrast. This is Team Assisted Individualization, or TAI (Slavin, 1985), an individualized mathematics program for the upper elementary grades. In TAI, students work in four-member heterogeneous learning teams. Students work within their teams on programmed materials appropriate to their own level of preparedness, check one another's work against answer sheets, help one another with problems, and take care of all management concerns. The teams are rewarded based on the progress of each team member through the individualized sequence of units. Since the students themselves take responsibility for all checking and routine management, the teacher is free to spend all period teaching groups of students drawn from the different teams who are performing at about the same level; students typically receive 10 to 20 minutes of direct instruction every class period. The team incentive, found in previous research to be a powerful motivator (see chapter 5; Slavin, 1983a,b), provides ample motivation for students to proceed at a rapid rate with high accuracy and to help one another to master difficult concepts. This incentive may produce high levels of engagement, perhaps enough to counterbalance the time needed to engage in checking or management-related activities.

Research on TAI has clearly established that when direct instruction and team incentives are added to an individualized program, achievement is accelerated. In six field experiments evaluating the program, the mean grade equivalent gain in computations on standardized tests was twice as great for TAI classes as that for control groups (Slavin, 1985; Slavin & Karweit, 1985; Slavin, Leavey, & Madden, 1984; Slavin, Madden, & Leavey, 1984). A component analysis of TAI by Cavanaugh (1984) found that the team incentive system was important to the success of the program.

The contrast of the results of TAI to those of earlier individual models suggests that individualization is not inherently ineffective, but can be made effective if in addition to providing appropriate levels of instruction, it also provides adequate direct instruction (quality of instruction) and enhanced incentives for learning. Attention to all four elements of effective instruction turned out in this case to be necessary to produce a positive effect on student achievement.

Ability Grouping   The most common means schools use to attempt to provide students with appropriate levels of instruction is some form of ability grouping, particularly assignment to classes according to general performance level (ability group class assignment). Of course, the idea behind ability grouping is that if student heterogeneity is reduced, the teacher will be able to accommodate instruction to students' needs; however research on ability grouped class assignment has found few if any positive effects on student achievement (see chapters 6 and 7; Oakes, 1987; Slavin, 1987b).

One problem with ability grouped class assignment is that if a general measure of ability or performance level is used to separate students into different classes, imperfect correlations between the general measure and student performance in any particular subject ensure that a good deal of heterogeneity will remain in the ability grouped class in whatever subject is being taught (Goodlad & Anderson, 1963). For example, grouping students by IQ, composite achievement, and/or teacher judgment will leave substantial heterogeneity in reading level, mathematics skills, and so on. However, studies have failed to find any correlation between class homogeneity and student achievement (e.g., Justman, 1968), and even grouping arrangements that create very narrow bands of ability have been found to be ineffective (Goldberg, Passow, & Justman, 1966). Apparently, reducing class heterogeneity is not in itself an effective means of increasing student achievement, even though it is likely to have at least some impact on appropriate levels of instruction.

However, here again there are tradeoffs involved. Ability grouped class assignment probably incurs costs in incentive for students assigned to low achieving groups. First, teachers have low expectations for low achieving classes, and students are likely to "live down" to those low expectations (Good & Marshall, 1984). By the fact of being assigned to low classes, students are likely to perceive themselves as having little academic potential. Second, low achievers are unlikely to see good models for achievement-oriented behavior within their segregated groups, further reducing the incentive to engage in such behavior. Because the adequacy of incentives are hypothesized to impact both on efficiency of instruction and on engaged time, any detrimental effects on incentive are especially likely to reduce student achievement.

An interesting contrast to ability grouped class assignment is the Joplin Plan (see chapter 6; Floyd, 1954; Slavin, 1987b), a grouping method in which students remain in heterogeneous classes all day except in reading. During reading time, students are regrouped according to reading level but without regard to age. For example, a fifth grade, first semester reading class might have some fourth, some fifth, and some sixth grade students, all reading at the same level.

Research on the Joplin Plan and on closely related forms of nongraded plans consistently finds positive effects on student achievement. Slavin (1987b) estimated the effect size in reading at .44, and a similar effect was found in one study of mathematics (Hart, 1962).

The difference between ability grouped class assignment and the Joplin Plan can be explained in terms of the QAIT model. First, the problems of incentive in ability grouped class assignment are largely averted in the Joplin Plan. Students are in heterogeneous classes most of the day, so their primary identification is with a class that contains positive peer models and for which teachers and students have high expectations. During reading time, low achievers are still grouped with (younger) high achievers, so the problems of managing uniformly low-achieving classes are averted.

In general, the Joplin Plan eliminates the use of reading groups, or at least reduces the number of reading groups. This is likely to affect both quality of instruction and time. Students are sure to receive more direct instruction and less seatwork in a situation with few reading groups than in a situation with the typical three or more. Not only has independent seatwork in reading been criticized as being meaningless busy work for many students (see, for example, Anderson, Brubaker, Alleman-Brooks, & Duffy, 1985) but time-on-task has been found to be low during unsupervised seatwork (Anderson, Evertson, & Brophy, 1979; Stallings & Kaskowitz, 1974).

Finally, the Joplin Plan is likely to do a much better job of obtaining truly homogeneous reading classes than does ability grouped class assignment. In the Joplin Plan, students are assigned to reading classes according to reading level, and are consistently reassessed and reassigned if necessary. The possibility of providing appropriate levels of reading instruction is much greater than in ability grouped class assignment, where factors other than reading level almost always enter into class assignments and where changing students' class assignments is rare.

CONCLUSIONS

The foregoing examples illustrate that many elements of school and classroom organization must be taken into account to understand the effects of any organizational arrangement. Many other cases of this kind exist. The theory presented here does not lead to any particular course of action in the creation of effective school and classroom organizational plans, but rather serves to focus the attention of researchers and practitioners on *multiple* variables involved in organizational practices.

The chapters in this volume carry out the themes raised here. In chapter 2, Thomas Good reviews research on the elements of effective lessons, issues of *quality* of instruction, and in chapter 3, Nancy Karweit discusses time-on-task, an issue of *quantity* of instruction. Chapters 4 and 5 review research on two specific models of classroom organization, respectively mastery learning and cooperative learning. Chapter 6 discusses research on within-and between-class grouping plans in elementary schools, including ability grouping, mastery learning, departmentalization, and cooperative learning. In chapter 7, Jeannie Oakes considers tracking in secondary schools, without doubt the most critical grouping issue at that level of schooling. Gaea Leinhardt and William Bickel then discuss in chapter 8 school and classroom organizational practices designed to meet the needs of low achieving students, in particular special and remedial programs. In chapter 9, Gary Natriello discusses the school and classroom uses of grades and other evaluations to motivate students to achieve, and chapter 10 reviews research on the controversial issue of class size and student achievement. These chapters each approach school and classroom organization from different theoretical perspectives, but all have in common an emphasis on the complexity of school and classroom organization, the idea that changing any one organizational element has consequences for all the other elements. As a group, these chapters extend our understanding of those aspects of effective instruction beyond the teaching act itself, the elements of school and classroom organization that provide the context within which good teaching will lead to optimum learning for all students.

REFERENCES

Abrami, P. C., Leventhal, L., & Perry, R. P. (1982). Educational seduction. *Review of Educational Research, 52,* 446–462.

Anderson, L. M., Brubaker, N. L., Alleman-Brooks, J., & Duffy, G. G. (1985). A qualitative study of seatwork in first-grade classrooms. *Elementary School Journal, 86,* 123–140.

Anderson, L. M., Evertson, C., & Brophy, J. (1979). An experimental study of effective teaching in first-grade reading-groups. *Elementary School Journal, 79,* 193–223.

Anderson, R. C., & Hidde, J. L. (1971). Imagery and sentence learning. *Journal of Educational Psychology, 62,* 81–94.

Atkinson, J. W., & Birch, D. (1978). *Introduction to motivation* (2nd ed.). New York: Van Nostrand.

Austin, J. D. (1978). Homework research in mathematics. *School Science and Mathematics, 79,* 115–122.

Ausubel, D. P. (1960). The use of advanced organizers in the learning and retention of meaningful verbal material. *Journal of Educational Psychology, 51,* 267–272.

Barr, R., & Dreeben, R. (1983). *How schools work.* Chicago: University of Chicago Press.

Barringer, C., & Gholson, B. (1979). Effects of type and combination of feedback upon conceptual learning by children: Implications for research in academic learning. *Review of Educational Research, 49,* 459–478.

Barth, R. (1979). Home-based reinforcement of school behavior: A review and analysis. *Review of Educational Research, 49,* 436–458.

Belgard, M., Rosenshine, B., & Gage, N. L. (1971). Effectiveness in explaining: Evidence on its generality and correlation with pupil rating. In I. Westbury & A. Bellack (Eds.), *Research into classroom processes: Recent developments and next steps.* New York: Teachers College Press.

Berlyne, D. E. (1965). Curiosity and education. In J. D. Krumboltz (Ed.), *Learning and the educational process.* Chicago: Rand McNally.

Block, J. H., & Burns, R. B. (1976). Mastery learning. In L. S. Shulman (Ed.), *Review of research in education (Vol. 4)*. Itasca, IL: F. E. Peacock.

Bloom, B. S. (1976). *Human characteristics and school learning*. New York: McGraw-Hill.

Brophy, J. E. (1979). Teacher behavior and its effects. *Journal of Educational Psychology, 71*, 733–750.

Brophy, J. (1981). Teacher praise: A functional analysis. *Review of Educational Research, 51*, 5–32.

Brophy, J. E., & Evertson, C. M. (1974). *Process–product correlations in the Texas teacher effectiveness study: Final report* (Research Rep.No. 74-4). Austin: University of Texas, Research & Development Center for Teacher Education.

Brophy, J. E., & Good, T. L. (1986). Teacher behavior and student achievement. In M. C. Wittrock (Ed.), *Handbook of research on teaching* (3rd ed.). New York: McMillan.

Carroll, J. B. (1963). A model of school learning. *Teachers College Record, 64*, 723–733.

Cavanagh, B. R. (1984). *Effects of interdependent group contingencies on the achievement of elementary school children*. Unpublished doctoral dissertation, University of Maryland.

Cooley, W. W., & Leinhardt, G. (1980). The instructional dimensions study. *Educational Evaluation and Policy Analysis, 2*, 7–25.

Dalis, G. T. (1970). Effect of precise objectives upon student achievement in health education. *Journal of Experimental Education, 39*, 20–23.

Dunkin, M. (1978). Student characteristics, classroom processes, and student achievement. *Journal of Educational Psychology, 70*, 998–1009.

Dunkin, M. J., & Biddle, B. J. (1974). *A study of teaching*. New York: Holt, Rinehart, & Winston.

Floyd, C. (1954). Meeting children's reading needs in the middle grades: A preliminary report. *Elementary School Journal, 55*, 99–103.

Frederick, W., & Walberg, H. (1980). Learning as a function of time. *Journal of Educational Research, 73*, 183–194.

Gold, R. M., Reilly, A., Silberman, R., & Lehr, R. (1971). Academic achievement declines under pass–fail grading. *Journal of Experimental Education, 39*, 17–21.

Goldberg, M. L., Passow, A. H., & Justman, J. (1966). *The effects of ability grouping*. New York: Teachers College Press.

Good, T., & Marshall, S. (1984). Do students learn more in heterogeneous or homogeneous groups? In P. Peterson, L. C. Wilkinson, & M. Hallinan (Eds.), *The social context of instruction: Group organization and group processes* (pp. 15–38). New York: Academic Press.

Goodlad, J. I., & Anderson, R. H. (1963). *The nongraded elementary school* (rev. ed.). New York: Harcourt, Brace, & World.

Gregory, I. D. (1975). A new look at the lecture method. *British Journal of Education Technology, 6*, 55–62.

Guskey, T. R., & Gates, S. L. (1985, April). *A synthesis of research on group-based mastery learning programs*. Paper presented at the annual convention of the American Educational Research Association, Chicago.

Hales, L. W., Bain, P. T., & Rand, L. P. (1971, February). *An investigation of some aspects of the pass–fail grading system*. Paper presented at the annual meeting of the American Educational Research Association, New York.

Hart, R. H. (1962). The nongraded primary school and arithmetic. *The Arithmetic Teacher, 9*, 130–133.

Hartley, S. S. (1977). Meta-analysis of the effects of individually paced instruction in mathematics. *Dissertation Abstracts International, 38*, 4003A. (University Microfilms No. 77–29, 926)

Hayes, L. (1976). The use of group contingencies for behavioral control: A review. *Psychological Bulletin, 83*, 628–648.

Horak, V. M. (1981). A meta-analysis of research findings on individualized instruction in mathematics. *Journal of Educational Research, 74*, 249–253.

Justman, J. (1969). Reading and class homogeneity. *Reading Teacher, 21*, 314–316.

Kaplan, R. M., & Pascoe, G. C. (1977). Humorous lectures and humorous examples: Some effects upon comprehension and retention. *Journal of Educational Psychology, 69*, 61–65.

Karweit, N. (1976). A reanalysis of the effect of quantity of schooling and achievement. *Sociology of Education, 49*, 236–246.

Karweit, N. L. (1981). Time in school. *Research in Sociology of Education and Socialization, 2*, 77–110.

Leighton, M. S., & Slavin, R. E. (1988, April). *Achievement effects of instructional pace and systematic instruction in elementary mathematics.* Paper presented at the annual convention of the American Educational Research Association, New Orleans.

Leinhardt, G., & Bickel, W. (1987). Instruction's the thing wherein to catch the mind that falls behind. *Educational Psychologist, 22*, 177–207.

Leinhardt, G., & Pallay, A. (1982). Restrictive educational settings: Exile or haven? *Review of Educational Research, 52*, 557–578.

Litow, L., & Pumroy, D. K. (1975). A brief review of classroom group-oriented contingencies. *Journal of Applied Behavior Analysis, 8*, 341–347.

Madden, N. A., & Slavin, R. E. (1983). Mainstreaming students with mild academic handicaps: Academic and social outcomes. *Review of Educational Research, 84*, 131–138.

Maddox, H., & Hoole, E. (1975). Performance decrement in the lecture. *Educational Review, 28*, 17–30.

Marliave, R., Fisher, C., & Dishaw, M. (1978). *Academic learning time and student achievement in the B-C period.* Far West Laboratory for Educational Research and Development. Technical Note V-29.

Miller, R. L. (1976). Individualized instruction in mathematics: A reveiw of research. *The Mathematics Teacher, 69*, 345–351.

Natriello, G. (1987). The impact of evaluation processes on students. *Educational Psychologist, 22*, 155–175.

Oakes, J. (1985). *Keeping track: How schools structure inequality.* New Haven, CT: Yale University Press.

Oakes, J. (1987). Tracking in secondary schools: A contextual perspective. *Educational Psychologist, 22*, 120–153.

O'Leary, K. D., & O'Leary, S. G. (1972). *Classroom management: The successful use of behavior modification.* New York: Pergamon.

Peckham, R. D., & Roe, M. D. (1977). The effects of frequent testing. *Journal of Research and Development in Education, 10*, 40–50.

Redfield, D.L., & Rousseau, E. W. (1981). A meta-analysis of experimental research on teacher questioning behavior. *Review of Educational Research, 51*, 237–245.

Rosenshine, B. V., & Stevens, R. J. (1986). Teaching functions. In M. C. Wittrock (Ed.), *Third handbook of research on teaching.* Chicago: Rand McNally.

Rowan, B., & Miracle, A. (1983). Systems of ability grouping and the stratification of achievement in elementary schools. *Sociology of Education, 56*, 133–144.

Rowe, M. B. (1974). Wait-time and rewards as instructional variable, their influence on language, logic, and fate control: Part one: *Journal of Research in Science Teaching, 11*, 81–94.

Slavin, R. E. (1977, April). *A new model of classroom motivation.* Paper presented at the annual convention of the American Educational Research Association, New York.

Slavin, R. E. (1980). Effects of individual learning expectations on student achievement. *Journal of Educational Psychology, 72*, 520–524.

Slavin, R. E. (1983a). *Cooperative learning.* New York: Longman.

Slavin, R. E. (1983b). When does cooperative learning increase student achievement? *Psychological Bulletin, 94*, 429–445.

Slavin, R. E. (1984). Component building: A strategy for research-based instructional improvement. *Elementary School Journal, 84*, 255–269.

Slavin, R. E. (1985). Team-Assisted Individualization: Combining cooperative learning and individualized instruction in mathematics. In R. E. Slavin, S. Sharan, R. Hertz-Lazarowitz, C. Webb, & R. Schmuck (Eds.), *Learning to cooperate, cooperating to learn* (pp. 177–209). New York: Plenum.

Slavin, R. E. (1986). The Napa evaluation of Madeline Hunter's ITIP: Lessons learned. *Elementary School Journal, 87,* 165–171.

Slavin, R. E. (1987a). Mastery learning reconsidered. *Review of Educational Research, 57,* 175–213.

Slavin, R. E. (1987b). Ability grouping and student achievement in elementary schools: A best-evidence synthesis. *Review of Educational Research, 57,* 293–336.

Slavin, R. E. (1988). *Educational psychology: Theory into practice. (2nd ed.).* Englewood Cliffs, NJ: Prentice–Hall.

Slavin, R. E., Karweit, N. L. (1985). Effects of whole-class, ability-grouped, and individualized instruction on mathematics achievement. *American Educational Research Journal, 22,* 351–367.

Slavin, R. E., Leavey, M., & Madden, N. A. (1984). Combining cooperative learning and individualized instruction: Effects on student mathematics achievement, attitudes, and behaviors. *Elementary School Journal, 84,* 409–422.

Slavin, R. E., Madden, N. A., & Leavey, M. (1984). Effects of Team Assisted Individualization on the mathematics achievement of academically handicapped and non-handicapped students. *Journal of Educational Psychology, 76,* 813–819.

Smith, L. R., & Cotten, M. L. (1980). Effect of lesson vagueness and discontinuity on student achievement and attitudes. *Journal of Educational Psychology, 72,* 670–675.

Stallings, J. A., & Kaskowitz, D. (1974). *Follow-through classroom observation evaluation 1972–73.* Menlo Park, CA: Stanford Research Institute.

Stallings, J., & Krasavage, E. M. (1986). Program implementation and student achievement in a four-year Madeline Hunter Follow Through project. *Elementary School Journal, 87,* 117–138.

Wilson, R. R., & Nachtigal, P. (1986). *Final Report: Cotopaxi/Westcliffe Follow Through Project.* Office of Educational Research and Improvement, Grant No. 400-81-0039.

Winne, P. H. (1979). Experiments relating teachers' use of higher cognitive questions to student achievement. *Review of Educational Research, 49,* 13–50.

II CLASSROOM INSTRUCTION: QUALITY AND QUANTITY

2 Teaching the Lesson

Thomas L. Good
University of Missouri-Columbia

Jere Brophy
Michigan State University

TEACHING THE LESSON

Group lessons are by far the most common instructional format in American classrooms. The popularity of this format is likely to continue, and hence teachers need to know how to utilize this structure appropriately. Even innovative or alternative instructional programs involve group-based lessons to some extent. Considering that teachers are charged with educating classes of twenty to forty students, they will have to use some variation of the traditional instruction-recitation-seatwork format, either with an entire class or with small groups (as in beginning reading instruction).

In this chapter, we draw upon classroom research (some experimental, but most correlational), linking elements of instruction within this traditionally favored format to student achievement gain in order to identify a model for presenting group lessons. We also show how this model has been adjusted to various teaching contexts in three different classroom experiments. Finally, by incorporating research on child development and student motivation, we present an expanded model that stresses the relationship between active teaching and active learning. We believe that this model will be useful for planning instruction across a broad range of classroom teaching situations, although we recognize that no single model is appropriate for all situations. What constitutes effective instruction varies with the subject matter, students, and other factors.

Subject Matter

Although there are similarities, there are also important differences in what constitutes an effective problem-solving lesson in mathematics, laboratory activity in chemistry, or history lesson. The types of learning required to achieve instructional objectives must be taken into account when designing lessons.

Gagné and Briggs (1979), for example, have identified five different capabilities that might represent the intended instructional outcomes of lessons: intellectual skills (concepts, principles, rules), cognitive strategies (thinking and problem-solving strategies), information (facts), attitudes, and motor skills. These authors assume that different "conditions of learning" must be established for each of these five types of learning. Thus, although they expect that a basic set of nine "instructional events" will be included in any well designed instruction, they also expect that these instructional events will take different forms depending on the nature of the learner capabilities that the instruction is designed to develop (see Table 2.1).

The purpose of this paper is not to discuss curricular goals and decisions that a teacher must make in adapting instructional materials for classroom use. However, we do want to mention this topic briefly to underline its importance and to note that teachers need to decide what content they will offer in a lesson and the level at which they will present that content. Although much of the elementary curriculum is dictated by district guidelines and standard textbook series, a teacher may have to adjust a standard lesson designed for an "average" sixth-grade class according to the aptitude and/or motivation of students in a particular class. If teachers' instructional goals differ from those of the textbook, it is especially important that they modify assignments. For example, the textbook may emphasize a product approach to writing (mechanics, neatness, correct margins); whereas, a teacher may be much more interested in writing processes (finding a topic, generating thoughts, arranging ideas).

Developmental Considerations in Lesson Design

It is difficult to create lessons that are effective for all of the students in a class or group, because students differ in ability, reading level, possession of relevant background information and vocabulary, content interests, and preferences for different types of lessons and assignments. Often it will be necessary to supplement group lessons with enrichment assignments for some students and remedial work with others.

These individual differences within a class are merely variations on larger themes established by students' more general levels of cognitive development, which have important implications for decisions concerning what to teach and how to teach it effectively. It is beyond the scope of this chapter to discuss cognitive development in detail (see Brophy & Willis, 1981 or Good & Brophy, 1986), but a few comments on developmental differences as they relate to lesson design are in order.

Children in the early elementary grades are still primarily preoperational in their thinking. Although it is true that most children exhibit at least some capaci-

TABLE 2.1

Instructional Events and the Conditions of Learning They Imply for Five Types of Learned Capabilities

Instructional Event	Type of Capability				
	Intellectual Skill	Cognitive Strategy	Information	Attitude	Motor Skill
1. Gaining attention	Introduce stimulus change: Variations in sensory mode				
2. Informing learner of objective	Provide description and example of the performance to be expected	Clarify the general nature of the solution expected	Indicate the kind of verbal question to be answered	Provide example of the kind of action choice aimed for	Provide a demonstration of the performance to be expected
3. Stimulating recall of prerequisites	Stimulate recall of subordinate concepts and rules	Stimulate recall of task strategies and associated intellectual skills	Stimulate recall of context of organized information	Stimulate recall of relevant information skills and human model identification	Stimulate recall of executive subroutine and part skills
4. Presenting the stimulus material	Present examples of concept or rule	Present novel problems	Present information in propositional form	Present human model demonstrating choice of personal action	Provide external stimuli for performance including tools or implements
5. Providing learning guidance	Provide verbal cues to proper combining sequence	Provide prompts and hints to novel situation	Provide verbal links to a larger meaningful context	Provide for observation of model's choice of action, and of reinforcement received by model	Provide practice with feedback of performance achievement
6. Eliciting the performance	Ask learner to apply rule or concept to new examples	Ask for problem solution	Ask for information in paraphrase, or in learner's own words	Ask learner to indicate choices of action in real or simulated situations	Ask for execution of the performance

(continued...)

(Table 2.1 continued)

Instructional Event	Intellectual Skill	Cognitive Strategy	Information	Attitude	Motor Skill
7. Providing feedback	Confirm correctness of rule or concept application	Confirm originality of problem solution	Confirm correctness of statement of information	Provide direct or vicarious reinforcement of action choice	Provide feedback on degree of accuracy and timing of performance
8. Assessing performance	Learner demonstrates application of concept or rule	Learner originates a novel solution	Learner restates information in paraphrased form	Learner makes desired choice of personal action in real or simulated situation	Learner executes performance of total skill
9. Enhancing retention and transfer	Provide spaced reviews, including a variety of examples	Provide occasions for a variety of novel problem solutions	Provide verbal links to additional complexes of information	Provide additional varied situations for selected choice of action	Lerner continues skill practice

Source: From Gagné and Briggs (1979). Principles of Instructional Design (2nd ed.). New York: Holt, Rinehart and Winston, p. 166.

ty for operational thinking by age five or six, most do not become functionally operational (develop stable operational structures and use operational thinking most of the time) until they are seven or eight. Thus, preoperational thinking predominates until about third grade for many children, and beyond this point for some.

Three general kinds of learning seem most appropriate for preoperational students: (a) development of knowledge about familiar and observable phenomena, (b) exploration and manipulation of concrete objects, and (c) learning and practice of basic knowledge and skills (the traditional Three Rs). Ideally, these tool skills will be taught in an integrated way that stresses explanation for meaningful understanding and opportunities for realistic application (Anderson, Hiebert, Scott, & Wilkinson, 1985; Hooper & DeFrain, 1980); however, it must be recognized that younger students have only limited abilities to transfer and generalize their learning and that basic knowledge and skills must be mastered to the point of automaticity. This will mean considerable time spent in drill and practice activities (Greeno, 1978). In addition, younger students are especially dependent on their teachers for direct instruction. They require demonstration, explanation, elicitation of responses to monitor their comprehension, correction as necessary, and continued practice to mastery (Brophy & Good, 1986).

During the preoperational years, good demonstrations and visual aids are needed to provide students with concrete models to imitate. The students can learn relatively easily if taught this way, but may have difficulty following purely verbal instruction. If tasks are lengthy or complex, they will need to be broken into subtasks that can be mastered and practiced in sequences that gradually lengthen as the ultimate task is learned. Follow-up assignments should be divided into modular units that can be presented, corrected, and discussed separately, and they should contain models for imitation and other learning aids that can help overcome short attention spans and difficulty in following purely verbal instructions. Worksheets, for example, might use lines and spacing designed to help students keep things separate from one another, boxes or lines to indicate where responses should be placed, and arrows to indicate where to go next.

This does not mean that teachers should avoid teaching learning-to-learn skills, independent work skills, integrative concepts, or strategies for self-regulated learning (how to read for understanding; how to evaluate information and integrate it with information from other sources; how to budget time and plan activities to accomplish complex tasks). It does mean that these concepts and skills cannot be assumed. They develop slowly during the preoperational years and the early concrete operational years. As children become operational and begin to master tool skills, they begin to read for pleasure and knowledge (not just to practice reading) and to use math skills for solving problems of personal interest (such as computing batting averages or money transactions). When students reach this point, they are ready for instruction in new subject areas, using methods that rely on the tool skills.

As students become operational and show evidence of inductive and deductive reasoning, teachers can place more emphasis on understanding and integrating concepts. Children now can do more verbalizing about academic content, self-monitoring of their comprehension, and independent work on complex projects. However, all of this must be kept within the concrete operational level. Attempts to teach highly abstract content using purely verbal methods will fail altogether or produce only superficial memorizations of material that is not really understood (Murray, 1978; Renner et al., 1976).

Students in the middle elementary school grades can work out elaborate mathematics or scientific experiments if they can carry out the operations physically or at least approximate them by drawing sketches. They also can respond meaningfully to questions about the reasons for historical events or events occurring in a story read during class, if these reasons were made clear in the presentation or involve situations that students can understand by putting themselves in the place of the characters in the story. However, the material must be familiar enough for students to comprehend if they are to understand.

Students who are in the stage of concrete operations will benefit from question sequences that require them to express themselves verbally. In working with students at this stage, teachers should both expect and foster verbal communication of concerns and questions, and should patiently encourage them to elaborate or rephrase questions that are too cryptic or ambiguous for the teachers to understand clearly. This will socialize children to express their needs verbally and at the same time give them practice in doing so.

Students at the concrete operational level need personalized treatment of human events in science and social studies that stresses the actions of key individuals with reference to motivational systems that the students can comprehend. For example, complex political and economic rivalries might be presented as contests between individuals or countries, because students can understand the motivations involved in trying to win a contest. Many students would not understand such concepts if they were presented only at an abstract level and described in an impersonal way, using terms such as ''spheres of influence,'' or ''import-export ratio.''

Beginning around the eighth grade, students who are entering the formal operations stage can understand largely abstract material; however, several cautions should be noted. First, although students show development of formal operations during the secondary school years, a great many of them never develop formal operations to the point where they can be used with efficiency in thinking and problem solving (Martorano, 1977; Neimark, 1975). They may memorize algebraic formulas and answer practice exercises on worksheets correctly, for example, but never really understand the formulas so as to be able to apply them to ''far transfer'' problems or to activate them when they would be useful for solving problems that arise in their lives outside of school. Second, even for students with efficient formal operations, learning is almost always easier if it is aided by imagery, diagrams, examples, or other forms of presentation that involve concrete operations (Cox & Matz, 1982; Renner et al., 1976).

To the extent that students do possess formal operations, a teacher can present knowledge in logical sequences involving articulation of general principles and then move toward specifics, stressing deductive logic. In other words, material can be organized and presented systematically and learning can be facilitated through the use of integrative concepts that promote conceptual understanding and general assimilation. This is how most highly abstract bodies of knowledge are taught, particularly those that are inherently organized in a logical way (as in logic, mathematics, or science courses). In earlier stages, this integrative level of knowledge was the last to develop, appearing only after students had mastered many facts and skills separately and then gradually assimilated them into increasingly larger schemes.

In summary, developmental stages have important implications for instruction. Younger students' attention spans are shorter, so they generally need relatively short lessons and frequent review. Older students can benefit from longer assignments, more complex choices, and more independent work. Preoperational students need numerous concrete examples; formal operational students can work with abstractions and learn propositionally.

STUDENT MOTIVATION VARIABLES

Research on motivation is important and helps to identify preconditions that teachers need to consider when planning lessons. For the most part, motivation concepts are more diffuse and more relative than developmental variables. Still, any teacher who wants to teach a lesson well will have to consider motivational variables. In this section, we provide a framework that teachers can utilize as they consider means by which to help students develop interest in learning key concepts and skills (motivating students to learn the curriculum as defined by the teacher) as well as to help students to develop and pursue their own interests (self-regulated learning).

Student Motivation

Several preconditions are essential if any motivational strategy is to work in the classroom. These are discussed briefly here; for more extensive discussion see Brophy, 1987; Good and Brophy, 1987.

Supportive Environment.   Students need opportunities to learn and to receive appropriate encouragement and support of their learning efforts. Clearly, some students need more encouragement and support than others; however, because anxious or alienated students are unlikely to develop motivation to learn academic content, it is important that a businesslike emphasis on teaching and learning the curriculum occurs within a relaxed and supportive atmosphere. Students should feel comfortable taking intellectual risks because they know they will not be embarrassed or criticized if they make a mistake. Students in classrooms that are appropriately supportive may realize that some failure is apt to be associated with any attempt to learn new and challenging material and that one can learn from initial failure as long as appropriately useful and specific feedback follows (Rohrkemper & Corno, 1988).

Appropriate Challenge or Difficulty.   Activities should be at an appropriate level of difficulty for the students. Tasks are of appropriate difficulty when the students know clearly enough what to do and how to do it so that they can achieve high levels of success if they apply reasonable effort.

Meaningful Learning Objectives.   Students will not be motivated to learn if presented with pointless or meaningless activities. Activities should be selected with worthwhile academic objectives in mind. That is, they should teach some knowledge or skill that is worth learning either in its own right or as a step toward some higher objective. Activities such as the following do *not* meet this criterion: continued practice on skills that have already been mastered thoroughly; memorizing lists for no good reason; looking up and copying definitions of terms that are never used in readings or assignments; or reading material that is not presented in enough detail or integrated well enough to allow the students to clearly understand it.

Moderation and Variation in Strategy Use.   Motivational strategies can be overused in two respects. First, the need for such strategies varies with the situation. When content is unfamiliar and its value or its meaningfulness is not obvious to students, significant motivational effort involving several of the strategies to be described may be needed. In contrast, little or no special motivation may be needed when the activity involves things that students are already eager to learn. Thus, motivational efforts can be counterproductive if they are used when they are not needed, go on too long, or are carried to extremes. Second, any particular motivational strategy may lose its effectiveness if used too often or too routinely. Thus, teachers should master and use a variety of motivational strategies rather than rely on just one or two. With these four preconditions in mind, let us consider the motivational strategies that various authors suggest.

Motivational Strategies

Maintaining Success Expectations.   Much of the best-known research on motivation has focused on expectancy issues. Research on achievement motivation (Dweck & Elliott, 1983) has established that effort and persistence are greater in individuals who set goals of moderate difficulty (neither too hard nor too easy), seriously pursue these goals rather than treat them as mere "pie-in-sky" hopes, and concentrate on achieving success rather than on avoiding failure.

Although it is difficult to specify how these conceptual approaches are related to any *single* lesson, it is clear that teachers need to encourage students to develop the following perceptions and attributional inferences concerning their performance at school if students are to come to regulate their own learning.

1. *Effort-outcome covariation.* Students need to recognize that there is a predictable relationship between the level of effort they invest in a task and the level of success they can expect (Cooper, 1979).

2. *Internal locus of control.* Students should believe that they have the potential to control their success, at least to some extent, rather than believing that their performance is determined by external factors that they cannot control (Stipek & Weiss, 1981).

3. *Concept of self as origin rather than pawn.* Students need to recognize that they can bring about desired outcomes through their own actions (deCharms, 1976).

4. *Sense of efficacy or competence.* Students must believe that they have the ability to succeed on a task if they choose to invest the necessary effort (Weisz & Cameron, 1985).

5. *Incremental concept of ability.* Students should perceive academic ability as a potential that is developed continually through learning rather than as a fixed capacity that predetermines and limits what can be accomplished.

Meaningful Progress. We think of teaching any particular lesson as a stage in a sequence of several lessons, each building on the previous one. It is important to realize that the levels of success that students are likely to achieve on a particular task depend not only on the difficulty of the task itself, but on the degree to which the teacher prepares them for that task through advance instruction and assists their learning efforts through guidance and feedback. A task that would be too difficult for students if they were left to their own devices might be just right to learn through active instruction by the teacher followed by supervised practice and the exchange of ideas with other students. In fact, contemporary theorists believe that instruction should focus on what is called the zone of proximal development (Vygotsky, 1978), which refers to the range of knowledge and skills that students are not yet ready to learn on their own but could learn with help from teachers.

Teach Goal Setting and Performance Appraisal. Students' reactions to their own performance will depend not so much on their absolute levels of success but on their perceptions of what they have achieved. Some students may not fully appreciate their own accomplishments unless helped to identify appropriate standards to use in judging their progress. The process begins with *goal setting*. Research indicates that setting goals and making a commitment to reach these goals increase performance (Bandura & Schunk, 1981). Goal setting is especially effective when it focuses on proximal outcomes, states a specific target success level, and involves a reasonable but challenging goal (difficult but reachable).

Goal setting is not enough by itself; there must also be goal commitment. Students must take the goals seriously and commit themselves to trying to reach them. It may be necessary to negotiate goal setting with some students, or at least to provide them with guidance and stimulate them to think about their performance potential. One way to do this is to provide a list of potential goals and ask students to commit themselves to particular goals (and associated levels of effort).

It is also essential that students receive help in assessing progress toward established goals by using appropriate standards for judging success. In particular, students may need to learn to compare their work with absolute standards or with their own previous performance rather than with the performance of others. Some students require specific, detailed feedback concerning both the strengths and the weaknesses of their performance (Elawar & Corno, 1985).

Help Students to Recognize Effort–Outcome Linkages

The following strategies are useful for developing an internal locus of control and a sense of efficacy in students and for helping them to recognize that they can achieve success if they put forth reasonable effort.

Modeling.   Teachers can model beliefs about effort–outcome linkages by talking to students about teachers' own learning and skill development and by demonstrating strategies (thinking aloud) as they search for a way to solve a problem.

Portray Effort as Investment Rather Than Risk.   Students need to be made aware that learning may take time and involve confusion or mistakes, but that persistence and careful work can eventually yield knowledge and skill mastery. Furthermore, students should realize that such mastery not only represents success on a particular task, but provides them with knowledge or skills that will make them more capable of handling higher-level tasks in the future.

Portray Skill Development as Incremental and Domain-Specific.   Students need to know that their intellectual abilities are open to improvement rather than fixed and limiting and that they possess a great many such abilities. In short, students must realize that success depends not just on general ability but on possession and use of specific knowledge and strategies.

Focus on Mastery.   In monitoring performance and giving feedback, teachers should stress the quality of students' task engagement and the degree to which they are making continuous progress toward mastery rather than comparisons with how other students are doing (McColskey & Leary, 1985). Teachers should perceive students' mistakes as learning opportunities, not just as failures. Students' errors should lead to remedial or additional instruction followed by practice. Hence, students should see that their efforts (even if they are wrong in the short run) lead to useful feedback that can help them achieve desirable goals.

RESEARCH ON TEACHING LESSONS TO GROUPS

It seems intuitively obvious that for attaining a certain learning objective with a particular group of students, some teachers will be more successful than others and some instructional methods will be more effective than others. Yet, until about 1970, not much research was available on relationships between teacher behavior and student outcomes, and the findings that did exist were confusing or contradictory. For a time, in fact, it was commonly stated that learning outcomes depended almost entirely on student factors and that the differences between teachers or teaching methods were trivial. The picture began to change in the late 1960s and early 1970s, due largely to increased educational research, particularly research on teacher behavior and its effects.

Teacher Behavior and Student Achievement

In the 1970s, a data base began to accumulate that indicated that some teachers and teaching methods consistently produced better results than others. This work led to a series of correlational and experimental studies that linked teacher behavior to student achievement gain in basic skills (reading and mathematics). This program of research has often been described as process-product research because the studies using this paradigm attempt to relate classroom *processes* (especially teacher behaviors such as enthusiasm, clarity, etc.) to student *products* or accomplishments (e.g., scores on standardized achievement tests). This research supports several conclusions about effective basic skills instruction (Brophy & Good, 1986). Among the factors consistently related to student achievement are: positive teacher expectations, student opportunity to learn material, good classroom organization and management, appropriate curriculum pacing, active teaching, teaching to mastery, and a supportive learning environment.

Positive Teacher Expectations.   Teachers whose classes make good learning gains generally accept responsibility for teaching their students. These teachers not only believe that their students can learn; they also believe that they (the teachers) are capable of teaching successfully. If students do not learn something the first time, teachers with appropriate expectations are willing to teach it again. Furthermore, if the regular curriculum materials are not adequate, they obtain additional resources for helping students to master material.

Opportunity to Learn.   Several studies have shown that amount learned is related to opportunity to learn, whether measured in terms of pages of curriculum covered or percentage of test items taught. When teachers allocate most of their available time to instruction, their students spend many more hours each year on academic tasks than do students of teachers who are less concerned about promoting students' achievement.

Classroom Management and Organization.   Achievement gains are greater when teachers organize their classrooms as effective learning environments and use group management approaches that maximize student engagement in academic activities. In these classrooms, academic activities run smoothly, transitions are brief and orderly, and little time is spent getting organized or dealing with inattention or resistance.

Appropriate Curriculum Pacing.   Achievement gains are greater when teachers move through the curriculum rapidly but in small steps that minimize unnecessary student frustration and allow continuous progress.

Active Teaching.   Teachers who obtain good achievement gain actively instruct their students; they demonstrate skills, explain concepts, conduct participatory and practice activities, explain assignments, and review when necessary. They teach academic content to students rather than relying principally on the curriculum materials to do so; however, they do not stress only facts or skills; they also emphasize concepts and understanding.

Teaching to Mastery.   Following active instruction on new content, these teachers provide opportunities for students to practice and apply the material. They monitor each student's progress and provide feedback and remedial instruction as needed, making sure that material is mastered. This appears to be essential in teaching basic tool skills or any material that is hierarchically sequenced so that success at any level usually requires not only mastery of skills taught earlier but also the ability to apply them to new situations.

A Supportive Learning Environment.   Despite their strong academic focus, teachers who elicit good achievement gain maintain pleasant, friendly classrooms and are perceived as enthusiastic, supportive instructors.

MODELS OF LESSON ORGANIZATION

Direct Instruction Model

Rosenshine and Stevens's (1986) review of studies relating teacher behavior to student achievement led them to conclude that effective teachers engage in direct instruction that includes the following behaviors:

1. Begin with a short review of previous, prerequisite learning.
2. Provide a short statement of goals for the current lesson.
3. Present new material in small steps, with student practice after each step.
4. Give clear and detailed instructions and explanations.
5. Provide a high level of active practice for all students.
6. Ask a large number of questions, check for student understanding, and obtain responses from all students.
7. Guide students during initial practice.
8. Provide systematic feedback and corrections.
9. Provide explicit instruction and practice for seatwork exercises and, where necessary, monitor students during seatwork.

Rosenshine and Stevens combined several different models to form a generic model for teaching lessons in subjects that are well structured. They report that six fundamental instructional functions are associated with direct teaching:

1. Review, check previous day's work (and reteach, if necessary)
2. Present new content/skills
3. Guided student practice (and check for understanding)
4. Feedback and correctives (and reteach, if necessary)
5. Independent student practice
6. Weekly and monthly reviews

Presentation and guided practice—two of the functions they discuss—are presented in greater detail in Table 2.2.

Active Teaching Model

Researchers associated with the Missouri Mathematics Program have used the concept of active teaching to describe the instruction that they found to be associated with high achievement gain in mathematics classes. They prefer the term "active teaching" to the more popular but narrower term "direct instruction" because the former represents a broader concept of effective teaching. Both terms imply that the teacher spends a great deal of time actively instructing

TABLE 2.2
Two Instructional Functions: Presentation and Guided Practice

Presentation

    Provide short statement of objectives
    Provide overview and structuring
    Proceed in small steps but at a rapid pace
    Intersperse questions within the demonstration to
      check for understanding
    Highlight main points
    Provide sufficient illustrations and concrete examples
    Provide demonstrations and models
    When necessary, give detailed and redundant instructions
      and examples

Guided Practice

    Initial student practice takes place with teacher
      guidance
    High frequency of questions and overt student practice
      (from teacher and/or materials)
    Questions are directly relevant to the new content or
      skill
    Teacher checks for understanding (CFU) by evaluating
      student responses
    During CFU teacher gives additional explanation, process
      feedback, or repeats explanation--where necessary
    All students have a chance to respond and receive feed-
      back; teacher insures that all students participate
    Prompts are provided during guided practice (where
      appropriate)
    Initial student practice is sufficient so that students
      can work independently
    Guided practice continues until students are firm
    Guided practice is continued (usually) until a success
      rate of 80% is achieved

Note. This table was taken from material that appeared in Rosen-
shine and Stevens (1986). Teaching functions. In M. C. Wittrock
(Ed.), Handbook of research on teaching (3rd ed., pp. 376-391).
New York: Macmillan.

the students in whole-class or small-group lessons and circulating to monitor their work on assignments. However, active teaching connotes a broader philosophical base than direct instruction. In active teaching, the initial style can be inductive or deductive, and student learning can be teacher-initiated or self-initiated (especially if thorough critique and synthesis follow student learning attempts).

The concept of active teaching can be applied not only to teacher-led instruction but also to instruction that occurs within a variety of organizational structures, such as the student-team learning that may follow teacher-led instruction (e.g., Peterson, Janicki, & Swing, 1981; Slavin & Karweit, 1985). Although it always implies that instruction is planned with particular learning outcomes in mind, the concept of active teaching also implies that instruction will become less direct as students mature and develop increased ability to direct their own learning, as attention shifts from cognitive to affective outcomes, and as the class moves through units and shifts from focus on lower-level knowledge and skill outcomes to higher-level application, analysis, synthesis, and evaluation outcomes (Good,1979).

THREE EXAMPLES OF ACTIVE TEACHING

To illustrate active teaching—and to show how it must be adapted to differences in grade level, subject matter, and group setting—we discuss three recent experimental studies that examined teaching effects.

Missouri Mathematics Program.   Building mostly on their own earlier correlational work, Good and Grouws (1979) developed the instructional model shown in Table 2.3 for fourth-grade mathematics classes. The model is similar to traditional fourth-grade mathematics instruction in many ways, although it is more systematic. Note that it includes guidelines for time allocation to ensure that mathematics is taught for about 45 minutes each day, and that it calls for supplementing classroom instruction with homework assignments. Although the model advocates that students work primarily individually on seatwork and homework, it also requires a great deal of active instruction by the teacher. New concepts are presented in detail during the development portion of the lesson, and the teacher both makes sure that students know how to do the assignment before releasing them to work individually and reviews the assignment with them the next day. This schedule of instruction and opportunity for practice with feedback, along with frequent testing, helps to ensure continuous progress.

Several studies have examined the effects of the Missouri Mathematics Program (see Brophy & Good, 1986; Good, Grouws, & Ebmeier, 1983). There is consistent evidence that implementation of the program is generally good. In one study, 19 of 21 treatment teachers implemented most of the program elements. A major exception in the Good and Grouws (1979) study was development, which was no more extensive in the treatment than in the control classes. Gains on standardized achievement tests were notable. In a few months, the treatment group increased from the 27th to the 58th percentile on national norms, and the teachers who had the highest implemtation scores produced the best results. Subsequent analyses indicated that main effects on achievement were complicated by interactions with teacher (four types) and student (four types) characteristics (Ebmeier & Good, 1979). That is, although students' achievement generally improved after the treatment, certain types of students in certain teachers' classrooms benefitted more than did other students.

First-Grade Reading Instruction.   Anderson, Evertson, and Brophy (1979) developed a set of guidelines, based on correlational research, for first-grade teachers to use during an experiment on small-group reading instruction. These

TABLE 2.3
Summary of Key Instructional Behaviors

Daily review (First 8 min except Mondays)

1. Review the concepts and skills associated with the homework
2. Collect and deal with homework assignments
3. Ask several mental computation exercises

Development (About 20 min)

1. Briefly focus on prerequisite skills and concepts
2. Focus on meaning and promoting student understanding by using lively explanations, demonstrations, process explanations, illustrations, and so on
3. Assess student comprehension using

   a. Process/product questions (active interaction)
   b. Controlled practice

4. Repeat and elaborate on the meaning portion as necessary

Seatwork (About 15 min)

1. Provide uninterrupted successful practice
2. Momentum--keep the ball rolling--get everyone involved, then sustain involvement
3. Alerting--let students know their work will be checked at the end of the period
4. Accountability--check the students' work

Homework assignment

1. Assign on a regular basis at the end of each math class except Friday's
2. Should involve about 15 min of work to be done at home
3. Should include one or two review problems

Special reviews

1. Weekly review/maintenance

   a. Conduct during the first 20 min each Monday
   b. Focus on skills and concepts covered during the previous week

2. Monthly review/maintenance

   a. Conduct every fourth Monday
   b. Focus on skills and concepts covered since last monthly review.

Source: Good and Grouws (1979). The Missouri mathematics effectiveness project: An experimental study in fourth-grade classrooms. Journal of Educational Psychology, 75, 821-829.

principles (revised to reflect the findings of the experiment) appear in Table 2.4. The revised model (Anderson, Evertson, & Brophy, 1982) is similar to that of Good and Grouws in that it includes time allocation guidelines and an emphasis on active instruction from the teacher followed by opportunities to practice and receive feedback. There are several important differences due to subject matter and grade level, however. First, first-grade reading is typically taught in small groups to facilitate individualized overt practice with feedback (as noted previously, early elementary students typically need such practice, and this is much

TABLE 2.4
Principles of Small-Group Instruction in Elementary Schools

General Principles

1. Reading groups should be organized for efficient, sustained focus on the content.

2. All students should be not merely attentive but actively involved in the lesson.

3. Questions and tasks should be easy enough to allow the lesson to move along at a brisk pace and the students to experience consistent success.

4. Students should receive frequent opportunities to read and respond to questions and should get clear feedback about the correctness of their performance.

5. Skills should be mastered to overlearning, with new ones gradually phased in while old ones are being mastered.

6. Although instruction takes place in the group setting, monitor each individual and provide whatever instruction, feedback, or opportunities to practice are necessary.

Specific Principles

Programming for continuous progress

1. Time. Across the year, reading groups should average 25-30 minutes each day. The length will depend on student attention level, which varies with time of year, student ability, and the skills being taught.

2. Academic focus. Successful reading instruction includes not only organization and management of the reading group itself (discussed below), but also effective management of students who are working independtly. Provide these students with: appropriate assignments; rules and routines to follow when they need help or information (to minimize their need to interrupt you as you work with your reading group); and activities when they finish their work.

3. Pace. Both progress through the curriculum and pacing within specific activities, should be brisk, producing continuous progress achieved with relative ease (small steps, high success rate).

4. Error rate. Expect to get correct answers to about 80% of your questions in reading groups. More errors can be expected when students are working on new skills (perhaps 20-30%). Continue with practice and review until smooth, rapid, correct performance is achieved. Review responses should be almost completely (perhaps 95%) correct.

Organizing the group

1. Seating. Arrange seating so that you can work with the reading group and monitor the rest of the class at the same time.

2. Transitions. Teach the students to respond immediately to a signal to move into the reading group (bringing their books or other materials) and to make quick, orderly transitions between activities.

3. Getting started. Start lessons quickly once the students are in the group (have your materials prepared beforehand).

Introducing lessons and activities

1. Overviews. When presenting a new word, do not merely say the word and move on. Usually, you should show the word and offer phonetic clues to help students learn to decode.

(continued...)

(Table 2.4 continued)

3. Work assignments. Be sure that students know what to do and how to do it. Before releasing them to work on activities independently, have them demonstrate how they will accomplish these activities.

Insuring everyone's participation

1. Ask questions. In addition to having the students read, ask them questions about the words and materials. This helps keep students attentive during classmates' reading turns and allows you to call their attention to key concepts or meanings.

2. Ordered turns. Use a system, such as going in order around the group, to select students for reading and answering questions. This insures that all students participate and simplifies group management by eliminating handwaving and other attempts by students to get you to call on them.

3. Minimize call-outs. In general, minimize student call-outs and emphasize that students must wait their turns and respect the turns of others. Occasionally, you may want to allow call-outs, to pick up the pace or encourage interest, especially with low achievers or students who do not normally volunteer. If so, give clear instructions or devise a signal to indicate that you intend to allow call-outs at these times.

4. Monitor individuals. Be sure that everyone, but especially slow students, is checked, receives feedback, and achieves mastery. Ordinarily this will require questioning each student and not relying on choral responses.

Teacher questions and student answers

1. Academic focus. Concentrate your questions on academic content; do not ask numerous questions about personal experiences. Most questions should be about word recognition or sentence or story comprehension.

2. Word-attack questions. Include word-attack questions that require students to decode words or identify sounds within words.

3. Wait for answers. In general, wait for an answer if the student is still thinking about the question and may be able to respond. However, do not continue waiting if the student seems lost or is embarrassed or if you are losing the other students' attention.

4. Give needed help. If you think the student cannot respond without help but may be able to reason out the correct answer if you do help, simplify the question, rephrase the question, or give clues.

5. Give the answer when necessary. When the student is unable to respond, give the answer or call on someone else. In general, focus the attention of the group on the answer and not on the failure to respond.

6. Explain the answer when necessary. If the question requires one to develop a response by applying a chain of reasoning or step-by-step problem solving, explain the steps necessary to arrive at the answer in addition to giving the answer.

When the student responds correctly

1. Acknowledge correctness (unless it is obvious). Briefly acknowledge the correctness of responses (nod positively, repeat the answer, say "right," etc.) unless it is obvious to the students that their answers are correct (such as during fast-paced drills reviewing old material).

(continued...)

(Table 2.4 continued)

2. Explain the answer when necessary. Even after correct answers, feed-back that emphasizes the methods used to get answers is often approp-riate. Onlookers may need this information to understand why the answer is correct.

3. Follow-up questions. Occasionally, you may want to address one or more follow-up questions to the same student. Such series of rela-ted questions can help the student to integrate relevant informa-tion. Or you may want to extend a line of questioning to its log-ical conclusion.

Praise and criticism

1. Praise in moderation. Praise only occasionally (no more than 10% of correct responses). Frequent praise, especially if nonspecific, is probably less useful than more informative feedback.

2. Specify what is praised. When you do praise, specify what is being praised if this is not obvious to the student and the onlookers.

3. Correction, not criticism. Routinely inform students whenever they respond incorrectly, but in ways that focus on the academic content and include corrective feedback. When it is necessary to criticize (typically only about 1% of the time when students fail to respond correctly), be specific about what is being criticized and about desired alternative behaviors.

Source: From Anderson, Evertson, and Brophy (1982). Principles of small-group in-struction in elementary reading. Occasional Paper No 58. East Lansing: Institute for Research on Teaching, Michigan State University.

easier to accomplish in small groups, even though this complicates classroom management).

Many of the principles in the Anderson et al. (1982) model deal with the organization and management of groups, not just with content instruction. This is because first graders are still learning student role behaviors that fourth graders have long since mastered, so that first-grade teachers have to be more concerned about maintaining students' attention and controlling the timing and nature of their contributions to the lesson. Another difference is that the principles in Table 2.4 focus on the teacher's interactions with individual students, even though the instruction takes place within a group context. In contrast, the principles in Table 2.3 more clearly exemplify a group (in this case, whole class) approach to instruction. Here, dealings with individuals are mostly minor variations on the main theme established by the group instruction rather than primary concerns.

In an experimental study, Anderson, Evertson, and Brophy (1979) found that the treatment was implemented unevenly. The best-implemented principles were those calling for frequent individualized opportunities for practice, minimal cho-ral responses, ordered turns, frequent sustaining feedback, and moderate use of praise. It is important that these well-implemented principles also correlated with student achievement. Other parts of the program were not as well implemented, including suggestions about beginning with an overview, giving clear explana-tions, or repeating new words. In general, the Anderson et al. (1979) data provide strong support for the notion of active teaching and proactive management. Specifcally, student achievement was greater in classrooms where more time was spent in reading groups, students received active instruction, and class-room management was more adequate (e.g., less time was spent dealing with misbehavior; transitions were shorter, etc.). Anderson, Evertson, and Brophy (1982) revised and reorganized their guidelines for first-grade reading-group instruction based on findings from their empirical research.

These examples illustrate that even basic skills instruction in the elementary grades must be adapted to the subject matter, the students, and other contextual factors. Thus, it is important to stress that research linking teacher behavior to student outcomes does not yield rules or simple answers to complex issues of teaching and learning (Good & Brophy, 1987; Shulman, 1986; Zumwalt, 1986). Although classroom research continues to develop support for instructional principles of varying generality, there appear to be no specific instructional behaviors that are ideal for all types of students and situations. Among other things, the amount of teaching and the degree to which students work independently or cooperatively will vary significantly with instructional intent. Variation in orga-nizational format and the role of the teacher is illustrated in the following example.

Cooperative Integrated Reading and Composition Program (CIRC). Mad-den, Slavin, Stevens and Farnish (1986) have developed the CIRC program for teaching students reading and writing skills. CIRC embodies some of the con-cepts of active teaching but calls for considerably more student self-learning and peer instruction. For example, in one aspect of their program—The Writer's Workshop —these authors recommend that each lesson have a definite structure. Each hour of instruction begins with a mini-lesson organized to provide structure and motivation for the Writer's Workshop. Following the mini-lesson, students are allowed to write for 30 to 40 minutes. During this time, students may have conferences with one another or with the teacher to receive feedback or help in resolving problems. The workshop ends with a 10-to 15-minute sharing and "celebration" time during which students read their writing to the entire class.

These mini-lessons are similar to the development stage discussed in the Missouri Mathematics Program. For example, Madden et al. (1986) recommend that teachers actively teach such topics as brainstorming for topics, conducting peer revision conferences, narrowing a topic, interviewing a peer, writing good leads, making transitions, eliminating run-ons, and various aspects of language usage and writing mechanics. Also consistent with the notion of active teaching, these researchers recommend that teachers show the practical value of informa-tion and actively model writing activities for students. Teachers are thus encour-aged to share their own writing with students and to provide them with various drafts of manuscripts showing how the teachers edit their own writing. Teachers are also encouraged to bring in examples of writing by published authors and to discuss various usages of writing (newspapers,etc.).

TABLE 2.5
Steps in the Completion of a Composition in the Writer's Workshop

---

Step 1: Topic Selection

Student may request interview with teammate.
Teacher-student conference available at the teacher's option.

Step 2: Prewriting

Student may request interview with teammate.
Teacher-student conference available at the teacher's option.

Step 3: Drafting

Student may request interview with teammate.
Teacher-student conference available at the teacher's option.

Step 4: Revising

After formal peer conferences have begun (about a month into the
    program), students meet with a teammate and complete a peer
    revision form.
Agreed-upon revisions are made.
Composition placed in teacher's box for review. (Student works on
    other writing until receiving teacher's response.)
Teacher-student conference held.
Appropriate revisions made and discussed with teacher.

Step 5: Editing

Student completes edit form. Necessary corrections are made.
Teammate completes edit form. Necessary corrections are made.
Composition placed in teacher's box for review. (Student works on
    other writing until receiving teacher's response.)
Teacher-student conference held. Lesson completed if needed.
Appropriate corrections made and reviewed by teacher.
Any additional mechanical or spelling errors corrected by teacher.

Step 6: Publication

Student writes final draft, incorporating any teacher-made
    corrections.
Cover attached.
Title, author's name, and date of publication written on cover.
Title, author's name, and date of publication placed on class
    publication list.
Publication placed on appropriate shelf.

Source: Madden, Slavin, and Stevens (1986). Cooperative integrated reading and
composition. (CIRC). Teacher's Manual. Baltimore: Center for the Social Organization of Schools, Johns Hopkins University.

In the CIRC program, students assume a much more active role in the learning process than they do in many direct instructional programs (Table 2.5 describes some of their responsibilities).

In general, experimental results examining the CIRC program show that it can have significant effects on student achievement; however, the effects are greater in certain areas than in others. For example, experimental students did better than control students on tests of reading comprehension, language expression, and language mechanics; however, there were no differences between control and experimental subjects in vocabulary. In the area of writing, experimental students did better than control students on a test of ideas, although there were no

differences between control and experimental students' organization and mechanics. The field experiments conducted by Stevens, Madden, Slavin and Farnish, (1987) indicate that when principles from research on classroom organization, active teaching, and motivation are used in a cooperative learning program,
student achievement in reading and writing can be increased.

As we emphasized previously, there is no single preferred way to organize a
lesson; however, we believe that active teaching, opportunity to practice, and
active student learning are important components of any lesson format. The
emphasis on any one component will undoubtedly vary with regard to the age of
the students and the instructional objectives pursued.

TEACHING THE LESSON: A MODEL

Our current framework or model for conceptualizing teaching a lesson is similar
in many respects to the models of Rosenshine and Stevens (1986) and Good,
Grouws, and Ebmeier (1983) because it incorporates the results of recent teacher
effects research. However, it differs in subtle but important ways because it also
builds on studies of *child development* and *student motivation*. The model in
Table 2.6 calls for meaningful presentation, assessment of student understanding, a decision about whether student learning is sufficiently complete to allow
meaningful practice or application, the opportunity for meaningful practice, and
the chance to integrate new knowledge with prior understandings.

MEANINGFUL PRESENTATION

Integrating Student and Curriculum Variables

Because we have already discussed issues involved in selecting subject matter
content, students' cognitive and motivational level, and related implications for
classroom practice, our comments here are brief. If teaching is to be successful,
it is critical that lesson content be matched to students' cognitive levels and that
appropriate motivational conditions be included in the lesson. Checklists are not
sufficient to gauge the effectiveness of a lesson. That is, it is not sufficient that
the teacher simply use imagery, examples, and models; it is essential that such
examples be *appropriate* for students. Examples that call for inferential thinking
on the part of the student may be irrelevant or inappropriate for students who are
still preoperational; however, the same example may facilitate learning for students who are capable of formal operational thought. It is also important that
lessons be conducted in classrooms that are supportive and that work be perceived by students as meaningful, for students need to have the disposition to do
appropriate work as well as the cognitive capacity.

TABLE 2.6
Presenting the Large-Group Lesson: Seven Tasks

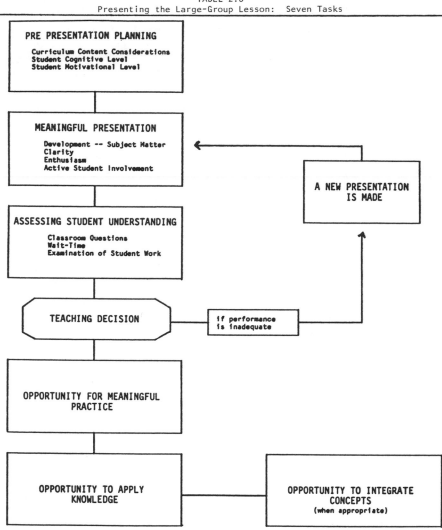

PRE PRESENTATION PLANNING

Curriculum Content Considerations
Student Cognitive Level
Student Motivational Level

MEANINGFUL PRESENTATION

Development -- Subject Matter
Clarity
Enthusiasm
Active Student Involvement

A NEW PRESENTATION
IS MADE

ASSESSING STUDENT UNDERSTANDING

Classroom Questions
Wait-Time
Examination of Student Work

TEACHING DECISION

If performance
is inadequate

OPPORTUNITY FOR MEANINGFUL
PRACTICE

OPPORTUNITY TO APPLY
KNOWLEDGE

OPPORTUNITY TO INTEGRATE
CONCEPTS
(when appropriate)

Development Portion of A Lesson

Subject-matter content must be presented in a *meaningful way* if students are to understand and to retain key concepts. Here we discuss the role of development in the Missouri Mathematics Program as an example of the need to consider subject-matter content as well as student variables. In the Missouri Mathematics Program, the aspect of the lesson that involves teacher presentation of new subject matter is called *development*. This part of the lesson is devoted to increasing comprehension of skills, concepts, and other facets of the mathematics curriculum (Good et al., 1983). For example, in teaching skills, instruction focusing on why an algorithm works, how certain skills are interrelated, what properties characterize a given skill, and means of estimating correct answers would be considered part of development. In teaching concepts, developmental activities would include initial instruction designed to help students distinguish certain concepts from others and associate labels with concepts. Attempts to extend ideas and to facilitate transfer of ideas, particularly to practical situations, are also part of development. Thus, in development, teachers facilitate the meaningful acquisition of an idea by learners.

During the development stage of the lesson, the teacher attempts to instruct students in ways that enable them to *understand* the concepts that they are working on rather than simply to memorize routines and procedures. Teachers who teach effective development lessons frequently demonstrate relationships between mathematical concepts. For example, a teacher might say: "5 × 2 = 10. Or, I could say this the long way; I could say 2 + 2 + 2 + 2 + 2, couldn't I? That's a long way. What's another way to arrange these?" By explaining that 5 × 2 is the same as 2 + 2 + 2 + 2 + 2, the teacher not only assesses students' prerequisite skills but also reminds students of the relationship between addition and multiplication. In the active teaching model, there is a continuing effort to illustrate what concepts are being studied and how those concepts relate to previously learned concepts.

It is sometimes assumed that active teaching means lecturing. Although there are times when teachers will provide information in a lecture format, the most important part of active teaching involves the teacher discussing material with students. Although the teacher may plan an active role in this discussion, students are encouraged to interpret information and to act on it. For example, consider the following situation in which students have paper clips on their desks and are trying to understand division with remainders. The teacher might say, "Picture in your mind what's going to happen if I try to sort them in groups of three. What's going to happen, Suzi?"

Through such questions and concrete activities, the teacher encourages students to visualize the various groups and remainders that are possible and to think about what division is. The students are likely to understand both the mechanics and the process of division because the teacher does a good job of using language and symbols as well as concretely representing the general concept of division with remainders. When teachers consider students' cognitive development and provide appropriate concepts and materials via clear and enthusiastic presentations, they allow students to think actively and to understand material.

In studies in elementary schools, Good and his colleagues found that many teachers do not regularly include much development in their mathematics lessons. This is unfortunate, because development is one means by which students understand mathematical ideas and their practical applications. In their current work, these researchers emphasize the role of development in a successful mathematics program. Part of the focus is on communicating criteria for evaluating development so that teachers can think more systematically about instruction (see Table 2.7 for a description of these criteria). Teachers are given the opportunity to discuss the criteria for development by applying them to videotapes of mathematics teaching and by writing original development lessons and exchanging those lessons with other teachers. Hence, teachers gain experience in building a theory of teaching—a set of beliefs and practices—that they can use to help students understand mathematics (Good & Grouws, 1987).

The research by Good, Grouws, and Ebmeier (1983) suggests that although the cycle of presentation followed by teacher-directed practice followed by individual seatwork is usually found in elementary mathematics lessons, the *quality* of that cycle varies widely. That is, some teachers place a premium on understanding, whereas others offer primarily practice with little attention to understanding. Thus, programs of instruction that seem the same superficially may have different underlying structures and varied effects. In this sense, the Missouri Mathematics Program has yielded a model that focuses on the quality of active teaching rather than merely on its form. Again, the emphasis on development in the Missouri Mathematics Program has been discussed to illustrate the need to think about how particular subject-specific content can best be taught meaningfully.

We have discussed the need to (a) match lesson content to students' cognitive levels, (b) provide appropriate motivation, and (c) present subject-matter meaningfully. We now discuss two teacher style variables that are associated with good presentations—clarity and enthusiasm.

Clarity

Clear teacher presentations are essential if students are to understand concepts and assignments. Does the teacher communicate the objectives of the lesson clearly? Do lessons begin with introductions and end with summaries, have organization that provides structure and highlights main points, and otherwise provide sufficient clarity to enable students to follow them without confusion?

McCaleb and White (1980) identify five aspects of clarity that seem to be important when analyzing the quality of teachers' presentations during group lessons:

1. *Understanding.* This is a prerequisite to clarity and involves matching the information to be learned to the learners' present knowledge. Does the teacher:
   a. Determine students' familiarity with the information presented?
   b. Use terms that are unambiguous and within the students' experience?
   c. Clarify and explain terms that are potentially confusing?

TABLE 2.7
Criteria for the Development Lesson

Attending to prerequisites. In mathematics an understanding of most new
concepts and processes is bason upon previously learned ideas and skills,
although the prerequisite ideas/skills vary depending on what is to be
learned. For example, a pupil would be unlikely to understand the notion
of a prime number without some knowledge of factors. Similarly, profic-
iency in using the traditional long division algorithm is not possible
without subtraction skills.

Attending to relationships. Mathematics is composed of a large body of logically consistent, closely related ideas. To teach it as a collection of
isolated facts to be memorized (as is often done) is a disservice to the
learner and to the discipline. Relationships among mathematical ideas
are numerous and the development portion of the lesson provides the teacher
with an opportunity to emphasize the meaning and interpretation of mathematical ideas. Some mathematical relationships are simple, such as the
doing-undoing relationship between addition and subtraction, or the relationship between angle measure and side length of a triangle. Other relationships are more complex: Is the product of two numbers greater than
their sum? Is there always a "next" fraction as there is with whole numbers? As part of development the teacher must bring into focus the inter-
relatedness of mathematical ideas.

Attending to representation. Mathematical formulas, theorems, processes,
and indeed, most of the mathematics, are a step removed from the physical
world. This level of generality of mathematics contributes to its power,
because any single mathematical idea or process can accurately represent
a great variety of real-world phenomena. For example, a fraction like
1/4 can convey important information on an advertisement, recipe card,
gauge, sales brochure, timesheet, and so on. The abstract nature of mathematics, which enables it to serve as a model for widely diverse physical
phenomena, may also create substantial impediments to learning. This is
especially true if the teacher presents the mathematical concept in its
abstract form without giving examples of its concrete representation. When
development is done well, students are frequently exposed to a variety of
representations of the mathematical ideas being learned.

Generality of concepts. Teachers often do not fully explain the general
applicability of a mathematical idea or process to students, even within
the limits of the students' ability. For example, teachers can explain
that the method used to find the sum of the angles of a quadrilateral
(divide it into triangles) works equally well for finding the sum of the
angles of any polygon. Similarly, the term vertex applies to all poly-
gons and not just to triangles, as it is sometimes introduced. Clearly,
only a few of the applications of a mathematical idea should be introduced in the initial discussion of the idea, with additional applications
considered as the idea is developed and reviewed. Ideally, over time, a
concept or skill should be developed in as general a setting as possible
rather than artificially confined to a narrow set of conditions.

Attending to language. Teachers should use precise terminology when talking
about mathematical ideas. Terms like divisor, numerator, and factor
should be used frequently so that students begin to understand and appreciate the language of mathematics. Confusing terminology or inconsistency
in expression makes it difficult for students to learn mathematical ideas.
The terms that are routinely used by mathematicians should be used in the
classroom so that students learn to discuss mathematical ideas in a practical way.

Note: We identify five components that we believe to be important parts of development.
It should be understood that not all components of development will necessarily occur in
any particular lesson...likewise, the existence of one component does not guarantee that
development is taking place. However, the above criteria provide a useful way of thinking
about the role of development in students' mathematical learning. Material adapted from
Good, Grows, and Ebmeire (1983). New York: Longman.

2. *Structuring*. This involves organizing material to promote a clear presentation: stating the purpose, reviewing main ideas, and providing transitions between sections. Does the teacher:
   a. Establish the purpose of the lesson?
   b. Preview the organization of the lesson?
   c. Include internal summaries and a final review?

3. *Sequencing*. This involves arranging information in an order conductive to learning, typically by gradually increasing the difficulty or complexity of material. Does the teacher order the lesson in a logical way, appropriate to the content and the learners?

4. *Explaining*. This refers to explaining principles and relating them to facts through examples, illustrations, or analogies. Does the teacher:
   a. Define major concepts?
   b. Give examples to illustrate these concepts?
   c. Use examples that are accurate and concrete as well as abstract?

5. *Presenting*. This refers to volume, pacing, articulation, and other speech mechanics. Does the teacher:
   a. Articulate words clearly and project speech loudly enough?
   b. Pace the various sections of the presentation at rates conducive to understanding?
   c. Support the verbal content with appropriate nonverbal communication and visual aids?

Others have written more extensively about some of the aspects of clarity identified by McCaleb and White. For example, Ausubel's (1963) concept of advance organizers is useful in thinking about how to structure presentations. Advance organizers, previews, or statements concerning instructional objectives help to characterize the nature of a learning task for students before instruction begins. For example, as a preview to a lesson describing 20 penalties that can occur during hockey games, a physical education instructor could say: "Today, we are going to discuss penalties that might be called during hockey games. We will discuss the differences between minor and major penalties and describe 15 minor penalties and five major penalties. At the end of the period, I will show you 20 slides and ask you to name the penalty each illustrates and state whether it is major or minor."

Advance organizers give students a structure to which they can relate the specifics that they will hear or read about. Students can expand this structure as they identify relevant concepts and information. Without such a structure, the material may seem fragmented, much like listening to a random list of unrelated sentences. A clear explanation of the nature of the assignment helps students to focus on the main ideas because students are more likely to find what they need if they know what to look for. Thus, students can be more selective and better organized as they attend to teacher presentations.

The advance organizer provides an abstract structure of the knowledge that is to be gained in a particular unit. For example, Berliner (1987) provides the following example of an advance organizer for teaching a unit on ecology to fifth graders. After defining ecology, he suggests the appropriateness of saying something like the following, "We are going to study ecosystems, systems of relationships. Keep in mind what you have heard about acid rain, because acid rain is a good example of how some factor far away can influence what goes on close to home. We will look at systems in balance and systems disturbed by factors like acid rain. We will look at cycles like the rain cycle and chains of interrelated events like the food chain. We will talk of change in nature, how slow it is to get things back to balance once they are disturbed, how cycles and chains, once broken, are hard to repair. And in our discussions of balance, harmony, change cycles, chains, and disturbances, we will talk about people—modern, urban, industrial, factory-working, car-driving people—and their contributions to balanced systems and disturbed systems " (pp. 285-286).

Teachers should tell students what they will be expected to learn from a lecture and why it is important for them to know this information. After the information is presented, teachers should summarize the main points in a few simple sentences. Providing a clear introduction and summary takes little planning and presentation time but can make a big difference in the degree to which students remember essential facts and concepts (Luiten, Ames, & Ackerson, 1970; Schuck, 1981).

For extended presentations, periodic internal summaries of subparts may be needed in addition to a major summary at the end. Rosenshine (1968) discusses the value of internal summaries, particularly the rule-example-rule approach, in which a summary statement is given both before and after a series of examples. He also stresses the importance of explaining links—prepositions or conjunctions—that indicate when the teacher is giving the cause, means, or purpose of an event or an idea. Words and phrases such as *because, in order to, if, then, therefore,* and *consequently* make explicit the causal linkages of phrases or sentences in ways that might not be clear without such language. For example, consider the following sentences:

1. Chicago became the major city of the midwest and the hub of the nation's railroad transportation system.
2. Because of its central location, Chicago became the hub of the nation's railroad transportation system.

The first example presents the relevant facts but does not make explicit the linkage between them, as the second example does. If asked, "Why did Chicago become the hub of the transportation system?'', most students taught with the second example would respond, ''Because of its central location,'' but many students taught with the first example would respond, ''Because it is a big city,'' or in some other way that would indicate failure to appreciate the linkage between a city's geographical location and its role in a nation's transportation system.

In addition to these organization factors, presentations or questions can lack clarity because of vague or confusing language. Smith and Land (1981) review several studies indicating that the effectiveness of presentations is reduced by the presence of ''vagueness terms'' and ''mazes.'' They provide a brief example indicating how vagueness terms can distract from the intended content of a message. The vagueness terms are italicized:

> This mathematics lesson *might* enable you to understand a *little* more about some things we *usually* call number patterns. *Maybe* before we get to *probably* the main idea of the lesson, you should review *a few* prerequisite concepts. *Actually,* the first concept you need to review is positive integers. *As you know,* a positive integer is any whole number greater than zero. (p. 38)

Mazes refer to false starts or halts during speech, redundantly spoken words, or tangles of words. The mazes are italicized in the following example:

> The mathematics lesson will *enab* . . . will get you to understand *number, ah* patterns. Before we get to the *main idea of the,* main idea of the lesson, you need to review *four conc* . . . four prerequisite concepts. A positive *number* . . . integer is any whole *integer, ah,* number greater than zero. (p. 38)

Enthusiasm

When teachers are enthusiastic about their subject matter, students are likely to pay attention and develop enthusiasm on their own. Ultimately, students are also more likely to achieve at higher levels (Rosenshine & Furst, 1973). In particular, young people develop interest through modeling others, including teachers. If teachers appear to enjoy knowledge in general and specific subject matter in particular, students are more likely to develop similar interests. In fact, students and observers are prone to overvalue enthusiasm and to rate enthusiastic instructors highly even when their presentations lack substance or clarity (McCaleb & White, 1980). Our argument is that lessons need to have both enthusiasm and substance.

Enthusiasm is a general teacher characteristic that is difficult to describe in specific terms. However, qualities such as alertness, vigor, interest, movement, and voice inflection are important. Enthusiastic teachers are alive; they show surprise, suspense, joy, and other feelings in their voices; and they make material interesting to students by relating it to students' experiences and showing that they themselves are interested in it.

There are at least two major aspects of enthusiasm. The first is conveying sincere interest in a subject. This involves modeling, and even shy teachers should be able to demonstrate interest. The other aspect is vigor, or dynamics. Teachers who lack a dynamic voice and manner can compensate with other techniques. For example, three days in advance, the teacher can announce that, "On Thursday, we will role-play the Scopes Trial." This can be followed with information that builds interest and suspense. During the intervening days, this will help to provide motivation for activities planned as preparation for the "big event." The teacher can ask students to imagine themselves in the places of historical persons: "Put yourself in the place of William Jennings Bryan and analyze the feelings, values, and attitudes of people in that small Tennessee town. What arguments would you advance? What types of witnesses (pastors, medical experts, whomever) would you use?" Seatwork and homework assignments could also be related to the project: "Tomorrow we will select jurors for the trial. Before doing this, we need to find out the basis on which the prosecutor and defense attorneys can reject witnesses . . ."

Of course, teachers must be enthusiastic about everyday topics and lessons as well, not just those related to special events. This is done by continually modeling enthusiasm in the very process of teaching: calling attention to new information or skills, presenting tasks as positive challenges rather than unwelcome chores, challenging students to test themselves when they try to solve problems or apply new skills, and personalizing information by showing how it relates to students' everyday lives and interests.

ASSESSING STUDENT UNDERSTANDING: TEACHER QUESTIONING

Our major intent in this chapter has been to convey information about the presentation part of teaching lessons. However, we want to make a few comments about assessing student understanding, because teachers sometimes overlook this critical part of a lesson. Instruction—even "good" instruction—does not always lead to student understanding. No matter how competent or well prepared a teacher is, or how well content is delivered, it is always possible that at least some students will misunderstand. Effective teachers recognize this and work hard to build up communication systems that allow them to determine whether students have mastered material. There are many ways to assess student learning after lessons are completed (homework, tests, etc.), and Rosenshine and Stevens (1986) have summarized various ways teachers can assess student performance during lessons. Here we discuss the role of questions in order to illustrate the importance of checking for student understanding.

Teacher questioning contributes to the effectiveness of lessons by providing information about student comprehension and by stimulating students to respond actively to the content by putting it in their own words; practicing it; or analyzing, synthesizing, or evaluating it. Process-outcome research indicates that the frequency of academic questions teachers ask is correlated with students' achievement gains (Brophy & Good, 1986). There are at least two reasons for this. First, teachers who have high rates of academic questions usually have well-organized and well-managed classes and spend most of their time actively teaching students during academic activities. Conversely, teachers with low rates of academic questions often either are poorly organized or choose to spend considerable time pursuing nonacademic goals. Thus, among other things, high frequencies of academic questions indicate that a class is spending most of its time in learning-related activities. A second reason for the relationship with achievement gain is that teachers who ask academic questions frequently supplement lectures, demonstrations, reading, and seatwork activities with recitations, discussions, and other opportunities for students to express themselves orally. These not only add variety buy also appear to be valuable strategies for accomplishing instructional objectives, especially higher-level cognitive objectives.

Sources of advice to teachers frequently claim that divergent questions are categorically better than convergent questions, high- level or complex questions better than low-level or simple questions, and thought questions better than fact questions. Research linking the number and percentages of the questions that teachers ask at varying cognitive levels to student achievement gains does not support these categorical claims. The results are mixed, with some studies revealing a positive relationship between the number or percentage of high-level questions and student achievement gain, some indicating a negative relationship, and most indicating no significant relationship at all (Brophy & Good, 1986).

Logical considerations suggest that such mixed findings should not be surprising, because we should expect different forms of questioning to be appropriate in various instructional situations, depending on such factors as grade level, subject matter, and (especially) instructional objectives. For example, teachers might ask questions to see if students are ready for an impending discussion, to arouse their interest, or to stimulate critical thinking. A good question for arousing interest might not be a good question for assessing learning. Similarly, if teachers wish to stimulate students to suggest possible applications of an idea, then sequences that begin with higher-level questions and proceed through lower-level follow-up questions would be appropriate. However, if teachers wish to call students' attention to relevant facts and then stimulate them to integrate these facts and draw conclusions, a series of lower-level questions followed by higher-level questions would be called for. With these important considerations in mind, we will discuss some characteristics of good questions. More detailed information about questioning strategies can be found in Good and Brophy (1986, 1987) and Groisser (1964).

Characteristics of Good Questioning

Clarity. Groisser (1964) contends that questions should precisely describe the specific points or issues to which students are to respond. Vague questions can be responded to in many ways (too many), and their ambiguous nature confuses students. Vague questions often result in wasted time as students ask the teacher to clarify or rephrase. The usefulness of clear and highly focused questions has been shown in some experimental situations (Rosenshine, 1968; Wright & Nuthall, 1970). Although questions should alert students about how they should respond, this does not mean that the teacher cues the answer; it means only that the teacher communicates the specific question to which the student is asked to respond.

Purpose. Purposeful questions help achieve the lesson's intent. Question series that are not planned in advance are seldom purposeful (this is why it is useful to write out questions that will be asked during class discussion). Teachers who improvise most of their questions will ask many irrelevant and confusing questions that work against achievement of their own goals.

Thought Provoking. Good questions are thought provoking. Especially in discussions, questions should arouse strong, thoughtful responses from students, such as "I never thought about that before", or "I want to find the answer to that question." Discussion questions should force students to think about facts and to integrate and apply them. Such questions should help students to clarify their ideas and to analyze or synthesize facts in addition to listing them.

Factual Questions. Factual questions often are needed to see if students possess information basic to the discussion or to bring out relevant facts before posing higher-level questions. Other questions should require students to use the information rather than just recite it and should motivate them to respond. This is especially true as students move into the upper elementary and secondary grades.

Question Sequences. If questions are intended to facilitate learning, and not merely to function as oral test items, they should be asked in carefully planned *sequences* in which teachers integrate each answer (or ask students to integrate each answer) with the previous discussion before moving to the next question. Initial questions should lead students to identify or review essential facts. These questions can be followed with ones that ask students to refine their understanding of the information and apply the knowledge to real or hypothetical problems. Planning will help insure an orderly progression through the sequence of objectives. Of course, it is not necessary that teachers adhere rigidly to a prepared sequence of questions. Other worthwhile topics may be opened up by pupil questions, and these should be pursued.

We believe that logical thinking about sequences of questions indicates that emphasis only on the cognitive level of questions is misplaced. At a certain point in a class discussion, factual questions are important. At other times, questions of value are essential and factual questions are inappropriate. Although there are few empirical data on this point, researchers who wish to understand and improve instruction should attempt to study the interconnectedness of questions— the extent to which *sequences* of questions lead to meaningful understanding on the part of students.

Wait-time.   Good questioning allows students sufficient time to think about and respond to questions. Rowe (1974a, 1974b) reported data that at the time seemed remarkable: after asking questions, the teachers she observed waited less than one second before calling on someone to respond. Furthermore, even after calling on a student, they waited only about a second for the student to give the answer before supplying it themselves, calling on someone else, or rephrasing the question or giving clues. Such findings suggest that teachers minimized the value of their questions by failing to give students time to think.

Rowe followed up these observations by training teachers to extend their wait-times from less than one second to three to five seconds. Surprisingly, most of the teachers found this difficult to do, and some never did succeed. However, in the classrooms of teachers who extended their wait-times to three to five seconds, the following desirable changes occurred: (a) increase in the average length of student responses; (b) increase in unsolicited but appropriate student responses; (c) decrease in failures to respond; (d) increase in speculative responses; (e) increase in student-to-student comparisons of data; (f) increase in statements that involve drawing inferences from evidence; (g) increase in student-initiated questions; and (h) a greater variety of verbal contributions to lessons by students.

Subsequent research (reviewed in Tobin, 1983a, 1983b) replicates these findings. In particular, this research verifies that increasing wait-time leads to longer and higher-quality student responses to teacher questions and to participation by a greater number of students. These effects are most notable on the less able students in a class.

Subsequent research has shown that teachers can wait too long as well as too short a time and that wait-time has to be adjusted to the cognitive demands of the question. Interactions featuring mostly lower-level questions should move at a quicker pace with shorter wait-times compared to interactions featuring higher-level questions, because pace and wait-time should depend on the objectives of an activity (Good & Brophy, 1987). Thus, a fast pace and short wait-times are appropriate for drill or review covering specific facts. However, if questions are intended to stimulate students to think about material and formulate original responses rather than merely to repeat information from memory, it is important to allow time for these effects to occur. When a slow pace and thoughtful responding are desired, teachers should not only adjust their wait-times but make objectives clear to students. Unless cued, some students may not realize that they are supposed to formulate an original response rather than search their memories for facts, and some may think that the teacher is looking for speed rather than the quality of response. This is another instance where clarity of teacher intentions may help students to be more active learners.

Question A Range of Students.   Students will learn more if they are actively involved in group-based lessons than if they sit passively day after day without participating. We all know reticent students who rarely participate in discussions but still get excellent grades, but most students benefit from opportunities to practice oral communication skills, and distributing response opportunities helps keep students attentive and accountable. Also, teachers who restrict their questions primarily to a small group of active (and usually high-achieving) students are likely to communicate undesirable expectations to the other students (Good & Brophy, 1987) and generally to be less aware and less effective teachers.

Feedback About Responses

Students should receive information about the correctness or incorrectness of their responses. This is especially important for low achievers. In general, evaluation is important both to motivate students and to produce learning. Feedback lets students know how they are doing or how much progress they have made.

Unless it is understood that no response indicates correctness, teachers should give some sort of response every time students answer questions. Evaluation need not be long or elaborate, although sometimes it will have to be. Often a head nod or a short comment like ''right'' is all that is needed to tell students that they are on the right track. Also, teachers do not always have to provide feedback personally. They can give students answer sheets so that they can assess their own work or allow students to check one another's responses. As simple as this advice is, it is often violated in classroom practice and unfortunately, it is often the low-achieving students who do not receive comments about the adequacy of their responses (Brophy & Good, 1974).

Demanding Student Performance

There is clear evidence that some teachers are likely to stay with students who have difficulty answering questions and to try to elicit improved responses (by repeating the question, asking a new question, calling for clarification, etc.). Other teachers are much more likely to give up (by providing the answer or calling on another student), especially when interacting with low-achieving students. The behavior of the latter teachers is unfortunate but understandable; when teachers are trying to maintain momentum and to involve all students in class discussions it can be difficult to take the time to interact at length with the original respondent. Teachers need to balance the needs of individual students with those of the class as a whole.

Much more research needs to be completed in this area to clarify how teachers can respond to individuals in a group setting. We believe that it is generally a good idea for teachers to sustain their interactions with low-achieving students. Because teachers typically ask questions to stimulate students' thinking and ability to present evidence and to share information in public settings, it makes sense to stay with and to elicit additional information from students when they give incorrect answers (Brophy & Good, 1986). Following student failure, teachers should indicate that the answer was incorrect and attempt to elicit an improved response by rephrasing the question or giving clues. Such attempts are likely to be successful when teachers have the time to listen and to work with students.

However, the same caveats noted earlier concerning wait-time apply here as well. That is, teachers can probably sustain too often as well as too infrequently, and sustaining has to be adjusted to the cognitive demands of a task. In general, if teachers are looking for a specific, factual answer and the student does not know the answer, it makes little sense to keep probing for it. However, if higher-order thinking (e.g., inference) is called for, it seems especially important to wait for low-achieving students to formulate an answer and to provide multiple opportunities for students to respond. Frequency of being called on is probably less important than the quality of interaction (when called on) for students with limited academic skills and low self-confidence. It is important to build up in these students the expectation that they can and will perform and that they must think about the *content* of an academic task rather than how to avoid it.

The general background and ability of a class can be used as a tentative way of thinking about appropriate instruction. For example, Brophy and Evertson (1976) report that in high-SES classes, it was important for teachers to be sure that more assertive students did not dominate lessons (e.g., by calling out answers) so that hesitant students had the opportunity to respond. However, they report that it was generally not useful for teachers to sustain interactions when these high-SES students could not answer the original question. Considering that most questions were factual and that most of the student were happy to respond if they could, probing in these circumstances would have amounted to a waste of time.

In contrast, probing for improved responses was effective in low-SES classes. Brophy and Evertson hypothesized that many students in these classrooms were anxious or lacked confidence even when they knew the answers. Hence, it was important for teachers to work for any kind of response from incommunicative students and to try to improve the responses of students who spoke up but gave incorrect or incomplete answers. In these situations, giving clues (particularly phonics clues in reading) or rephrasing the question to make it easier were more successful strategies than waiting silently or merely repeating the original question. Thus, in low-SES classrooms it was important for teachers to encourage students to respond and to think about the actual academic content being presented.

Similar distinctions have been noted by other investigators as well. For example, Larrivee and Algina (1983) found that teachers' attempts to improve the incorrect responses of mainstreamed pupils resulted in greater student involvement in assigned learning tasks.

Moving on to Follow-Up Activities

As noted previously, teachers might ask questions for a variety of instructional purposes in addition to assessing student understanding; however, most lessons involve some presentation of new content to students, followed by questioning to assess the students' understanding. In these lessons, teachers will need to use the quality of the students' responses to questions as the basis for deciding whether or not they have mastered the new content. If they have, the teacher can then move on to follow-up activities that provide the students with opportunities to practice, apply, or integrate what they have been learning. If students' responses to the teacher's questions have not been satisfactory, the teacher will need to revert to a presentation mode, preferably by making a new or more elaborated presentation of the content rather than merely by repeating essentially the same presentation made earlier. Considering that students did not adequately understand this presentation the first time it was made, it appears that more or better examples are needed, that the presentation needs to be subdivided and elaborated more thoroughly, or that some other adjustments must be made to increase its clarity and comprehensibility.

It is important that teachers' decisions about whether or not to move on to follow-up activities be informed by valid and comprehensive information about students' understanding of content. This implies asking students open-ended questions that call for them to supply facts from memory or (better yet) formulate more substantive and lengthy responses in their own words. Students' success in answering such open-ended questions provides a basis for teacher confidence that the students understand the content, whereas correct answers to questions that merely require students to answer yes or no or to choose between two provided alternatives are highly susceptible to guessing and thus provide less reliable evidence of understanding. In addition to asking questions that call for substantive responses, teachers should call on nonvolunteers as well as volunteers, and in particular, should be sure to call on several of the lower achievers in the group (those who are most likely to be confused or to misunderstand). If teachers only call on volunteers to assess student understanding, and especially if these volunteers are primarily high achievers, the assessment will be invalid because it will be based on an unrepresentative sample that makes students' understanding appear to be much greater than it actually is.

Assessing Long-Term Student Goals

The emphasis in this section has been on the need to assess students' progress on immediate lesson goals. It is also important for teachers to use some instructional strategies that help students improve their learning-how-to-learn skills and to assess the extent to which students think and show self-reliance. Although most assessment of student comprehension should focus on immediate lesson objectives, it is essential that teachers also assess long-term academic goals. Teachers who carefully plan assessment can assess immediate learning in a way that facilitates the more general and long-term ability of students to make decisions successfully about their own learning and to evaluate their performance.

Active Student Learning

We have pointed out that successful teachers are active in the classroom, providing appropriate motivation, instruction, and resources to students. However, students must also be active learners, learning not only how to respond successfully to the challenges and questions teachers raise, but also to raise their own questions and to use teachers and other resources as they pursue self-defined goals. Thus, teachers need to help students acquire skills for independent learning and practice those skills in problem-solving and critical-thinking exercises. Weinstein and Mayer (1986) identify five general types of learning strategies that teachers should help students to acquire. Here, we emphasize strategies that can take place during *group-based lessons*. Periodically, during normal lessons, teachers should assess the extent to which students use and benefit from these strategies.

1. *Rehearsal strategies* involve repeating material either by saying or writing it or by focusing attention on key parts of it. For example, in attempting to learn information presented in a text, rehearsal might involve repeating key terms aloud, copying the material, or underlining important parts.

2. *Elaboration strategies* include making connections between the new material and more familiar material. Hence, following a teacher presentation, students might want to paraphrase, summarize, create analogies, and attempt to describe how new information relates to existing knowledge. Teachers who give students outlines of their presentations may facilitate students' use of elaboration strategies by providing them with the opportunity to take notes that go beyond verbatim repetition, to have time to write their own questions in the margin, etc.

3. *Organizational strategies* require students to impose structure on material that has been presented by subdividing it into parts and identifying superordinate/subordinate relationships. Students should be encouraged to create diagrams or show relationships among concepts. For example, in a social studies class the teacher might present information initially along historical timelines.

Students then might be encouraged to reorganize the material in terms of common problems or key concepts.

4. *Comprehension-monitoring strategies* include remaining aware of what one is trying to accomplish during a learning task, keeping track of the strategies one uses and the degree of success achieved with them, and adjusting behavior accordingly. One of the reasons that we believe that teachers need to be clear in their presentations is that clarity enables students to develop criteria for monitoring their own learning. Students who are uncertain about what they are trying to accomplish will have difficultly being active learners. Comprehension-monitoring strategies include noting and taking action when one does not understand something, self-questioning to check understanding, and modifying strategies if necessary. Hence, during group lessons teachers should encourage students to raise questions about material and also ask students how they can be certain that they understood a presentation. Although it is important for the teacher to check for comprehension, students should be directly involved in this process. Teachers who regularly ask students questions such as, "How can be we sure that we understand the material?" and "What new questions will we want to raise?" help students to be active learners.

5. *Affective strategies* involve eliminating undesirable affect when preparing to learn. They include establishing and maintaining motivation, focusing attention, maintaining concentration, managing performance anxiety, and managing time effectively. These strategies can be developed in students by teachers who model these important traits and who systematically encourage students to develop capacities for managing their own time. Students should understand that they can make important decisions about listening, taking notes during lectures, and about using their time productively during seatwork.

Thus, we believe it to be important that teachers not only assess students' understanding of lesson content but also monitor students' progress on long-term issues associated with self-regulated learning. The ways in which teachers attempt to monitor student progress in the short run can also help students achieve other important developmental goals. Corno and Rohrkemper (1985) in particular stress the need for teachers to teach students specific strategies for becoming autonomous learners who can regulate and evaluate their own learning.

SUMMARY AND CONCLUSIONS

Building on research in child development, student motivation, and (especially) linkages between teacher behavior and student achievement gain, we have developed a model (Table 2.6) of group lessons featuring active instruction by teachers. The model includes seven elements, of which two are discussed in detail here: (a) selecting content and organizing its presentation to maximize understanding and active learning by students; and (b) using strategies for questioning students that support instructional goals and yield valid information about the nature and level of students' understanding of content.

The model applies primarily to aspects of instruction that focus on lower-level knowledge and skills. This is not as stringent a limitation as it might appear, because most instruction is directed to such objectives. Specifically, the model would apply to any instruction in any body of knowledge or set of skills that has been sufficiently well articulated so that: (a) it can be presented systematically, and then (b) practiced or applied during activities that call for student performance that, (c) can be evaluated, and (d) can be given corrective feedback (if the performance is incorrect or imperfect). This includes not only basic knowledge and skills in any subject matter but also certain higher-level activities such as reading comprehension and study skills, mathematics problem solving, and scientific experimentation. Thus, if we take into account both the knowledge and skills that are taught because they are considered to be important in their own right and the knowledge and skills that are taught because they are prerequisites to accomplishment of high-level objectives, we can say that the model applies to most of what is taught in school.

On the other hand, the model (at least the content presentation and checking for understanding aspects described here) would not apply to teacher behavior during activities designed primarily to create a process rather than a product (debate, discovery, discussion, role play, simulation, etc.) or during activities that call for students to discover or invent their own responses rather than to follow a prescribed process to reach a predetermined outcome (interpretation of poetry or other literature, creative writing, artistic expression, etc.). To date, not much scientific information is available on effective strategies for accomplishing such higher-level cognitive outcomes with students. It seems obvious, however, that such objectives will not be achieved if all classroom time is allocated to activities with lower-level objectives. Thus, in addition to actively instructing students by presenting information, demonstrating skills, conducting recitations, and supervising practice on assignments designed to develop mastery of basic knowledge and skills, teachers will also need to schedule debates, discussions, simulation activities, book reviews, research projects, creative writing assignments, problem-solving activities, or assignments calling for development or construction of products; or provide other opportunities for students to apply, analyze, synthesize, or evaluate what they have learned.

Our discussion of the model might be slightly misleading in that it focuses on content rather than skills and speaks of assessing student understanding primarily with reference to oral questioning/recitation. Thus, we wish to emphasize that we used these terms for clarity and economy of presentation and did not intend to restrict the model to content (knowledge) instruction. The model also applies to skills instruction, and it is understood that presentations during such lessons involve skill demonstration in addition to verbal explanation. Also, checking for understanding might involve boardwork, behavioral performance, or leading the class in working through worksheets or assignments, in addition to questions calling for oral responses.

Another way that the model could be somewhat misleading is through its suggestion that lesson implementation is a linear process that always begins with content presentation, then moves to assessment of student understanding, and so on. This is not always the case in practice, where many variations occur that violate the linear sequence implied in this model. Teachers will sometimes use higher-level analysis or evaluation questions as a way to introduce new content, for example, or even will begin with an application activity that assumes prior mastery of the content to be taught (as a way to assess existing knowledge, give the students a preview of how the knowledge will be used, and help make them aware of what they do not know and thus more able to appreciate the value of the knowledge when they learn it). Instruction will often include previews in the form of advance organizers or statemtnts of learning goals that help students to prepare for meaningful learning activities.

A nonlinear form of lesson presentation frequently seen in elementary and junior high school classes is interactive teaching, in which the teacher works through the content with the students in ways that involve rapid movement back and forth between content presentation and questioning. For example, the teacher may read a paragraph in a social studies text (or have a student read it), ask questions designed to ensure that students grasp the main ideas, and then provide students with opportunities to paraphrase the material in their own words. In the process of asking these questions and providing feedback to the students' answers, however, teachers do not merely repeat what was in the paragraph but elaborate on it by providing additional examples, connecting it to current events or to material studied earlier in the course, providing more detail about something described only sketchily in the text, and so on. Similar combinations of presentation, questioning, and elaboration on content occur during boardwork in mathematics, during reading of stories from basal readers, and when teachers are leading their classes in working through content in science and social studies.

The general principles articulated in the model probably apply just as much to these hybrid lesson forms as they do to the more linear form outlined in Table 2.6, but there is reason to believe that these mixed forms embody additional principles that are important for optimizing instruction in particular subject matter and for certain types of students. Thus, although the model and its associated principles are useful as far as they go, a great deal of additional conceptualization and research are needed to identify key aspects of the different forms that lessons take at various grade levels and in different subject-matter areas, and to develop better understanding of why particular forms are optimal in certain teaching situations. Thus, in addition to progressing from a focus on global aspects of teaching toward a focus on more specific issues involved in teaching particular subject matter to particular types of students, research on teacher effects will need to identify the similarities and differences between effective teaching in various contexts. Eventually, such research should yield not only more specific guidelines for instruction, but more powerful models and associated explanatory theories describing classroom teaching. We need not just one model, but several that depict effective teaching in common instructional situations (and their variations).

For now, however, the present model is useful as a heuristic for conceptualizing and planning lessons and as a reminder that effective instruction includes attention not only to clarity and organization of subject matter presentations, but also to the need to match content to students' cognitive development and to stimulate students to process information actively (by teaching them to use relevant cognitive strategies and to display metacognitive awareness and self-regulation of learning efforts as they do so). In summary, an effective lesson does not merely present content to students but helps them to learn it systematically, so that the result is not mere rote memorization but meaningful and self-regulated learning.

ACKNOWLEDGMENT

We acknowledge logistical support provided by the Center for Research in Social Behavior, University of Missouri-Columbia, and the Institute for Research on Teaching, Michigan State University. We especially thank Diane Chappell, Teresa Hjellming, Patricia Shanks, and June Smith for typing the manuscript and Gail Hinkel for editing it.

REFERENCES

Anderson, L., Evertson, C., & Brophy, J. (1979). An experimental study of effective teaching in first-grade reading groups. *Elementary School Journal, 79,* 193–223.

Anderson, L., Evertson, C., & Brophy, J. (1982). *Principles of small-group instruction in elementary reading.* East Lansing, MI: Institute for Research on Teaching, Michigan State University (Occasional Paper No. 58).

Anderson, R., Hiebert, E., Scott, J., & Wilkinson, I. (1985). *Becoming a nation of readers: The report of the Commission on Reading.* Washington, DC: National Institute of Education.

Ausubel, D. (1963). *The psychology of meaningful verbal learning: An introduction to school learning.* New York: Grune & Stratton.

Bandura, A., & Schunk, D. (1981). Cultivating competence, self-efficacy, and intrinsic interest through proximal self-motivation. *Journal of Personality and Social Psychology, 41,* 586–598.

Berliner, D. C. (1987). But do they understand? In V. Richardson-Koehler (Ed.), *Educators' handbook: A research perspective* (pp. 285–286). New York: Longman.

Brophy, J. (1987). On motivating students. In D. Berliner & B. Rosenshine (Eds.), *Talks to teachers.* New York: Random House.

Brophy, J., & Evertson, C. (1976). *Learning from Teaching: A Developmental Perspective.* Boston: Allyn and Bacon.

Brophy, J., & Good, T. (1974). *Teacher–student relationships: Causes and consequences.* New York: Holt, Rinehart and Winston.

Brophy, J., & Good, T. (1986). Teacher behavior and student achievement. In M. C. Wittrock (Ed.), *Handbook of research on teaching* (3rd ed.) (pp. 328–375). New York: Macmillan.

Brophy, J., & Willis, S. (1981). *Human development and behavior.* New York: St. Martin's Press.

Cooper, H. (1979). Pygmalion grows up: A model for teacher expectation communication and performance influence. *Review of Educational Research, 49,* 389–410.

Corno, L., & Rohrkemper, M. (1985). Self-regulated learning. In R. Ames & C. Ames (Eds.), *Research in motivation in education* (Vol.2). Orlando, FL: Academic Press.

Cox, W., & Matz, R. (1982). Comprehension of school prose as a function of reasoning level and instructional prompting. *Journal of Educational Psychology, 74,* 77–84.

deCharms, R. (1976). *Enhancing motivation: Change in the classroom.* New York: Irvington.

Dweck, C., & Elliott, E. (1983). Achievement motivation. In P. Mussen & E. Hetherington (Eds.), *Handbook of child psychology, IV: Socialization, personality and social development.* New York: Wiley.

Ebmeier, H., & Good, T. (1979). The effects of instructing teachers about good teaching on the mathematics achievement of fourth-grade students. *American Educational Research Journal, 16,* 1–16.

Elawar, M. C., & Corno, L. (1985). A factorial experiment in teachers' written feedback on student homework: Changing teacher behavior a little rather than a lot. *Journal of Educational Psychology, 77,* 162–173.

Gagné, R., & Briggs, L. (1979). *Principles of instructional design* (2nd ed.). New York: Holt, Rinehart and Winston.

Good, T. (1979). Teacher effectiveness in the elementary school: What we know about it now. *Journal of Teacher Education, 30,* 52–64.

Good, T., & Brophy, J. (1986). School effects. In M.C. Wittrock (Ed.), *Handbook of research on teaching* (3rd ed.), (pp. 570–602). New York: Macmillan.

Good, T., & Brophy, J. (1987). *Looking in classrooms* (4th ed.). New York: Harper & Row.

Good, T., & Grouws, D. (1979). The Missouri Mathematics Effectiveness Project: An experimental study in fourth-grade classrooms. *Journal of Educational Psychology, 71,* 355–362.

Good, T., & Grouws, D. (1987, June). Increasing teachers' understanding of mathematical ideas through inservice training. *Phi Delta Kappan, 68,* 778–783.

Good, T., Grouws, D., & Ebmeier, H. (1983). *Active mathematics teaching.* New York: Longman.

Greeno, J. (1978). Natures of problem-solving abilities. In W. Estes (Ed.), *Handbook of learning and cognitive processes* (Vol. 5). Hillsdale, NJ: Lawrence Erlbaum Associates.

Groisser, P. (1964). *How to use the fine art of questioning.* New York: Teachers' Practical Press.

Hooper, F., & DeFrain, J. (1980). On delineating distinctly Piagetian contributions to education. *Genetic Psychology Monographs, 101,* 151–181.

Larrivee, B., & Algina, J. (1983). *Identification of teaching behaviors which predict success for mainstreamed students.* Paper presented at the annual meeting of the American Educational Research Association, Montreal.

Luiten, J., Ames, W., & Ackerson, G. (1970). A meta-analysis of the effects of advance organizers on learning and retention. *American Educational Research Journal, 17,* 211–218.

Madden, R., Stevens, R., Slavin, R., & Farnish, A. (1986). *Cooperative integrated reading and composition (CIRC), teacher's manual.* Baltimore, MD: Johns Hopkins University, Center for the Social Organization of Schools.

Martorano, S. (1977). A developmental analysis of performance on Piaget's formal operation tasks. *Developmental Psychology,13,* 666–672.

McCaleb, J., & White, J. (1980). Critical dimensions in evaluating teacher clarity. *Journal of Classroom Interaction, 15,* 27–39.

McColskey, W., & Leary, M. (1985). Differential effects of norm-referenced and self-referenced feedback on performance expectancies, attributions, and motivation. *Contemporary Educational Psychology, 10,* 275–284.

Murray, F. (1978). Teaching strategies and conservation training. In A. Lesgold, J. Pellegrino, S. Fokkema, & R. Glaser (Eds.), *Cognitive psychology and instruction.* New York: Plenum.

Neimark, E. (1975). Intellectual development during adolescence. In F. Horowitz (Ed.), *Review of child development research* (Vol. 4). Chicago: University of Chicago Press.

Peterson, P., Janicki, T., & Swing, S. (1981). Ability x treatment interaction effects on children's learning in large group and small group approaches. *American Educational Research Journal, 18,* 453–473.

Renner, J., Stafford, D., Lawson, A., McKinnon, J., Friot, E., & Kellogg, D. (1976). *Research on teaching and learning with the Piaget model.* Norman: University of Oklahoma Press.

Rohrkemper, M., & Corno, L. (1988). Success and failure on classroom tasks: Adaptive learning and classroom teaching. *Elementary School Journal, 88,* 297–312.

Rosenshine, B. (1968). To explain: A review of research. *Educational Leadership, 26,* 275–280.

Rosenshine, B., & Furst, N. (1973). The use of direct observation to study teaching. In R. Travers (Ed.), *Second handbook of research on teaching.* Chicago: Rand McNally.

Rosenshine, B., & Stevens, R. (1986). Teaching functions. In M. C. Wittrock (Ed.), *Handbook of research on teaching* (3rd ed.) (pp. 376–391). New York: Macmillan.

Rowe, M. (1974a). Pausing phenomena: Influence on quality of instruction. *Journal of Psycholinguistic Research, 3,* 203–224.

Rowe, M. (1974b). Wait-time and rewards as instructional variables, their influence on language, logic, and fate control: Part I: Wait-time. *Journal of Research in Science Teaching, 11,* 81–94.

Schuck, R. (1981). The impact of set induction on student achievement and retention. *Journal of Educational Research, 74,* 227–232.

Shulman, L. (1986). Paradigms and research programs in the study of teaching: A contemporary perspective. In M. C. Wittrock (Ed.), *Handbook of research on teaching* (3rd ed.) (pp. 3–36). New York: Macmillan.

Slavin, R., & Karweit, N. (1985). Effects of whole class, ability grouped, and individualized instruction on mathematics achievement. *American Educational Research Journal, 22*(3), 351–367.

Smith, L., & Land, M. (1981). Low-inference verbal behaviors related to teacher clarity. *Journal of Classroom Interaction, 17,* 37–42.

Stevens, R.J. Madden, N. A., Slavin R. E., & Farnish, A. M. (1987). Cooperative integrated reading and composition: Two field experiments. *Reading Research Quarterly, 22,* 433–454.

Stipek, D., & Weiss, J. (1981). Perceived personal control and academic achievement. *Review of Educational Research, 51,* 101–137.

Tobin, K. (1983a). The influence of wait-time on classoom learning. *European Journal of Science Education, 5*(1), 35–48.

Tobin, K. (1983b). Management of time in classrooms. In B. Fraser (Ed.), *Classroom management.* Bentley, Australia: Western Australian Institute of Technology.

Vygotsky, L. (1978). *Mind in society: The development of higher psychological processes.* (M. Cole, V. John-Steiner, S. Scribner, & E. Souberman, Eds.). Cambridge: Harvard University Press.

Weinstein, C., & Mayer, R. (1986). The teaching of learning strategies. In M. C. Wittrock (Ed.), *Handbook of research on teaching* (3rd ed.) (pp. 315–327). New York: Macmillan.

Weisz, J., & Cameron, A. (1985). Individual differences in the students' sense of control. In C. Ames & R. Ames (Eds.), *Research on motivation in education. Vol. II: The classroom milieu.* Orlando, FL: Academic Press.

Wright, C., & Nuthall, G. (1970). Relationships between teacher behaviors and pupil achievement in three experimental elementary science lessons. *American Educational Research Journal, 7,* 477–491.

Zumwalt, K. (Ed.).(1986). *Improving teaching.* (The 1986 ASCD Yearbook). Alexandria, VA: Association for Supervision and Curriculum Development.

3 Time and Learning: A Review

Nancy Karweit
Center for Research on
Elementary and Middle Schools
The Johns Hopkins University

INTRODUCTION

Time in school and student time-on-task became educational "hot topics" following the appearance of *A Nation At Risk* in 1983 (National Commission on Excellence in Education, 1983). That report recommended extending the school term from 180 to 200 or 220 days and lengthening the school day from five or six hours to seven. Although a great deal of interest in and legislative proposals concerning school time were generated, little significant change in the amount of school time actually resulted. In fact, recent increases in school time that have occurred, were put into place prior to the *Nation At Risk* report.

The educational reform movement thus did not produce major changes in opportunity time for learning. The school term is still about 180 days.[1] The school day is still roughly six hours in most places.[2]

The educational reform movement's focus on time appears to have been recently redirected from these original proposals to increase mandated opportunity time to proposals to improve the efficiency of time use in schools and classrooms. This redirection is based on the assumption that there is adequate time for learning, but that it is inappropriately used. In short, the verdict seems to be that more time is not the answer; better use of the existing time is. A recent National Education Association (NEA) report concludes that "School improvement efforts that focus on making better use of existing instructional time are

---

[1]The District of Columbia has 184 days in the school year, whereas Ohio has 182. The remaining states have 175 to 180 days.

[2]Texas has a 7 hour school day. Tennessee has a 6.5 to 7 hour day.

likely to be both more effective and more cost effective than increasing the quantity of instructional time'' (1987, p. 5).

What research evidence supports and does not support this view? Because time use can be altered and can be monitored, it is an especially important factor for educational improvement. It is therefore important that the research on time and learning be understood and the implications for practice spelled out. The purpose of this review is to contribute to such an understanding.

Research efforts focusing on time can be divided into three major areas: *theoretical* studies of time and learning, *descriptive* studies of the allocation and use of time and *effect* studies that measure the importance of various time factors for learning. This review focuses primarily on descriptive studies of time use and on empirical studies estimating the effect of time on learning. The discussion here of the theoretical work centers only on issues which have major implications for the interpretation of research results.

The landmark theoretical study of time and learning is Carroll's forumlation of a model of school learning (Carroll, 1963). Carroll represented the relationship between time and learning by the model:

$$\text{learning} = \frac{f \text{ (time actually spent)}}{\text{(time needed)}}$$

Carroll's model is the starting point for recent examinations of time and learning. Yet, it is important to note that recent studies, while acknowledging Carroll's model, do not in fact pay attention to *both* time spent and time needed. Virtually all recent examinations of the effect of school time focus exclusively on time spent. This is a significant omission in the empirical work that must be kept in mind in reviewing the results.

A second issue that needs to be considered in interpreting these studies of time and learning is the measurement and conceptualization of learning time. Many investigations of learning time have used such global measures as days in the school year to assess the effect of time spent. From a measurement point of view, these global measures are not satisfactory because they do not accurately reflect the amount of learning time a student actually experiences. Two students may be in school the same number of days, but have dramatically different amounts of active instructional time depending on classroom practices and individual factors. Recognizing this accuracy problem, more recent studies have relied on measures of student attention to assess the effect of time spent. Student attention is a more accurate measure of active learning time, but it is an imperfect measure of policy purposes. This is because student engagement is the consequence of many different decisions, policies, and practices. Our policies and practices manipulate causes or sources of time-on-task and not time-on-task in and of itself. We need to understand how time-on-task is related to these alterable practices and policies. If we know that student attention and achievement are related in a certain way, we still don't know very much until we also know how time-on-task is related to specific elements of time usage we can change, such as the amount of instructional time or the length of the school day.

To assess the importance of time for learning we need to use proximal measures of time, such as student attention. To assess the policy importance of time for learning we need to know how these proximal measures are related to the manipulable features of classrooms and schools. Consequently, studies of time and learning need to focus both on global and proximal measures of learning time and on the process connecting these measures.

Active learning time: Process

The amount of time a child is actively engaged in learning is the result of a complex chain of legal, institutional and individual decisions as well as characteristics of the students themselves. Figure 3.1 traces the processes that create active learning time. The figure starts with state laws and suggests how different factors transform legislated time into actual amounts of active learning time. Two schools may begin with identical mandated opportunity time, but end up with student active learning times that differ by a factor of 2 : 1 or 3 : 1. Figure

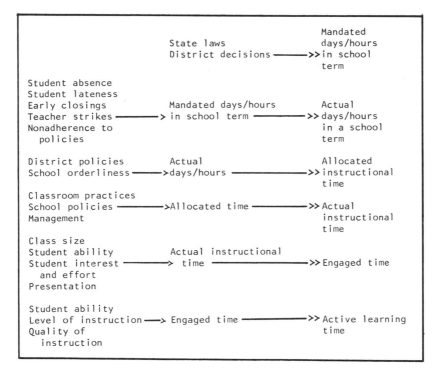

FIG. 3.1.   Disaggregation of active learning time into parts and causes.

FACTOR	RANGE	TYPICAL	NOTES
Days and hours in the school year[a]	175-184 days 4-7 hours	180 days 6 hours	Present practices
Percentage of mandated time which is used[b]	75-95%	90%	Reduced due to student absence, early closings, late openings
Percentage of school day allotted to academic instruction[c]	60-80% school day	80% school day	Present practices differentiating academic and nonacademic times
Percentage of allotted time used for instruction[d]	50-90% allotted time	80% allotted time	School and classroom management practices
Percentage engaged time[e]	40-90% inst. time	80% inst. time	Individual and setting variations
Percentage appropriate engaged[f]	40-90% engaged time	80% engaged time	Individual and instruction factors

[a]Statistics on the length of school day and term provided by the Education Commission of the States.
[b]The low and high values for percentage of opportunity time used were derived from assuming in the high case an absence rate equivalent to sickness days only (6 days) and in the low case from an 80% attendance rate and a loss of an additional 5% of days/hours due to early closings, late openings, and student tardiness. This rate should also incorporate school days that are lost due to weather related closings and are not made up.
[c]The percentage of the day used for academic instruction was based on observational studies of elementary schools (Denham & Lieberman, 1980; Karweit, 1983) and data from the National Assessment of Educational Practice.
[d]The management time and procedural time came from observational data (Karweit & Slavin, 1984; Denham & Lieberman, 1980).
[e]The engagement rates came from Evertson (1980) study of attention in junior high classrooms.
[f]The active learning time is an estimate based on the success rates in the BTES (Denham & Lieberman, 1980) data.

FIG. 3.2. Range of values for components of active learning time.

3.2 estimates typical ranges of variables at each step in this process of whittling away legislated time for instruction.

Opportunity Time

Compulsory attendance laws mandate the ages between which students must attend school. The state laws are not uniform. Some states mandate a minimum exposure to schooling of only 9 years (Arizona and Mississippi), whereas others require 13 years (Hawaii, Kentucky, Ohio, South Carolina, Virginia, and

Wisconsin). Most states require attendance for 10 or 11 years. The beginning and ending ages are not uniform either, with 32 states requiring that attendance must begin by age 7 or 8, sixteen setting the age at 6 and three states requiring 5-year-olds to be in school (Delaware, South Carolina, and Virginia). Eight states require attendance until age 18. Of course, compulsory attendance laws set the minimum boundary for time in school with many students receiving appreciably more schooling than the minimum. Attendance at optimal prekindergarten and kindergarten programs and post secondary schooling continuation extend the amount of schooling for many students.

State laws also determine the days in the school year. The length of the school year has increased considerably over the last 100 years. In 1869 the average school year was 132.2 days; presently it is around 179 days. The length of the school year has also become increasingly uniform. In 1930, for example, Southerners attending school 147 days per year, whereas Northerners and Westerners attending 177 days per year. Rural students in the North and West attending 175 days per year, whereas urban students attended 181 days per year (Meyer, Tyack, Nagel, & Gordon, 1977, Table 6, p. 93). Many urban districts in the 1830s to 1840s had school terms of 220 days. Presently the average is 179 days with a range of 175 to 184 days.

Recent efforts at increasing the length of the school term have not been successful. The annual Gallup poll of the *Public's Attitude Towards the Public Schools* shows that a majority of the public oppose an increase in the school year (1982 - 53%; 1983 - 49%; 1984 - 50%). Teachers seem not too thrilled with the idea either; a majority of teachers polled nationwide were not in favor of a longer school term (or day). Some states have been sufficiently concerned about the negative effects on their tourism industry that they have enacted specific legislation to prohibit such extensions. Nor have educational researchers embraced the idea. Levin (1986) points out that extensions are not cost effective. Karweit (1983, 1985) questions the educational effectiveness of extending the school term. Unfortunately, there is limited empirical evidence to guide this discussion. Two counties in North Carolina did change their term to a 200-day, seven-hour term. One dropped the experiment because of local dissatisfaction; the results of the other experiment are not yet available (NEA, 1987).

The impetus for increasing the school year came largely from international time and learning comparisons. For example, the fact that Japan has a longer school term and higher achievement than the United States was interpreted to mean that the longer school term caused the achievement. There are several problems with this line of reasoning. First, examinations from the International Association for the Evaluation of Educational Achievement (IEA) do not in general support the findings that a longer school term is associated with greater achievement. For example, Japan leads the list in the 1981–1982 Second International Mathematics Study with a mean mathematics total score of 62, whereas Luxembourg trails with a total score of 37. The U.S. scored 45. Japan has 243 days per school term, Luxembourg has 216. In general, the international comparisons do not provide evidence of a strong link between achievement and time (Husen, 1972; Levin, 1983; NEA, 1987; Passow, 1975).

Secondly, even if we did find enormous correlations between time and learning in these cross national comparisons (which we do not), we would have to ask what this implies. We would still have to show that this correlations was due to differences in time itself and not due to differences that are masquerading as time. Although differences in time allocations may vary with achievement differences, manipulating time may not result in changes in achievement because time per se may not be the real cause of the differences. Nations that allocate more time to school may not do this by accident; school terms may be longer because these countries attach more importance to education as an activity. If greater support for education is the primary reason for achievement, manipulating an effect of this support—the amount of school time—will not necessarily change achievement.

Studies examining the effect of differences in the length of the school term and day within the United States suffer from these same interpretation difficulties. Wiley and Harnischfeger (1974) found impressive effects for the quantity of schooling (number of days times attendance times hours in the day) in an analysis using 40 Detroit schools that were a part of the Equality of Educational Opportunity Survey (EEOS). Karweit (1976) replicated their analysis using the remainder of the EEOS data (grades 3, 6, 9, and 12 with 2101, 2040, 768, and 647 schools respectively). Karweit's extended analysis did not find the same magnitude of effects as Wiley and Harnischfeger did for the original 40-school, selected sample. Even had the extended reanalyses found quantity of schooling to be significantly related to achievement, it would still be problematic to interpret differences in time as the cause of differences in achievement.

Mandated time is reduced by student absence, teacher work stoppages, early closings, late openings, and failure to make up days lost due to inclement weather. Student elective absence is probably one of the greatest factors reducing allocated time to the time actually used for learning. Daily attendance rates vary enormously by age and sex of the student (Levanto, 1973), by location of the school (Statistics of the State School Systems, 1978), by the size of the school (Lindsay, 1982), and by the grade organization of the school (e.g., middle school vs. junior high schools; see Slavin & Karweit, 1982). For most urban school districts, student absenteeism has been and continues to be a major educational disruption. In many urban secondary schools, more students may be absent than present on a given day (Karweit, 1973). For example, in Baltimore in 1983–1984, over one-third of the students were absent forty or more days. This high absenteeism creates serious problems for instructional time use. In addition to the obvious fact that absent students are not exposed to school instruction, there is the secondary consequence of their absence on the instructional time of their classmates, because teachers must take time to reintegrate the absent students into the classroom. Generally, research suggests negative effects of absence on grades or achievement (Butler, 1925; Crider, 1929; Finch & Nemzek, 1940; Karweit, 1973; Levanto, 1973; Odell, 1923; Rozelle, 1968; Ziegler, 1928). The direction of causality between absence and achievement is not clear; however, it is certainly true that low achievement and low grades are causes as well as outcomes of truancy.

Another way that the school term is shortened is by teacher strikes and by school closings due to financial or energy crises. Although the number of teacher strikes has decreased as contracts have become multi-year, specific school systems have a history of work stoppages. For example, Philadelphia has had three teacher strikes from 1973 to 1980, one lasting 51 days, one 6 days, and one 22 days. Other large city systems have been similarly embroiled in teacher strikes or financial crises necessitating early school closings. The loss of school days due to strikes, financial difficulties, and high student absence are often combined in urban school settings, and help produce markedly lower amounts of exposure to instruction for these students.

Instructional Time

The amount of time school is in session and the attendance of the students set the maximum amount of possible instructional time a student can receive. Within this maximum, the scheduling practices of schools and classrooms appear to differ, with no precise amount of time set aside for instructional and non-instructional activities. One study of elementary time use, the Beginning Teacher Evaluation Study (BTES; Cahen & Fisher, 1978) suggests that of the typical 6-hour school day, four hours are scheduled for instruction with the remaining time scheduled for lunch, recess, breaks, and non-instructional activities. Of the four hours scheduled for instruction, three are typically scheduled for academic activities, whereas the remaining hour is used for art, music, and physical education (Rosenshine, 1980).

The amount of time devoted to a particular topic also varies as classroom teachers have considerable autonomy to decide what topics and subjects to emphasize (Smith, 1977). For example, within one school in Maryland, the time allocated to mathematics instruction ranged from 2 hours and 50 minutes per week in one classroom to 5 hours and 55 minutes per week in another. Over a year's time, this weekly time difference means that some students receive over 100 hours more math instruction than their schoolmates (Karweit & Slavin, 1981). The ASCD study of allocated instructional time in 4th grade classrooms nationally indicates comparable ranges in allocated times.

Within the scheduled time, the curriculum is certainly not standard. The BTES study (Cahen & Fisher, 1978) for example, documents up to seven-fold differences in time allocation to specific content areas. Such differences could arise because the students already knew the material, because students were not prepared for it, or because the teacher thought it non-essential. Thus, the content of the curriculum may vary substantially from place to place, depending on individual teachers' perceptions of what is important to teach (Smith, 1977).

In secondary schools, there is considerable latitude in what courses must be taken to receive a secondary school diploma. Obviously, curricular track placement affects the choice of courses, but within each track there is still appreciable variation in formal and informal requirements for high school graduation. For example, a college preparatory program in one school may require two years of foreign language; in another school it may require none. For a particular student, the requirement of the college that he or she hopes to attend may be the most important determinant of what courses are taken.

The length of the school day and the amount of time to be scheduled for instructional and non-instructional activities comprise the broad framework for decisions concerning daily time use in classrooms. These scheduled times represent the maximum amount of in-school time for instruction. Several factors affect how much of this scheduled time is actually used for instruction. First, the time scheduled for instruction may be used for another purpose, such as a field trip, standardized testing, or special school assemblies. Second, the time scheduled may be routinely reduced by late starts or early endings. For example, in one math class in a Maryland school that was scheduled for the hour before lunch, the first ten minutes were typically used to collect lunch money, and the last ten were used to line the students up for lunch. Third, the manner in which classes are scheduled for instruction may reduce the amount of scheduled time. In particular, the change in recent years in many elementary schools from a self-contained classroom structure to a departmentalized structure reduces the amount of time available for instruction because it takes time to move students, especially young students, from one part of the school to another. These transition times typically come out of time once reserved for instruction.

Once instruction is under way, the actual minutes in which instruction is delivered depends on how the classroom is organized for instruction, including the grouping practices, the instructional strategies, the size and ability distribution of the class, and other factors such as the number and length of interruptions and the teacher's skill as a classroom manager.

Studies of the amount of instructional time used suggest that instruction may occupy at most 60 percent of the school day. Conant (1973) suggests that about 92 of the 300 minutes per school day were actually used for instruction. Park (1976) documents that somewhere between 21 to 69 percent of the school day was used for instruction in the classes he observed.

Cusick (1973) found that over 200 minutes of the school day in one high school were spent on procedural or maintenance tasks. Summarizing the lack of academic activity, Cusick states that ''the time spent actively engaged with some teacher over a matter of cognitive importance may not exceed twenty minutes a period for five periods a day. This is a high estimate. I would say that if an average student spent an hour to one-and-a-half hours involved on subject matter—that was a good day" (Cusick, 1973, p. 56).

Fredrick (1977) documents that interruptions, procedural activities, and other non-academic matters are extremely time consuming within the classroom. He points out that low-achieving classes are more likely than high-achieving classes to be involved in these non-academic uses of time.

Engaged Time

Given that instruction is actually taking place, the final determinant of learning time is the amount of time a student pays attention. Interest in student attention dates back at least to the studies of classroom and teacher efficiency in the 1920s. These early attention studies used group attention scores, obtained by watching the eye involvement of the student with the teacher, and were intended to rate teacher effectiveness. Shannon (1941) questioned this technique and conducted an experiment to test the fallibility of the connection between the attention measure and learning. An unfamiliar story was read to the class and attention was observed at the exact time that key ideas were presented. Examining the correlation between answers on multiple choice items designed to test these key ideas and attention during presentation, Shannon concluded that group attention scores were not valid indices of student learning or teacher effectiveness.

One reason for this may simply be that eye involvement of the student may be a misleading indicator of actual involvement. Students can have their eyes on the teacher and still not be paying attention. Overt measures of student attention made by behavioral observers cannot readily distinguish between this situation and the one in which the student is actually learning something. Covert measures at specific critical junctures, which ask the student to recall what the lesson was about (such as stimulated recall techniques), get around this problem. Anderson (1973) compared the estimates of on-taskness obtained with overt and covert measures and found a reasonable correspondence was influenced by the mode of instruction—agreement was highest during teacher lecture and lowest during seatwork.

Several observational studies suggest that students pay attention to instructional activities about seventy to seventy-five percent of the time. BTES observers coded whether a student was on- or off-task during instruction and obtained on-task behavior estimates of .70 and .73 for grade 2 mathematics and reading, respectively, and .73 and .75 for grade 5 mathematics and reading. Similarly, Karweit and Slavin (1981) report engagement rates of .78 during mathematics instruction for both their grade 2 and grade 5 samples. Good and Beckerman (1978) found rates between .66 and .78.

Students differ in the amount of time that they spend engaged in learning. We know little about individual characteristics related to high or low on-task behaviors, except for the influence of aptitude and sex of student. A positive association between intelligence or ability and on-task behavior has been documented many times (e.g., Lahaderne, 1967). Other studies have shown a positive correlation between pre-test score (e.g., Karweit & Slavin, 1981) and on-task behavior, which suggests the connection between on-task behavior and aptitude. In elementary schools, at least, girls have been found to be on-task more than boys. The scarcity of information about the relationship of individual factors to attention may simply reflect the view that the most important sources of student engagement are located elsewhere—such as in classroom organizational arrangements and teacher management practices.

In an observational study of fifth grade mathematics classes, Karweit and Slavin (1981) found that students' time-on-task varied markedly from day to day. Some of this variation may be due to differences in classroom organization or content of instruction, but not all of it. Certain periods of the year, such as before or after holidays, may show marked differences from other times of the year. Students may be more distractible on days when there is an important school event (for example, a school assembly or sports event). For older students, Mondays and Fridays may exhibit peculiar "warming up" and "winding down" patterns, as do adult work weeks.

The BTES study (Fisher et al, 1980) documents that some classes show average attentiveness rates of 50 percent, whereas others have averages as high as 90 percent. Teacher managerial competencies, the composition of the classroom and mode of instruction are some classroom factors affecting variations in on-task behavior. Because the *mode* of instruction is a manipulable feature of classroom organization, the differences in on-task behavior here are especially noteworthy. Rosenshine (1980), also using the BTES data, found that engagement was 70 percent during unsupervised seatwork and 84 percent during teacher-led discussion. These differences are of some consequence, because much of the time (about 70 percent) in elementary classrooms is spent doing seatwork.

Mandated school time is therefore converted to active learning time by a process that involves many different persons, decisions, and practices. The amount of time a student spends on learning will therefore depend on how these factors collectively operate. Because there are many links in this chain connecting opportunity for learning and active learning time, it is likely that the end result will vary from student to student and from classroom to classroom. In Fig. 3.3, we present optimistic, average, and pessimistic patterns of time usage to illustrate how different amounts of learning time can be created. These graphs suggest three conclusions about the allocation and use of time in school:

1. The amount of time mandated for school is fairly uniform.

2. The amount of active learning time experienced by different children is highly variable, depending upon school, classroom, teacher, instructional and individual student characteristics.

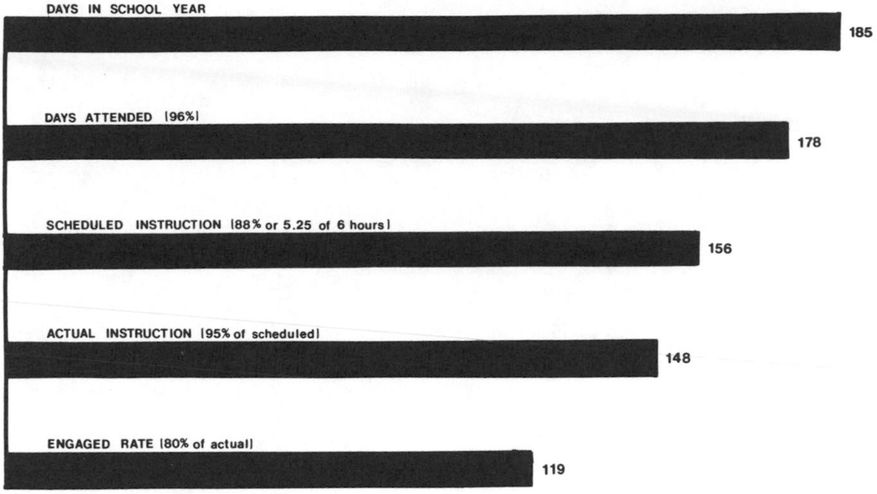

DAYS IN SCHOOL YEAR
185

DAYS ATTENDED (96%)
178

SCHEDULED INSTRUCTION (88% or 5.25 of 6 hours)
156

ACTUAL INSTRUCTION (95% of scheduled)
148

ENGAGED RATE (80% of actual)
119

FIG. 3.3a. Optimistic distribution of active instruction time.

DAYS IN SCHOOL YEAR
180

DAYS ATTENDED (95%)
171

SCHEDULED INSTRUCTION (83% or 5 of 6 hours)
143

ACTUAL INSTRUCTION (80% of scheduled)
115

ENGAGED RATE (70% of actual)
81

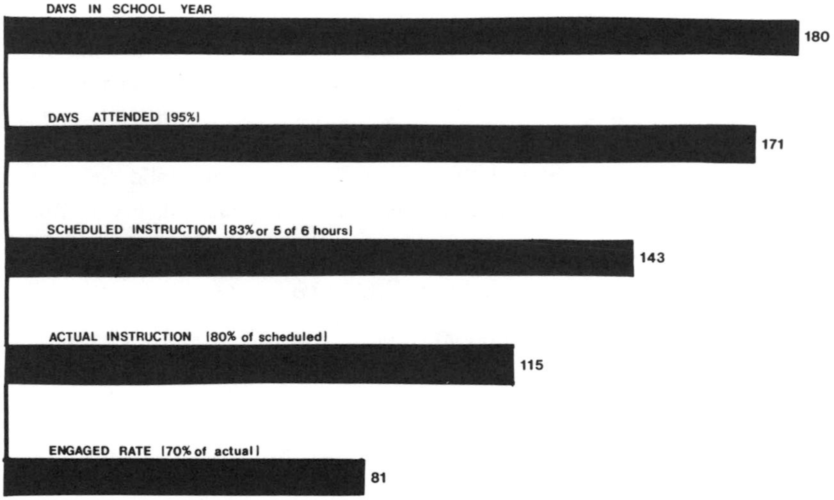

FIG. 3.3b. Average distribution of active instruction time.

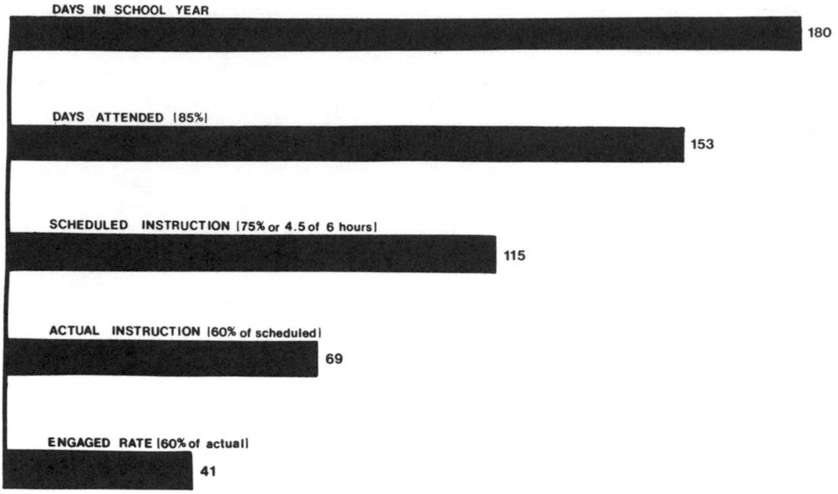

DAYS IN SCHOOL YEAR

180

DAYS ATTENDED (85%)

153

SCHEDULED   INSTRUCTION (75% or 4.5 of 6 hours)

115

ACTUAL   INSTRUCTION (60% of scheduled)

69

ENGAGED RATE (60% of actual)

41

FIG. 3.3c.   Pessimistic distribution of active instruction time.

3. Active learning time is at best only about 60 percent of allocated time and at worst may be less than a quarter of it.

TIME AND LEARNING

The preceding discussion has identified the sources and the extent of variation in student time-on-task. We now turn to an examination of the relationship of time and learning. Although there have been numerous studies that have examined the effect of such global measures as days in the school year or hours in the school day, we are primarily interested here in the relation between more proximal measures of time and learning, because these provide more valid and accurate measures of the construct of interest: student time actively engaged learning.

The Beginning Teacher Evaluation Study (BTES)

The Beginning Teacher Evaluation (BTES) is probably the most widely known study to examine the effects of time on learning. Because of the importance of this study and its findings, we address this study first and in some detail. Tables 3.1 through 3.4 present the results of the basic BTES analyses.

During the 6-year project, four separate samples were studied (known as Phase II, Phase III-A, Phase III-A Continuation, and Phase III-B). The last of these field studies is the one considered here. From a set of volunteer teachers, classrooms were selected that fell into the 30th to 60th percentile range on

TABLE 3.1

Regression Analyzing the Combined Effects of ALT Variables on Reading and Language Arts Achievement in Grade 2 BTES Survey B-C Period

Content Category for Postachievement, Preachievement, and Allocated Time	Post X (s.d.)	Intercept	Pre X (s.d.)	b	Alloc. Time X (s.d.)	b	Engaged Rate X (s.d.)	b	Low Error X (s.d.)	b	High Error X (s.d.)	b	Variances Pre Ach	Unique	Residual
Total Comprehension	11.5 (7.0)	3.57	6.8 (6.3)	.55	760.0 (319.8)	.0005	.74 (.10)		.50 (.18)	5.1	.02 (.03)	-10.0	.32	.03	.04
Decoding Blends and Long Vowels	24.7 (6.5)	6.33	18.9 (8.8)	.44	351.0 (255.9)	.0033		9.5		5.0		-31.7	.49	.09	.18
Decoding Variant Consonants	8.2 (4.8)	-.64	5.5 (5.5)	.22	50.1 (67.9)	.0056		4.7		7.9		-4.9	.12	.11	.12
Decoding Complex Patterns: Spelling Time	9.5 (5.0)	-2.17	6.2 (4.7)	.58	394.9 (303.3)	.0017		5.1		7.6		-11.6	.47	.12	.22
Word Structures: Meaningful Units	17.5 (5.0)	7.35	13.2 (5.6)	.0021	258.8 (184.5)	.0021		1.3		2.2		-4.4	.49	.01	.02
Word Structure: Syllables	5.4 (2.8)	1.85	3.0 (2.7)	.17	68.5 (81.5)	.0085		1.3		3.3		-9.0	.09	.13	.14
Total Reading	90.7 (30.4)	18.00	61.9 (32.1)	.68	4475.2 (1056.8)	.0013		20.6		22.1		-87.3	.68	.05	.15

TABLE 3.2
Regressions Analyzing the Combined Effects of ALT Variables
on Mathematics Achievement in Grade 2 BTES Survey B-C Period

Content Category for Postachievement, Preachievement, and Allocated Time	Post X s.d.	Intercept	Pre X s.d.	b	Alloc. Time X s.d.	b	Engaged Rate X s.d.	b	Low Error X s.d.	b	High Error X s.d.	b	Variances Pre Ach / Unique / Residual
Add and Subtract: No Regrouping	25.7 (6.7)	15.70	18.3 (8.2)	.35	449.7 (276.3)	-.0005	.70 (.12)	1.7	.50 (.21)	5.4	.05 (.07)	-1.9	.24 .04 .05
Add and Subtract: Speeded Test	16.7 (6.9)	.13	11.5 (6.2)	.56	54.3 (70.2)	.0148		5.5		11.0		-0.9	.35 .14 .22
Add and Subtract: With Regrouping	2.3 (7.5)	-5.10	-0.3 (3.0)	.59	272.6 (270.0)	.0010		6.6		4.7		6.4	.06 .03 .03
Computational Transfer	10.2 (5.6)	2.85	6.2 (4.9)	.59	401.6 (300.1)	.0014		0.3		5.6		1.3	.32 .04 .05
Place Value and Numerals	13.0 (6.4)	8.84	7.8 (5.4)	.79	309.6 (184.2)	-.0010		-2.9		1.2		-5.8	.47 .00 .01
Word Problems	6.8 (4.2)	2.73	4.3 (3.2)	.66	116.8 (107.9)	.0049		0.4		1.4		-8.0	.27 .05 .07
Money	7.4 (2.7)	3.21	5.2 (2.9)	.47	88.9 (101.2)	-.0005		1.8		1.7		-6.6	.34 .08 .13
Linear Measurement	8.1 (1.8)	4.56	7.3 (1.9)	.10	68.4 (76.4)	.0000		0.2		1.2		-2.2	.19 .04 .04
Fractions	4.7 (3.4)	2.65	6.2 (4.9)		70.9 (89.1)	.0126		-0.6		1.6		2.0	.05 .10 .11
Total Mathematics	94.9 (30.4)	17.52	61.5 (23.7)	.91	2242.8 (531.6)	.0005		15.3		19.8		-4.5	.58 .03 .08

TABLE 3.3
Regressions Analyzing the Combined Effects of ALT Variables
on Reading and Language Arts Achievement in Grade 5 BTES Survey B-C Period

Content Category for Postachievement, Preachievement, and Allocated Time	Post X s.d.	Intercept	Pre X s.d.	b	Alloc. Time X s.d.	b	Engaged Rate X s.d.	b	Low Error X s.d.	b	High Error X s.d.	b	Variances Pre Ach / Unique / Residual
Total Word Meaning	28.8 (12.4)	-5.42	23.6 (12.4)	.78	594.8 (232.0)	-.0019	.75 (.11)	23.6	.46 (.15)	-0.4	.01 (.02)	-30.8	.69 .08 .24
Total Comprehension	25.3 (12.7)	9.80	19.3 (12.7)	.81	1547.0 (1065.4)	.0026		-3.4		-0.7		-88.9	.66 .05 .16
Word Structure: Syllable	10.7 (5.6)	4.88	9.4 (6.0)	.51	99.6 (91.4)	-.0016		2.7		-0.7		-44.0	.35 .03 .05
Total Reading	71.4 (29.1)	8.57	57.8 (28.0)	.89	4341.0 (1429.5)	.0014		16.7		-11.7		-121.6	.77 .02 .07

TABLE 3.4

Regressions Analyzing the Combined Effects of ALT Variables on Reading and Language Arts Achievement in Grade 5 BTES Survey B-C Period

Content Category for Postachievement, Preachievement, and Allocated Time	Post X s.d.	Intercept	Pre X s.d.	b	Alloc. Time X s.d.	b	Engaged Rate X s.d.	b	Low Error X s.d.	b	High Error X s.d.	b	Variances Pre Ach Unique	Residual
Total Geometry	5.3 (4.8)	0.41	3.6 (3.9)	.34	144.4 (180.4)	.0016	.73 (.13)	6.1	.34 (.21)	-1.9	.03 (.06)	-12.7	.12 .06	.07
Total Multiplication	14.2 (5.2)	9.94	12.3 (6.6)	.36	388.9 (438.6)	.0007		-1.4		3.6		-18.7	.33 .08	.11
Multiplication: Speed Test: Basic Facts Time	21.5 (10.4)	-2.23	17.8 (9.0)	.92	28.2 (37.9)	-.0088		6.4		7.9		6.2	.65 .03	.10
Division	7.4 (5.5)	8.00	4.4 (5.1)	.59	579.1 (444.5)	.0010		-4.1		-0.5		-19.3	.30 .06	.08
Fractions	5.6 (4.9)	1.06	2.0 (4.0)	.55	728.3 (677.8)	.0027		3.7		-2.2		-13.8	.28 .23	.31
Computational Transfer	16.8 (4.8)	7.02	15.3 (4.6)	.73	146.5 (181.7)	-.0001		-2.6		2.9		-12.4	.58 .04	.10
Word Problems	3.7 (3.3)	2.56	2.1 (3.2)	.60	156.3 (194.7)	-.0007		0.0		0.3		-3.5	.38 .01	.01
Total Mathematics	87.7 (27.9)	13.96	70.0 (26.3)	.84	2349.9 (606.3)	.0062		1.5		2.4		-41.3	.69 .03	.10

reading and mathematics tests that were designed specifically for this study. Within these classrooms, six students (three males, three females) were selected for observation, producing a final sample of 139 second-grade students in 25 classrooms and 122 fifth-grade students in 21 classrooms. Achievement data were collected in October 1976, December 1976, May 1977, and September 1977. The inter-test period, October to December, is referred to as the A–B period. From December to May is referred to as the B–C period. The results from the B–C period are of primary interest here. During this 17-week period, time allocated to reading and mathematics instruction was documented in teachers' logs. Specific content categories within subject matters were coded (e.g., mathematics speed test, decoding consonant blends). The teachers recorded the allocated time per content and per student for each school day during the 85-day inter-test period.

Observations of the six selected students within a classroom took place for a complete day. In most instances, each classroom was observed about fifteen times. Targeted students were observed once every 4 minutes to gauge the activity, the content area, the student's engagement, and level of success.

The obtained engagement rate and success rates are global measures of student engagement during reading and language arts or mathematics and not during specific contents. Thus, engagement rates and percent easy and hard are the same within each grade by subject quadrant for a particular student.

The post- and pre-tests were designed especially for this study to test what was taught during the inter-test period. The allocated minutes are the number of minutes, from teachers' logs, that instruction occurred in the particular subtests. To convert these minutes into the number of minutes per day it is necessary to divide by the number of data days in the study. Although there were 85 possible data days during the B–C period, the actual number of days with data is appreciably smaller. For grade 2 reading, there were 71.5 data days, for grade 2 mathematics there were 65.6, for grade 5 reading there were 55.7 data days, and for grade 5 mathematics there were 52.8 data days. This loss of days came about either because scheduled instruction did not take place due to field trips or other events, or because observation did not take place.

The major findings of the BTES study that are of interest here are:

1. The amount of time that teachers allocate to instruction in a particular content area is positively associated with student learning in that content area.

2. The proportion of allocated time that students are engaged is positively associated with learning.

3. The proportion of time that reading or mathematics tasks are performed with high success is positively associated with student learning.

(Fisher, et al., 1980, p. 15).

Separate regression analyses for grades 2 and 5 for reading/language arts and mathematics were carried out, with the individual as the unit of analysis. Academic Learning Time (ALT) was entered into the regression as four separate variables—allocated time, engaged rate, percent of low-difficulty questions, and percent of high-difficulty questions. Then the contribution, unique and residual, to R square was compared to a regression predicting post-test by pre-test alone.[1]

Separate analyses were carried out for each grade for each sub-test using matched pre-test, time, and post-test measures or 29 different regressions (see Borg, 1980, Table 2.6, pp. 70–71). Summarizing the B–C period results, Borg indicates that 41 or 35 of the ALT variables had significant effects on achievement.

Primarily on the basis of these analyses, we are told that "a major finding of the study is that increases in Academic Learning Time are associated with increases in student achievement" (Fisher et al., 1980, p. 22).

These effects for time are likely to be overestimates, for several reasons (see Karweit, 1983). As noted earlier, because pre-achievement, engagement, and post-achievement are all highly correlated, controlling for pre-achievement is critical to remove ability effects from the correlation between engagement and post-achievement. However, partialing out the effect of a third variable from the correlation between two other variables does not completely remove the effect of the third variable when the intercorrelations are high and the reliability of the control variable is less than perfect (see Lord, 1960). In other words, because students who tend to be highly engaged are usually significantly higher in ability than minimally engaged classmates, controlling for ability will only partially remove ability effects from the engagement/post-achievement correlation. In fact, the use in the BTES of short, criterion-referenced pre-tests as control variables may exacerbate this problem, as such scales would likely to be less reliable than longer norm-referenced measures, such as IQ or standardized test scores. Further, use of "percent easy" and "percent hard" as part of ALT almost certainly inflates the uncontrolled effect of student ability on student achievement. Because these measures are derived from student responses to questions, more able students will obviously answer correctly more often than less able students.

---

[1]The calculations for unique and residual variance are detailed here. Given two regression models:

(1) POST = a+b1 (pre)

(2) POST = a+b1(pre)+b2(alloc)+b3(rate)+b4(low)+b5(high)

The difference between the R squared of these two models is the unique contribution to variance accounted for by ALT—allocated time, engaged rate, low and high error rate. This unique contribution divided by the proportion of variance unaccounted for by the pretest score is the residual variance. The residual variance thus indicates how much of the remaining variance was accounted for by the ALT variables.

The problem of under-controlling for prior achievement would be largely solved by analysis of class means rather than individual scores on all variables. Use of class means would focus the analysis on classroom practices rather than on student-to-student ability differences. "Percent easy" and "percent hard" for the whole class might be influenced by the overall class ability level, but less so than an individual student's "percent of correct answers" would be influenced by their own abilities. Class-level analyses were conducted in the BTES (Marliave, Fisher, & Dishaw, 1978), and in fact show even less consistent effects for time.

Other Studies of Time and Learning

Of course, the BTES is not the only study that purports to show that time-on-task is related to student learning, net of ability. The following section discusses several other time studies, in chronological order. Consult Table 3.5 for summaries of these studies.

Edminston and Rhoades' (1969) study, although not intended to address the issue of how pupil attention affects achievement, has often been cited to indicate the positive effects of time on achievement (see Bloom, 1976). They report the correlation between CAT general achievement and attention to be .58. Because this study did not control for ability or intelligence, partial correlations with this entering level controlled are not available. As an exercise, we assumed a hypothetical pre-test was given which correlated .7 with the post-test and .46 with attention. These values are typical correlations, observed in other studies. With these zero-order correlations, the partial correlation between post-test and attention becomes .40. Looking at the results in terms of the amount of variance accounted for by the attention variable indicates that attention accounts for about one percent of the residual variance. We cast Edminston and Rhoades' study in this framework to show that the presentation of the zero-order correlation of attention and achievement is deceptive, for it implies a more important effect that is indicated either by the partial correlation or by the increment to R square.

Lahaderne (1967) examined the effect of student attention on sixth grade reading and arithmetic achievement, controlling for IQ. Attention was measured by observer rating over a 3-month inter-test period. The partial correlations between attention and post-test score, controlling for IQ, were significant in three of the eight subtests, with a range of .26 to .31. How important are these effects in terms of variance accounted for? This determination requires making some assumptions about the zero-order correlations between IQ and post-test score, which Lahaderne does not report. She does, however, report the other correlations between attention, post-test score and IQ. Using the reported correlations, and the reported partials, we determined what the unreported correlations must have been. This estimated correlation matrix was then used to deter-

TABLE 3.5
Summary of Time-On-Task Effects on Achievement

Study	Post	Pre	Time	Sample	Correlations Pre	Post Time	Partial Time, Post	Variance Unique	Resid
Edmiston and Rhoades	CAT general achievement	---	attention	n = 94 high school seniors in one school system	$.70^a$	.46 / .58	.43	.01	.03
Lahaderne	Scott Foresman Reading	Kuhlman Anderson IQ	attention	n = 65 boys in 4 6th grade classes	$.62^b$	.48 / .51	.31	.03	.07
	Stanford Arithmetic	IQ	attention	"	$.85^b$	.48 / .53	.26	.04	.08
	Scott Foresman	IQ	attention	n = 62 girls in 4 6th grade classes	$.77^b$	.44 / .49	.26	.03	.07
Cobb	Stanford Reading	---	attention	n = 103 4th grade students in 5 classes in 2 schools	$.70^c$	.20 / .49	.43	.02	.07
	Stanford Arithmetic	---	attention	"	$.70^c$	.20 / .44	.16	.00	.00
Smith	STEP social Studies	CAT Nonverbal battery	allocated time	n = 68 5th grade classes	.69	.16 / .23	$.17^d$	.01	.03
Bell and Davidson	Teacher made Ach Test	IQ	attention	n = 23 classrooms of 4th, 5th, 6th grade students	.33	.07 / .25	$.27^e$	.00	.00
Evertson, Emmer, and Clements	English Content Specific	CAT	attention	n = 50 classrooms, junior high	.97	.25 / .29	$.20^f$	.00	.00
	Math	CAT	attention	n = 50 classrooms, junior high	.96	.31 / .39	$.34^f$	.00	.00
Karweit and Slavin	CTBS	CTBS	engaged minutes	n = 33 students in 6 classes, grade 2/3	.91	.30 / .42	$.38^g$	.03	.18
	CTBS	CTBS	attention	n = 62 students in 12 classes, grade 4/5	.89	.43 / .42	.09	.01	.03

mine the unique and residual variance accounted for by the attention measures. The unique contributions hover around .04, with a maximal residual variance accounted for of .08. Lahaderne's study is often cited as indicating the importance of time-on-task. In actuality, the partials were significant in three of eight cases examined and accounted for at most a residual variance of .08 and unique contribution of .04 in the three cases.

Cobb's (1972) study, which examined the relationship between concurrent achievement and attention measures, is also frequently cited. The attentiveness of 103 students in five fourth-grade classrooms was observed. The correlations between attention and achievement were reported to be .44 (reading) and .25 (arithmetic). To assess what the partial correlations might have been had an IQ or pretest been given, we set the correlation between this hypothetical covariate and attention to be .20. Using this derived correlation matrix, partial correlations for reading and arithmetic of .43 and .16 were obtained. These partials probably represent maximal effects, given the rather low estimate of the correlation between attention and pretest used. The unique amount of variance accounted for by the time measure was at most two percent. The attention score accounted for about six percent of the residual variance.

Smith (1979) used data from teachers' logs in a pre-test, time, post-test study of social studies achievement. The regressions indicated that allocated time was not a significant factor in post-test achievement. We computed the partial coefficient between allocated time and social studies achievement, with prior ability controlled, to be .17. In terms of the unique and residual variance explained, allocated time accounts for one and three percent respectively, hardly impressive indications of independent effects of time.

The independent effect of time-on-task on the achievement of 462 students in 23 classes was assessed in a study by Bell and Davidson (1976). The achievement tests were teacher-made and were specific to the content of instruction. Bell and Davidson used observational indices of time-on-task and additionally employed measures of IQ as a control variable. Analyses were carried out separately for the 23 classes. They report the partials between time and achievement, controlling for IQ, in each class. In only 3 of the 23 classes are these partials significant. Using the correlations supplied in the article and weighting these by the number of students in each classroom, we derived a weighted correlation matrix across the 23 classes. From this correlation matrix, an average partial correlation of .27 was obtained between post-test and attention, controlling for IQ. In terms of variance explained, the attention measure accounted for less than one percent of the variance both in terms of unique and residual variance.

The study of Everston, Emmer, and Clements (1980) provides data on the importance of time-on-task for achievement for junior high school students. Using content-specific English and math tests and controlling for CAT scores, the partial correlation of time-on-task and English score was computed to be .20, and was .34 for mathematics. The unit of analysis here was the class (n=150).

The unique and residual variance accounted for by the attention variable was less than one percent for both reading and mathematics.

Karweit and Slavin (1981) report the effects of student engaged time from a pre-test–observation–post-test design where the observation interval was about 3 months. Six mixed second- and third-grade classes and twelve mixed fourth- and fifth-grade classes comprised the sample. Within each class, the attentive behavior of six students was observed for a period of at least 10 consecutive school days.

An observation consisted of coding an activity, a response to the activity, and the content of instruction during repeated thirty-second intervals. The activities included teacher lecture, seatwork (with or without teacher involvement), and procedural activities. The coding scheme allowed multiple activities to be defined in one time frame, so that different activities in the classroom could be coded. For example, a group of students could be working with the teacher, while another group could be working independently on seatwork.

The response category was coded only during instruction. Thus, if a student were engaged in a procedural task (such as getting out a book or sharpening a pencil), on- and off-task responses were not coded. Behavior was coded as off-task only when the student was obviously not attending, for example whispering to another student, engaging in horseplay, sleeping, and so on. Content of instruction was noted by referring to the page number in the text or by recording a sample of seatwork or boardwork. Achievement was measured by the mathematics subtest of the CTBS and by chapter-specific tests. In regressions examining the effects of engaged minutes, inconsistent results were obtained. Significant engagement effects were found in grade 2/3 for the standardized tests, but not the chapter tests. Grade 4/5 had significant effects for the chapter tests, but not the standardized tests. Translating the regression results into the time required to increase achievement by .25 of a standard deviation indicates that a 10-minute increase in *engaged* minutes would be required for grade 2/3. Recalling that students are on-task about 70 percent of the time, for this increase to occur, instructional time would have to be increased from 46 to 65 minutes in this case.

Rephrasing the results of the study in this fashion suggests how likely (or unlikely) it is that *feasible* alterations in learning time can produce noticeable results. Quite sizeable changes in learning time would have to occur before having a detectable effect on achievement.

Summarizing the results of these studies of time-on-task and achievement, we found the engagement measures to be related to achievement in the range of .25 to .58. Once initial ability was controlled, the partial correlation between achievement and engagement was found to lie in the range of .09 to .43. In terms of the proportion of variance explained, the engagement variables were found to explain between one and ten percent of the unique variance in achievement outcomes.

Thus, looking at several studies of time-on-task and achievement, it is clear that the inconsistent effects of time variables on achievement (net of ability) are not unique to the BTES, but are generally found in studies examining these variables. This conclusion of the generally weak effects of time-on-task is clearly at odds with the conventional wisdom that equates more time with more learning. One might ask why it is worthwhile to quibble over the importance of such an apparently benign variable as time-on-task. After all, it is probably not injurious to children or schools to seek to increase time-on-task. Yet as researchers whose work eventually touches school practice, it is important that we be clear about where the important educational effects are situated. As the research on time-on-task has presently been cast, there is little evidence to suggest that increasing time for learning in and of itself will be an effective educational strategy. This conclusion is reinforced by the findings of the recent Follow-Through evaluations, especially the findings from the Cotopaxi, Colorado study (Blackadar & Nachtigal, 1986). Time-on-task was increased, but corresponding increases in achievement did not result. The authors conclude that "we can keep children on task but can't necessarily make them learn better." (Blackadar & Nachtigal, 1986, p. 60)

IMPLICATIONS OF TIME-ON-TASK RESEARCH FOR PRACTICE

It is useful to spell out in some detail what the findings of weak and inconsistent effects of time-on-task imply for educational practice. Otherwise, the inappropriate impression may be drawn that this review has concluded that time, like many other educational resources, is not important for educational achievement.

Carroll's model defines learning as the ratio of time spent to time needed. Most of our research has been overly preoccupied with opportunity time, a factor primarily affecting time spent. The question—"does more time increase learning?"—is primarily a question about time spent. But the answer—"it depends"—is primarily an answer about time needed. To the extent that time needed and time spent are roughly comparable, we should expect to see a strong relationship between time and learning. To the extent that time needed and time spent are not comparable, we should not expect to see a strong relationship between time and learning.

The findings of weak effects for time therefore suggest that time needed and time spent are out of harmony. The critical question remains why they are out of alignment, and what practical steps can be taken to bring them into alignment.

In many instances, the lack of alignment of time needed and time spent is due primarily to the fact that students need differing amounts of time to master a topic, but are given the same amount of time. That is, the instructional program fails to accommodate to differences in individual time needed. Estimates suggest that children can differ as much as 7 : 1 in time needed to learn (Gettinger, 1984). This ratio may be reduced somewhat by increasing the quality of instruction, but individual differences in time needed will clearly always be present (Arlin, 1984; Buss, 1976).

Time needed and time spent can also be out of phase because the school is not providing adequate instructional time. In all schools, there is simply a large portion of the school day that is taken up with matters other than instruction. Some part of this is unavoidable because schools are involved in services for children in groups. On the other hand, many schools simply do not think about how they schedule their activities and events in time. Concern with time and management of time may be seen as an overly rational and even inappropriate point of view for schools whose clientele are children.

The alignment difficulty that we are most concerned with is when time spent is grossly and perpetually below the time that is needed to make adequate progress. This can arise because time spent on instruction is only a tiny proportion of what is allocated and because inadequate preparation and poor instruction makes time needed very large. Such a situation may characterize many urban classrooms where excessive student absence, classroom disruption, and interruptions reduce time spent and family background, poverty, and inadequate instruction increase time needed. These schools thus have a double disadvantage with respect to time.

Blanket solutions—such as increasing the length of the school year—seek to align time needed and time spent by increasing time spent. This strategy is problematic. First of all, mandated opportunity time is related in an uncertain way to active learning time. In some situations, the increase of many days of instructional time may only produce a few minutes worth of increase in active learning time. Secondly, even when active learning time is added, learning will not result if the instruction is inappropriate for some or all students.

Blanket solutions—such as increasing the appropriateness of instruction— seek to align time needed and time spent by decreasing time needed. This strategy enacted by itself is also problematic. In many schools there is not adequate time for instruction. Appropriate instruction can only be effective if there is adequate and sustained time for it.

Schools need to be concerned with *both* time needed and time spent. A major organizational and instructional dilemma for schools is how to synchronize the time needed and time spent. As a starting point, schools should assess their existing time use patterns to determine whether there is adequate time for instruction. Comparison with typical use patterns, such as those in Fig. 3.2 and Fig. 3.3, can provide helpful guidelines. For example, schools that are above average on all usage factors probably will not benefit greatly from a program aimed at increasing opportunity time and should focus their energies more on improving the appropriateness of instruction. Schools that have very low amounts of instructional time, on the other hand, should identify why this is so and locate strategies for improvement that seem appropriate given their situation (Karweit, 1987).

For many schools, the solution to the time needed/time spent disharmony is not to provide more time in general, but to provide more time to some children some of the time. In order to do this schools need to have greater flexibility in the use of existing time. The problem is how to introduce flexibility while still maintaining accountability of time use.

To bring time needed and time spent into alignment, schools can either decrease time needed or increase time spent. The important conclusion from the time research is that both these factors have to be considered. The research on time has thus far been preoccupied with time spent. These research results do not support the conclusion that adding more time will necessarily increase achievement. In the search to understand the conditions under which this statement may or may not be true, the importance of considering time needed is clearly apparent. Future efforts at instructional improvement will be successful to the extent that both time needed and time spent are taken into account.

REFERENCES

Anderson, L. W. (1973). *Time and school learning*. Unpublished doctoral dissertation, University of Chicago.

Bell, M., & Davidson, C. W. (1976). Relationships between pupil on task performance and pupil achievement. *The Journal of Educational Research, 69*(5), 172–176.

Blackadar, A., & Nachtigal, P. (1986). *Cotopaxi/Westcliffe follow through project*. Final Report. Mid Continent Regional Educational Laboratory. Denver, Colorado.

Bloom, B. S. (1976). *Human characteristics and school learning*. New York: McGraw Hill.

Borg, W. (1980). Time and school learning. In C. Denham & A. Lieberman (Eds.), *Time to learn*. Washington, DC: National Institute of Education, pp. 571–593.

Buss, A. R. (1976). The myth of vanishing individual differences in Bloom's mastery learning. *Journal of Instructional Psychology, 3*(3), 4–14;20.

Butler, C. H. (1925). School achievement and attendance. *The School Review, 33*,450–452.

Cahen, L. S., & Fisher, C. W. (1978). *An analysis of instructional time in grade 2 mathematics*. Far West Laboratory for Educational Research and Development. San Francisco, California.

Carroll, J. B. (1963). A model for school learning. *Teacher's College Record, 64*, 723–733.

Cobb, J. A. (1972). Relationship of discrete classroom behaviors to fourth grade academic achievement. *Journal of Educational Psychology, 63*(1), 74–80.

Conant, E. H. (1973). *Teacher paraprofessional work productivity*. Lexington, MA: D.C. Health.

Crider, B. (1929). The effect of absence on scholarship. *School and Society, 30*, 27–28.

Cusick, P. A. (1973). *Inside high school*. New York: Holt, Rinehart, and Winston.

Denham, C., & Lieberman, A. (1980). *Time to learn*. Washington, DC: National Institute of Education.

Edminston, R. W., & Rhoades, B. J. (1969). Predicting achievement. *Journal of Educational Research, 51*, 177–180.

Evertson, C. M., Emmer, E. T., & Clements, B. S. (1980). *The junior high classroom organization study: Summary of training procedures and methodology*. (Report No. 6101) University of Texas at Austin, Research and Development Center for Teacher Education.

Finch, F. H., & Nemzek, C. L. (1940). Attendance and achievement in secondary school. *Journal of Educational Research, 34,* 119–126.

Fisher, C. W., Berliner, D. C., Filby, N. N., Marliave, R., Cahen, L.S., & Dishaw, M. M. (1980). Teaching behaviors, academic learning time and student achievement: An overview. In C. Denham & A. Lieberman (Eds.), *Time to learn.* Washington D.C.: Department of Health, Education, and Welfare, National Institute of Education.

Fredrick, W. C. (1977). The use of classroom time in high schools above or below the median reading score. *Urban Education, 11*(4), 459–464.

Gettinger, M. (1984). Measuring time needed for learning to predict learning outcomes. *Exceptional Children, 51*(3), 244–248.

Good, T. L., & Beckerman, T. M. (1978). Time on task: A naturalistic study in sixth grade classrooms. *The Elementary School Journal, 73,* 193–201.

Husen, T. (1972). Does more time in school make a difference? *Saturday Review, 55*(18), 266–279.

Karweit, N. (1973). *Rainy days and Mondays: An analysis of factors related to absence from school.* (Report No. 162). Baltimore, MD: Center for Social Organization of Schools.

Karweit, N. (1976). A reanalysis of the effect of quantity of schooling on achievement. *Sociology of Education, 49,* 236–246.

Karweit, N. (1983). Time-on-task: A research review. (Report 332), Baltimore, MD: Center for Social Organization of Schools.

Karweit, N. (1985). Should we lengthen the school term? *Educational Researcher, 14,* 6:9–15.

Karweit, N. (1987). *Practical implications of time-on-task research.* Unpublished manuscript.

Karweit, N., & Slavin, R. (1981). Measurement and modeling choices in studies of time and learning. *American Educational Research Journal, 18*(2), 157–171.

Lahaderne, H. M. (1967). Attitudinal and intellectual correlates of attention: a study of four sixth grade classrooms. *Journal of Educational Psychology, 59*(8), 320–324.

Levanto, J. (1973). *The identification and analysis of factors related to secondary school absenteeism.* Unpublished doctoral dissertation, University of Connecticut.

Levin, H. (1983). *About time for educational reform,* Stanford, CA: Stanford University, School of Education.

Levin, H. (1986). Are longer school sessions a good investment? *Contemporary Policy Issues, 4*(3), 63–75.

Lindsay, P. (1982). The effect of high school size on student participation, satisfaction, and attendance. *Educational Evaluation and Policy Analysis, 4*(1), 57–65.

Lord, F. M. (1960). Large sample covariance analysis when the control group is fallible. *Journal of American Statistical Association, 66,* 307–321.

Marliave, R., Fisher, C. W., & Dishaw, M. M. (1978). *Academic learning time and student achievement in the B–C period.* (Technical Note V–2a). Far West Laboratory for Educational Research and Development, San Francisco, CA.

Meyer, J., Tyack, D., Nagel, J., & Gordon, A. (1977). *Education as nation-building in America: Enrollments and bureaucratization in the American states, 1870–1930.* Stanford, University, Boys Town Center for the study of youth development, Stanford University.

National Commission on Excellence in Education (1983). *A nation at risk.* Washington, DC: U.S. Department of Education.

National Education Association (1987). *Extending the school day/year: Proposal and results* (Number 9). Washington, DC: National Education Association.

Odell, C. (1923). The effect of attendance upon school achievement. *Journal of Educational Research, 8,* 425–432.

Park, C. (1976). The Bay City experiment . . . As seen by the director. *The Journal of Teacher Education, 7*(2), 105.

Passow, H. (1975). *The national case study: An empiricial comparative study of twenty-one educational systems.* New York: Wiley.

Rosenshine, B. V. (1980). How time is spent in elementary classrooms. In C. Denham & A. Lieberman (Eds.), *Time to learn.* Washington, DC: National Institute of Education.

Rozelle, R. M. (1968). The relationship between absenteeism and grades. *Educational and Psychological Measurement, 28,* 1151–1158.

Shannon, J. R. (1941). Homogeneous grouping and pupil attention in junior high schools. *The Teacher's College Journal, 12,* 49–52.

Slavin, R., & Karweit, N. (1982). *School organizational vs. developmental effects on attendance among young adolescents.* Paper presented at the annual meeting of the American Educational Research Association, Washington, DC.

Smith, J. K. (1977). Teacher planning for instruction (Report No. 12). Chicago IL: University of Chicago, Studies of Educative Processes.

Smith, N. M. (1979). Allocation of time and achievement in elementary social structures. *Journal of Educational Research, 72,* 2312–2316.

Statistics of State School Systems & U.S. Department of Health, Education and Welfare (1978). Washington, DC: National Center for Educational Statistics.

Wiley, D., & Harnischfeger, A. (1974). *Explosion of a myth: Quantity of schooling and exposure to instruction, major educational vehicles* (Report no. 8). University of Chicago, Studies of Educative Processes.

Ziegler, C. (1928). School attendance as a factor in school progress. *Contributions to Education, No. 297.* Columbia University, Teachers College.

III ALTERNATIVE MODELS OF CLASSROOM ORGANIZATION

4 Achievement Effects of Group-Based Mastery Learning*

Robert E. Slavin
Center for Research on Elementary and Middle Schools
Johns Hopkins University

Over the past decade, mastery learning has been perhaps the most widely used and widely discussed innovation in classroom organization. Yet the effects of practical applications of mastery learning on student achievement in elementary and secondary schools have only recently begun to be understood. This chapter reviews the research on mastery learning as actually applied in schools.

Defining Mastery Learning

The term *mastery learning* refers to a large and diverse category of instructional methods. The principal defining characteristic of mastery learning methods is the establishment of a criterion level of performance held to represent "mastery" of a given skill or concept, frequent assessment of student progress toward the mastery criterion, and provision of corrective instruction to enable students who do not initially meet the mastery criterion to do so on later parallel assessments (see Bloom, 1976; Block & Anderson, 1975). Bloom (1976) also includes an emphasis on appropriate use of such instructional variables as cues, participation, feedback, and reinforcement as elements of mastery learning, but these are not uniquely defining characteristics; rather, what defines mastery learning approaches is the organization of time and resources to ensure that most students are able to master instructional objectives.

There are three primary forms of mastery learning. One, called the *Personalized System of Instruction* (PSI) or the Keller Plan (Keller, 1968), is used primarily at the post-secondary level. In this form of mastery learning, unit

---

*An earlier version of this chapter was published by Slavin (1987a).

objectives are established for a course of study and tests are developed for each. Students may take the test (or parallel forms of it) as many times as they wish until they achieve a passing score. To do this, students typically work on self-instructional materials and/or work with peers to learn the course content, and teachers may give lectures more to supplement than to guide the learning process (see Kulik, Kulik, and Cohen, 1979). A related form of mastery learning is *continuous progress* (e.g., Cohen, 1977), where students proceed through a hierarchical set of objectives at their own rates and are frequently regrouped according to their individual skills and needs. Continuous progress mastery learning programs differ from individualized models primarily in that they establish mastery criteria for unit tests and provide corrective activities to students who do not meet these criteria the first time, and in that instruction is provided by the teacher to small groups rather than relying on programmed, self-instructional materials.

The third form of mastery learning is called *group-based mastery learning,* or Learning for Mastery (LFM) (Block & Anderson, 1975). This is by far the most commonly used form of mastery learning in elementary and secondary schools. In group-based mastery learning the teacher instructs the entire class at one pace. At the end of each unit of instruction a "formative test" is given, covering the unit's content. A mastery criterion, usually in the range of 80–90% correct, is established for this test. Any students who do not achieve the mastery criterion on the formative test receive corrective instruction, which may take the form of tutoring by the teacher or by students who did achieve at the criterion level, small group sessions in which teachers go over skills or concepts students missed, alternative activities or materials for students to complete independently, and so on. In describing this form of mastery learning, Block and Anderson (1975) recommend that corrective activities be different from the kinds of activities used in initial instruction. Following the corrective instruction, students take a parallel formative or "summative" test. In some cases only one cycle of formative text-corrective instruction-parallel test is used, and the class moves on even if several students still have not achieved the mastery criterion; in others, the cycle may be repeated two or more times until virtually all students have gotten a passing score. All students who achieve the mastery criterion at any point are generally given an "A" on the unit, regardless of how many tries it took for them to reach the criterion score.

The most recent full-scale review of research on mastery learning was published more than a decade ago, by Block and Burns (1976); however, in recent years two meta-analyses of research in this area have appeared, one by Kulik, Kulik, and Bangert-Drowns (1986) and one by Guskey and Gates (1985, 1986). Meta-analyses characterize the impact of a treatment on a set of related outcomes using a common metric called *effect size,* the post-test score for the experimental group minus that for the control group divided by the control group's standard deviation (see Glass, McGaw & Smith, 1981). For example, an effect size of 1.0

would indicate that on the average, an experimental group exceeded a control group by one standard deviation; the average member of the experimental group would score at the level of a student in the 84th percentile of the control group's distribution.

Both of the recent meta-analyses of research on mastery learning report extraordinary positive effects of this method on student achievement. Kulik et al. (1986) find mean effect sizes of 0.52 for pre-college studies and 0.54 for college studies. Guskey and Gates (1985) claim effect sizes of 0.94 at the elementary level (grades 1–8), 0.72 at the high school level, and 0.65 at the college level. Further, Walberg (1984) reports a mean effect size of 0.81 for mastery learning in science and Lysakowski and Walberg (1982) estimated an effect size for cues, participation, and corrective feedback, principal components of mastery learning, at 0.97. Bloom (1984a) claims an effect size of 1.00 "when mastery learning procedures are done systematically and well" (p. 7), and has predicted that forms of mastery learning will be able to consistently produce achievement effects of "two sigma" (i.e., effect sizes of 2.00). To put these effect sizes in perspective, consider that the mean effect size for randomized studies of one-to-one adult tutoring reported by Glass, Cahen, Smith and Filby (1982) was 0.62 (see Slavin, 1984a). If the effects of mastery learning instruction approach or exceed those for one-to-one tutoring, then mastery learning is indeed a highly effective instructional method.

The purpose of this chapter is to review the research on the effects of group-based mastery learning on the achievement of elementary and secondary students in an attempt to understand the validity and the practical implications of these findings. The review uses a method for synthesizing large literatures called "best-evidence synthesis" (Slavin, 1986), which combines the use of effect size as a common metric of treatment effect with narrative review procedures. Before synthesizing the "best evidence" on practical applications of mastery learning, the following sections discuss the theory on which group-based mastery learning is based, how that theory is interpreted in practice, and problems inherent to research on the achievement effects of mastery learning.

Mastery Learning in Theory and Practice

The theory on which mastery learning is based is quite compelling. Particularly in such hierarchically organized subjects as mathematics, reading, and foreign language, failure to learn prerequisite skills is likely to interfere with students' learning of later skills. For example, if a student fails to learn to subtract, he or she is sure to fail in learning long division. If instruction is directed toward ensuring that nearly all students learn each skill in a hierarchical sequence, then students will have the prerequisite skills necessary to enable them to learn the later skills. Rather than accepting the idea that differences in student aptitudes will lead to corresponding differences in student achievement, mastery learning theory holds that instructional time and resources should be used to bring all students up to an acceptable level of achievement. Put another way, mastery learning theorists suggest that rather than holding instructional time constant and allowing achievement to vary (as in traditional instruction), *achievement level* should be held constant and *time* allowed to vary (see Bloom, 1968; Carroll, 1963).

In an extreme form, the central contentions of mastery learning theory are almost tautologically true. If we establish a reasonable set of learning objectives and demand that every student achieve them at a high level *regardless of how long that takes,* then it is virtually certain that all students will ultimately achieve that criterion. For example, imagine that students are learning to subtract two-digit numbers with renaming. A teacher might set a mastery criterion of 90% on a test of two-digit subtraction. After some period of instruction, the class is given a formative test, and let's say half of the class achieves at the 80% level. The teacher might then work with the "non-masters" group for one or more periods, and then give a parallel test. Say that half of the remaining students pass this time (25% of the class). If the teacher continues this cycle indefinitely, then all or almost all students will ultimately learn the skill, although it may take a long time for this to occur. Such a procedure would also accomplish two central goals of mastery learning, particularly as explicated by Bloom (1976): To reduce the variation in student achievement and to reduce or eliminate any correlation between aptitude and achievement. Since all students must achieve at a high level on the subtraction objective but students who achieve the criterion early cannot go on to new material, there is a ceiling effect built in to the procedure which will inherently cause variation among students to be small and correspondingly reduce the correlation between mathematics aptitude and subtraction performance. In fact, if we set the mastery criterion at 100% and repeated the formative test-corrective instruction cycle until all students achieved this criterion, then the variance on the subtraction test would be zero, as would the correlation between aptitude and achievement.

However, this begs several critical questions. If some students take much longer than others to learn a particular objective, then one of two things must happen. Either corrective instruction must be given outside of regular class time, or students who achieve mastery early on will have to spend considerable amounts of time waiting for their classmates to catch up. The first option, extra time, is expensive and difficult to arrange, as it requires that teachers be available outside of class time to work with the non-masters and that some students spend a great deal more time on any particular subject than they do ordinarily. The other option, giving enrichment or lateral extension activities while corrective instruction is given, may or may not be beneficial for these students. For all students mastery learning poses a dilemma, a choice between content coverage and content mastery (see Arlin, 1984a; Mueller, 1976; Resnick, 1977). It may often be the case that even for low achievers, spending the time to master each objective may be less productive than covering more objectives (see, for example, Cooley & Leinhardt, 1980).

Problems Inherent to Mastery Learning Research

The nature of mastery learning theory and practice creates thorny problems for research on the achievement effects of mastery learning strategies. These problems fall into two principal categories: Unequal time and unequal objectives.

Unequal Time.   One of the fundamental propositions of mastery learning theory is that learning should be held constant and time should be allowed to vary, rather than the opposite situation held to exist in traditional instruction. However, if the total instructional time allocated to a particular subject is fixed, then a common level of learning for all students is likely to require taking time away from high achievers to increase it for low achievers, a leveling process that would in its extreme form be repugnant to most educators (see Arlin, 1982, 1984b; Arlin & Westbury, 1976; Fitzpatrick, 1985; Smith, 1981).

To avoid what Arlin (1984b) calls a ''Robin Hood'' approach to time allocation in mastery learning, many applications of mastery learning provide corrective instruction during times other than regular class time, such as during lunch, recess, or after school (see Arlin, 1982). In short-term laboratory studies, the extra time given to students who need corrective instruction is often substantial. For example, Arlin & Webster (1983) conducted an experiment in which students studied a unit on sailing under mastery or non-mastery conditions for four days. After taking formative tests, mastery learning students who did not achieve a score of 80% received individual tutoring during times other than regular class time. Non-mastery students took the formative tests as final quizzes, and did not receive tutoring.

The mastery learning students achieved at twice the level of non-mastery students in terms of percent correct on daily chapter tests, an effect size of more than 3.0. However, mastery learning students spent more than twice as much time learning the same material. On a retention test taken four days after the last lesson, mastery students retained more than non-mastery students (effect size = .70). However, non-mastery students retained far more *per hour of instruction* than did mastery learning students (ES = -1.17). Similarly, Gettinger found that students who were given enough time to achieve a 100% criterion on a set of reading tasks achieved only 15.5% more than did students who were allowed an average of half the time allocated to the 100% mastery group.

In recent articles published in *Educational Leadership* and the *Educational Researcher,* Benjamin Bloom (1984a,1984b) noted that several dissertations done by his graduate students at the University of Chicago found effect sizes for mastery learning of one sigma or more (i.e., one standard deviation or more above the control group's mean). In all of these, corrective instruction was given outside of regular class time, increasing total instructional time beyond that allocated to the control groups. The additional time averaged 20–33% of the initial classroom instruction, or about one day per week. For example, in a two-week study in Malaysia by Nordin (1979) an extra period for corrective instruction was provided to the mastery learning classes, while control classes did other school work unrelated to the units involved in the study.

In discussing the practicality of mastery learning, Bloom (1984b) states that "the time or other costs of the mastery learning procedures have usually been very small" (p.9). It may be true that school districts could in theory provide tutors to administer corrective instruction outside of regular class time; the costs of doing so would hardly be "very small," but cost or cost-effectiveness is not at issue here. But as a question of experimental design, the extra time often given to mastery learning classes is a serious problem. It is virtually unheard-of in educational research outside of the mastery learning tradition to systematically allocate an experimental group more instructional time than a control group, except in studies of the effects of time itself. Presumably, any sensible instructional program would produce significantly greater achievement than a control method that allocated 20–33% less instructional time. Studies that fail to hold time constant across treatments essentially confound treatment effects with effects of additional time.

It might be argued that mastery learning programs that provide corrective instruction outside of regular class time produce effects that are substantially greater *per unit time* than those associated with traditional instruction. However, computing "learning per unit time" is not a straightforward process. In the Arlin and Webster (1983) experiment discussed earlier, mastery learning students passed about twice as many items on immediate chapter tests as did control students, and the time allocated to the mastery learning students was twice that allocated to control. Thus, the "learning per unit time" was about equal in both groups. Yet on a *retention* test only four days later, the items passed per unit time were considerably higher for the control group. Which is the correct measure of learning per unit time, that associated with the chapter tests or that associated with the retention test?

Many mastery learning theorists (e.g., Block, 1972; Bloom, 1976; Guskey & Gates, 1985) have argued that the "extra time" issue is not as problematic as it seems, because the time needed for corrective instruction should diminish over time. The theory behind this is that by ensuring that all students have mastered the prerequisite skills for each new unit, the need for corrective instruction on each successive unit should be reduced. A few very brief experiments using specially constructed, hierarchically organized curriculum materials have demonstrated that over as many as three successive one-hour units, time needed for corrective instruction does in fact diminish (Anderson, 1976; Arlin, 1973, Block, 1972); however, Arlin (1984a) examined time-to-mastery records for students involved in a mastery learning program over a 4-year period. In the first grade, the ratio of average time to mastery for the slowest 25% of students to that for the fastest 25% was 2.5 to 1. Rather than decreasing, as would have been predicted by mastery learning theorists, this ratio increased over the four year period. By the fourth grade, the ratio was 4.2 to 1. Thus, while it is theoretically possible that mastery learning procedures may ultimately reduce the need for corrective instruction, no evidence from long-term practical applications of mastery learning supports this possibility at present.

It should be noted that many studies of mastery learning do hold total instruction time more or less constant across experimental and control conditions. In discussing the "best evidence" on practical applications of mastery learning, issues of time for corrective instruction are explored further later.

Unequal Objectives. An even thornier problem posed by research on mastery learning revolves around the question of achievement measures used as dependent variables. Most studies of mastery learning use experimenter-made summative achievement tests as the criterion of learning effects. The danger inherent in the use of such tests is that they will correspond more closely to the curriculum taught in the mastery learning classes than to that taught in control classes. Some articles describing mastery learning experiments (e.g., Kersh, 1970; Lueckemeyer & Chiappetta, 1981) describe considerable efforts to ensure that experimental and control classes were pursuing the same objectives, and many studies administer the formative tests used in the mastery learning classes as quizzes in the control classes, which in theory should help focus the control classes on the same objectives. On the other hand, many other studies specified that students used the same texts and other materials but did not use formative tests in the control group or otherwise focus the control groups on the same objectives as those pursued in the mastery learning classes (e.g., Cabezon, 1984; Crotty, 1975).

The possibility that experimenter-made tests will be biased toward the objectives taught in experimental groups exists in all educational research that uses such tests, but it is particularly problematic in research on mastery learning, which by its nature focuses teachers and students on a narrow and explicitly defined set of objectives. When careful control of instructional methods, materials, and tests is not exercised, there is always a possibility that the control group is learning valuable information or skills not learned in the mastery learning group but not assessed on the experimenter-made measure.

Even when instructional objectives are carefully matched in experimental and control classes, use of experimenter-made tests keyed to what is taught in both classes can introduce a bias in favor of the mastery learning treatment. As noted earlier, when time for corrective instruction is provided within regular class time (rather than after class or after school), mastery learning trades *coverage* for *mastery* (see Anderson, 1985). The overall effects of this trade must be assessed using broadly based measures. What traditional whole-class instruction is best at, at least in theory, is covering material. Mastery learning proponents point out that material covered is not necessarily material learned. This is certainly true, but it is just as certainly true that material *not* covered is material *not* learned. Holding mastery learning and control groups to the same objectives in effect finesses the issue of instructional pace by only measuring the objectives that are covered by the mastery learning classes. If the control classes in fact cover more objectives, or could have done so had they not been held to the same pace as the mastery learning classes, this would not be registered on the experimenter-made test.

These observations concerning problems in the use of experimenter-made measures do not imply that all studies that use them should be ignored. Rather, they are meant to suggest extreme caution and careful reading of details of each such study before conclusions are drawn.

METHODS

This review uses a method called *best-evidence synthesis,* procedures described by Slavin (1986a) for synthesizing large literatures in social science. Best-evidence synthesis essentially combines the quantification of effect sizes and the systematic literature search and inclusion procedures of meta-analysis (Glass et al., 1981) with the description of individual studies and methodological and substantive issues characteristic of traditional literature reviews. In order to allow for adequate description of a set of studies high in internal and external validity, best-evidence synthesis applies well justified a priori criteria to select studies to constitute the main body of the review.

This section, ''Methods,'' outlines the specific procedures used in preparing the review, including such issues as how studies were located, which were selected for inclusion, how effect sizes were computed, how studies were categorized, and how the question of pooling of effect sizes was handled. For additional details on the review procedures, see Slavin, 1987a.

Literature Search Procedures

The first step in conducting the best-evidence synthesis was to locate as complete as possible a set of studies of mastery learning. Several sources of references were used. The ERIC system and Dissertation Abstracts produced hundreds of citations in response to the keywords ''mastery learning.'' Additional sources of citations included a bibliography of mastery learning studies compiled by Hymel (1982), earlier reviews and meta-analyses on mastery learning, and references in the primary studies. Papers presented at the American Educational Research Association meetings since 1976 were solicited from their authors. Dissertations were ordered from University Microfilms and from the University of Chicago, which does not cooperate with University Microfilms.

Criteria for Study Inclusion

The studies on which this review is primarily based had to meet a set of a priori criteria with respect to germaneness and methodological adequacy.

Germaneness.   To be considered germane to the review, all studies had to evaluate group-based mastery learning programs in regular (i.e., non-special) elementary and secondary classrooms. "Group-based mastery learning" was defined as any instructional method that had the following characteristics:

1.   Students were tested on their mastery of instructional objectives at least once every 4 weeks. A mastery criterion was set (e.g., 80% correct) and students who did not achieve this criterion on an initial formative test received corrective instruction and a second formative or summative test. This cycle could be repeated one or more times. Studies were included regardless of the form of corrective instruction used and regardless of whether corrective instruction was given during or outside of regular class time.

2.   Before each formative test, students were taught as a total group. This requirement excluded studies of individualized or continuous progress forms of mastery learning and studies of the Personalized System of Instruction. However, studies in which mastery learning students worked on individualized materials as corrective (not initial) instruction were included.

3.   Mastery learning was the only or principal intervention. This excluded comparisons such as those in two studies by Mevarech (1985a, 1985b) evaluating a combination of mastery learning and cooperative learning, and comparisons involving enhancement of cognitive entry behaviors (e.g., Leyton, 1983).

Methodological Adequacy.   Criteria for methodological adequacy were as follows:

1.   Studies had to compare group-based mastery learning programs to traditional group-paced instruction not using the feedback-corrective cycle. A small number of studies (e.g., Katims & Jones, 1985; Strasler & Rochester, 1982) that compared achievement under mastery learning to that during previous years (before mastery learning was introduced) were excluded, on the basis that changes in grade-to-grade promotion policies, curriculum alignment, and other trends in recent years make year-to-year changes difficult to ascribe to any one factor.

2. Evidence had to be given that experimental and control groups were initially equivalent, or the degree of non-equivalence had to be quantified and capable of being adjusted for in computing effect sizes. This excluded a small number of studies that failed to either give pretests or to randomly assign students to treatments.

3. Study duration had to be at least 4 weeks (20 hours). This restriction excluded a large number of brief experiments that often used procedures that would be difficult to replicate in practice (such as providing 1 hour of corrective instruction for every hour of initial instruction). The reason for this restriction was to concentrate the review on mastery learning procedures that could in principle be used over extended time periods.

4. At least two experimental and two control classes and/or teachers had to be involved in the study.

5. The achievement measure used had to be an objective assessment of objectives taught in control as well as experimental classes.

Computation of Effect Sizes

The size and direction of effects of mastery learning on student achievement are presented throughout this review in terms of effect size. Effect size, as described by Glass et al. (1981), is the difference between experimental and control post-test means divided by the control group's post-test standard deviation. However, this formula was adapted in the present review to take into account pre-test or ability differences between the experimental and control groups. If pre-tests were available, then the formula used was the difference in experimental and control *gains* divided by the control group's post-test standard deviation (see Slavin, 1987a, for more on this).

In the few cases in which data necessary for computing effect sizes were lacking in studies that otherwise met criteria for inclusion, the studies' results were indicated in terms of their direction and statistical significance.

RESEARCH ON ACHIEVEMENT EFFECTS
OF GROUP-BASED MASTERY LEARNING

What are the effects of group-based mastery learning on the achievement of elementary and secondary students? In essence, there are three claims that proponents of mastery learning might make for the effectiveness of mastery learning. These are as follows:

1. Mastery learning is more effective than traditional instruction *even when instructional time is held constant and achievement measures register coverage as well as mastery.*

This might be called the "strong claim" for the achievement effects of mastery learning. It is clear, at least in theory, that if mastery learning procedures greatly increase allocated time for instruction by providing enough additional time for corrective instruction to bring all students to a high level of mastery, then mastery learning students will achieve more than traditionally taught control students. But it is less obviously true that the additional time for corrective instruction is more productive in terms of student achievement than it would be to simply increase allocated time for the control students. The "strong claim" asserts that time used for corrective instruction (along with the other elements of mastery learning) is indeed more productive than time used for additional instruction to the class as a whole. It is important to note that this "strong claim" might not be endorsed by all mastery learning proponents. For example, Bloom (1976) notes that the "time costs (necessary to enable four-fifths of students to reach a level of achievement which less than one-fifth attain in non-mastery conditions) are typically of the order of ten to twenty percent additional time over the classroom scheduled time" (p. 5). However, Block and Anderson (1975) describe a form of mastery learning that can be implemented within usual time constraints, and in practice corrective instruction is rarely given during additional time.

Similarly, it is clear (in theory) that if students who experienced mastery learning are tested on the specific objectives they studied, they will score higher on those objectives than will students who were studying similar but not identical objectives. Further, it is likely that even if mastery learning and control classes are held to precisely the same objectives but the control classes are not allowed to move ahead if they finish those objectives before their mastery learning counterparts do, then the traditional model is deprived of its natural advantage, the capacity to cover material rapidly. A "fair" measure of student achievement in a mastery learning experiment would have to register both coverage and mastery, so that if the control group covered more objectives than the mastery learning group, its learning of these additional objectives would be registered. The "strong claim" would hold that even allowing control classes to proceed at their own rate and even using such an achievement measure, mastery learning would produce more achievement than control methods.

The best evidence for the "strong claim" would probably come from studies in which mastery learning and control classes studied precisely the same objectives using the same materials and lessons and the same amount of allocated time, but in which teachers could determine their own pace of instruction and achievement measures covered the objectives reached by the fastest-moving class. Unfortunately, such studies are not known to exist. However, a good approximation of these experimental design features is achieved by studies that hold allocated time constant and use standardized tests as the criterion of achievement. Assuming that curriculum materials are not specifically keyed to the standardized tests in either treatment, these tests offer a means of registering both mastery and coverage. In such basic skills areas as mathematics and reading, the standardized tests are likely to have a high overlap with the objectives pursued by mastery learning teachers as well as by control teachers.

2. Mastery learning is an effective means of ensuring that teachers adhere to a particular curriculum and students learn a specific set of objectives (the "curricular focus" claim).

A "weak claim" for the effectiveness of mastery learning would be that these methods focus teachers on a particular set of objectives that is held to be superior to those that might have been pursued by teachers on their own. This might be called the "curricular focus" claim. For example, consider a survey course on U.S. history. Left to their own devices, some teachers might teach details about individual battles of the Civil War; others might entirely ignore the battles and focus on the economic and political issues; and still others might approach the topic in some third way, combine both approaches, or even teach with no particular plan of action. A panel of curriculum experts might determine that there is a small set of critical understandings about the Civil War that all students should have, and they might devise a criterion-referenced test to assess these understandings. If it can be assumed that the experts' judgments are indeed superior to those of individual teachers, then teaching to this test may not be inappropriate, and mastery learning may be a means of holding students and teachers to the essentials, relegating other concepts they might have learned (which are not on the criterion-referenced test) to a marginal status. It is no accident that mastery learning grew out of the behavioral objectives/criterion-referenced testing movement (see Bloom, Hastings, & Madaus, 1971); one of the central precepts of mastery learning is that once critical objectives are identified for a given course, then students should be required to master those and only those objectives. Further, it is interesting to note that recent years the mastery learning movement has often allied itself with the "curriculum alignment" movement, which seeks to focus teachers on objectives that happen to be contained in district or state-level criterion-referenced minimum competency tests as well as norm-referenced standardized tests (see Levine, 1985).

The "curricular focus" claim, that mastery learning may help focus teachers and students on certain objectives, is characterized here as a "weak claim" because it requires a belief that any objectives other than those pursued by the mastery learning program are of little value. Critics (e.g., Resnick, 1977) point out with some justification that a focus on a well-defined set of minimum objectives may place a restriction on the maximum that students might have achieved; however, in certain circumstances it may well be justifiable to hold certain objectives to be essential to a course of study, and mastery learning may represent an effective means of ensuring that nearly all students have attained these objectives.

The best evidence for the "curricular focus" claim would come from studies in which curriculum experts formulated a common set of objectives to be pursued equally by mastery learning and control teachers within an equal amount of allocated time. If achievement on the criterion-referenced assessments were higher in mastery learning than in control classes, then we could at least make the argument that the mastery learning students have learned more of the *essential* objectives, even though the control group may have learned additional, presumably less essential concepts.

3. Mastery learning is an effective use of additional time and instructional resources to bring almost all students to an acceptable level of achievement (the "extra time" claim).

A second "weak claim" would be that given the availability of additional teacher and student time for corrective instruction, mastery learning is an effective means of ensuring almost all students a minimal level of achievement. As noted earlier, in an extreme form this "extra time" claim is almost axiomatically true. Leaving aside cases of serious learning disabilities, it should certainly be possible to ensure that virtually all students can achieve a minimal set of objectives in a new course if an indefinite amount of one-to-one tutoring is available to students who initially fail to pass formative tests. However, it may be that even within the context of the practicable, providing students with additional instruction if they need it will bring almost all to a reasonable level of achievement.

The reason that this is characterized here as a "weak claim" is that it begs the question of whether the additional time used for corrective instruction is the *best* use of additional time. What could the control classes do if they also had more instructional time? However, the "extra time" issue is not a trivial one, as it is not impossible to routinely provide corrective instruction to students who need it outside of regular class time. For example, this might be an effective use of compensatory (Chapter 1) or special education resource pull-outs, a possibility that is discussed later.

The best evidence for this claim would come from studies that provided mastery learning classes with additional time for corrective instruction and used achievement tests that covered all topics which could have been studied by the fastest-paced classes (e.g., standardized tests). However, such studies are not known to exist; the best existing evidence for the "extra time" claim is from studies which used experimenter-made achievement measures and provided corrective instruction outside of class time.

Evidence for the "Strong Claim"

Table 4.1 summarizes the major characteristics and findings of seven mastery learning studies that met the inclusion criteria discussed earlier, provided equal

TABLE 4.1

Equal-Time Studies Using Standardized Measures

Article	Grades	Location	Sample Size	Duration	Design	Treatments	Subjects	Effect Sizes by Group/Measure	Total
Elementary									
Anderson et al. (1976)	1-6	Lorain, Ohio	2 sch.	1 yr.	Students in matched ML, control schools matched on ability	ML-Followed Block (1971). Control-Untreated	Math		+.04
Kersh (1970)	5	Suburban Chicago	11 cl.	1 yr.	Teachers/classes randomly assigned to ML, control within each school	ML-Corr. inst. included reteaching, alternative mtls, peer tutoring. Formative tests given every 3-4 weeks. Control-Untreated.	Math	middle cl (-) lower cl (+)	0
Gutkin (1985)	1	Inner-city New York	41 cl.	1 yr.	Schools randomly assigned to ML, Control	ML-Formative tests given every month. Control-Untreated.	Reading		+.12
Katims et al. (1977)	upper elem	Inner-city Chicago	19 cl.	15 wks.	1 ML, 1 cont. class from each of 10 schools. Trts self-selected or principal imposed	ML-specific mtls provided. Control-Untreated.	Reading		+.25
Jones et al. (1979)	upper elem	Inner-city Chicago	4 sch.	1 yr.	2 ML schools matched with 2 control schools	ML-specific mtls provided. Control-Untreated.	Reading		+.09
Secondary									
Slavin & Karweit (1984)	9	Inner-city Philadelphia	25 cl.	25 wks.	Tchrs/classes randomly assigned to ML, cont.	ML-Formative tests given every 2-3 wks. Corr. inst. given by tchrs. Cont-Used same mtls, tests, procedures as ML except for corr. inst. & summative tests	General Math	Hi 0 Lo 0	+.02
Chance (1980)	8	Inner-city New Orleans	6 cl.	5 wks.	Students within each of 3 classes randomly assigned to ML or control	ML-Formative tests given every wk. Mast. crit. =80-90% Control-Used same mtls, tests, procedures as ML.	Reading	Hi 0 Av 0 Lo 0	0

Key: (+) Nonsignificant difference favoring ML
0 = No difference
(-) Nonsignificant difference favoring control

time for experimental and control classes, and used standardized measures of achievement. (For detailed descriptions of the individual studies, see Slavin, 1987a.)

Table 4.1 clearly indicates that the effects of mastery learning on standardized achievement measures are extremely small, at best. The median effect size across all seven studies is essentially zero (ES = +.04). The only study with a non-trivial effect size (ES = +.25), a semester-long experiment in inner-city Chicago elementary schools by Katims, Smith, Steele, and Wick (1977), also had a serious design flaw. Teachers were allowed to select themselves into mastery learning or control treatments or were assigned to conditions by their principals. It is entirely possible that the teachers who were most interested in using the new methods and materials, or those who were named by their principals to use the new program, were better teachers than were the control teachers. In any case, the differences were not statistically significant when analyzed at the class level, were only marginally significant (p = .071) for individual-level gains, and amounted to an experimental-control difference of only 11% of a grade equivalent.

One of the most important studies of mastery learning is the year-long Anderson, Scott, and Hutlock (1976) experiment briefly described earlier. This study compared students in grades 1–6 in one mastery learning and one control school in Lorain, Ohio. The study used both standardized tests and experimenter-made, criterion-referenced tests. The standardized tests were the Computations, Concepts, and Problem Solving scales of the California Achievement Test. The experimenter-made test was constructed by the project director (Nicholas Hutlock) to match the objectives taught in the mastery learning classes. Control teachers were asked to examine the list of objectives and identify any they did not teach, and these were eliminated from the test.

The results of the study were completely different for the two types of achievement tests. On the experimenter-made tests, students in the mastery learning classes achieved significantly more than did their matched counterparts at every grade level (mean ES = +.64). A retention test based on the same objectives was given three months after the end of the intervention period, and mastery learning classes still significantly exceeded control (ES = +.49). However, on the standardized tests, these differences were not registered. Mastery learning students scored somewhat higher than control on Computations (ES = +.17) and Problem Solving (ES = +.07), but the control group scored higher on Concepts (ES = −.12).

The Anderson et al. (1976) finding of marked differences in effects on standardized and experimenter-made measures counsels great caution in interpreting results of other studies which used experimenter-made measures only. In a year-long study of mathematics, it is highly unlikely that a standardized mathematics test would fail to register any meaningful treatment effect. Therefore, it must be assumed that the strong positive effects found by Anderson et al. (1976) on the experimenter-made tests are mostly or entirely due to the fact that these tests were keyed to the mastery learning classes' objectives. It may be that the control classes covered more objectives than the mastery learning classes, and that learning of these additional objectives was registered on the standardized but not the experimenter-made measures. A similar discrepancy between effects of mastery learning on standardized and experimenter-made measures was found in a year-long study of reading by Jones, Monsaas, and Katims (1979). A third study, which used standardized and experimenter-made math tests, found no effects on either measure (Kersh, 1970).

Overall, research on the effects of mastery learning on standardized achievement test scores provides little support for the "strong claim" that holding time and objectives constant, mastery learning will accelerate student achievement. The studies assessing these effects are not perfect; particularly when mastery learning is applied on a fairly wide scale in depressed inner-city schools, there is reason to question the degree to which the model was faithfully implemented. However, most of the studies used random assignment of classes or students to treatments, study durations approaching a full school year, and measures that registered coverage as well as mastery. Not one of the seven studies found effects of mastery learning that even reached conventional levels of statistical significance (even in individual-level analyses), much less educational significance. If group-based mastery learning had strong effects on achievement in such basic skills as reading and math, these studies would surely have detected them.

Evidence for the "Curricular Focus" Claim

Table 4.2 summarizes the principal evidence for the "curricular focus" claim, that mastery learning is an effective means of increasing student achievement of *specific* skills or concepts held to be the critical objectives of a course of study. The studies listed in the table are those that (in addition to meeting general inclusion criteria) used experimenter-made, criterion-referenced measures and apparently provided experimental and control classes with equal amounts of instructional time.

A total of nine studies met the requirements for inclusion in Table 4.2. Three of these (Anderson et al, 1976; Jones et al., 1979; Kersh, 1970) were studies that used both standardized and experimenter-made measures, and were therefore also included in Table 4.1.

Overall, the effects summarized in Table 4.2 could be interpreted as supporting the "curricular focus" claim. All but one (Kersh, 1970) of the studies found positive effects of mastery learning on experimenter-made, criterion-referenced measures. The median effect size is a moderate +.255. Two studies (Fuchs, Tindal, & Fuchs, 1985; Wyckoff, 1974) found that the effects of mastery learning were greatest for low achievers, as would be expected from mastery learning theory, and one (Kersh, 1970) found effects to be greatest for low-SES students.

TABLE 4.2

Equal-Time Studies Using Experimenter-Made Measures

Article	Grades	Location	Sample Size	Duration	Design	Treatments	Subjects	Effect Sizes by Group Measure		Total	Retention
Elementary											
Anderson et al. (1976)	1-6	Lorain, Ohio	2 sch.	1 yr.	See Table 4.1	See Table 4.1	Math	Posttest Retention (3 mo.)		+.64	+.49
Kersh (1970)	5	Suburban Chicago	11 cl.	1 yr.	See Table 4.1	See Table 4.1	Math			(-)	
Jones et al. (1979)	upper elem	Inner-city Chicago	4 sch.	1 yr.	See Table 4.1	See Table 4.1	Reading			+.18	
Wyckoff (1974)	6	Suburban Atlanta	4 cl.	9 wks.	Tchrs/classes randomly assigned to ML, control	ML-Mastery criterion 70%. Corr. Inst. was either reteaching to whole class or peer tutoring. Control-Used same mtls, tests, procedures as ML except for corr. inst. and summative tests.	Anthropology	Hi +.03 Lo +.58		+.24	
Fuchs et al. (1985)	1	Rural Minnesota	4 cl.	1 yr.	Students randomly assigned to ML, control	ML-Students tested on oral rdg. passages each wk. Whole rdg grp reviewed until 80% of students got at least 50 wpm correct. Control-students tested every 4-6 wks., all were promoted w/o corr. inst.	Reading	Hi (-) Lo +		+.20	
Elementary and Secondary											
Cabezon (1984)	3,6,8	Chile	46 cl.	1 yr.	Compared classes using ML to classes similar in SES, IQ.	ML-Not clearly specified Control-Untreated	Spanish Math	+.40 +.14	Gr3 +.47 Gr6 +.22 Gr8 +.12	+.27	

(continued...)

(Table 4.2 continued)

Article	Grades	Location	Sample Size	Duration	Design	Treatments	Subjects	Effect Sizes by Group Measure	Total	Retention
Secondary										
Leuckemeyer & Chiappetta (1981)	10	Suburban Houston	12 cl.	6 wks.	Students randomly assigned to ML, control. Pretest differences favored control.	ML-Formative tests given every 2 wks., followed by 2 days of corr. inst. (Criterion = 80%) Control-Used same mtls., tests, procedures as ML except for corr. inst. and summative tests	Human Physiology	Posttest Retention (4 wks.)	+.39	0
Dunkelberger & Heikkinen (1984)	9	Suburban Delaware	14 cl.	10 wks.	Students randomly assigned to ML, control classes. Tchrs taught ML & Control classes. Posttest given 4 mos. after end of implementation period.	ML-Students had to meet 80% criterion on repeatable tests to go on. Corrective activities available during free time. Control-Used same mtls, procedures, tests. Received detailed feedback and had same corrective mtls available during free time.	Chem./ Physics	Retention (4 mos.)		+.26
Mevarech (1986)	7	Israel	4 cl.	3 mos.	Students randomly assigned to ML, control classes.	ML-Students who did not reach 70% criterion on formative tests rec'd corr. inst. from tch or peers. Control-Used same mtls., tests as ML.	Algebra	Lo SES +1.78 Mid SES + .91 Hi SES + .66	+.90	

Key: + Significant difference favoring ML
(+)Nonsignificant difference favoring ML
(0)No difference
(-)Nonsignificant difference favoring control

However, the meaning of the results summarized in Table 4.2 is far from clear. The near-zero effects of mastery learning on standardized measures (Table 4.1) and in particular the dramatically different results for standardized and experimenter-made measures reported by Anderson et al. (1976) suggest that the effects of mastery learning on experimenter-made measures result from a shifting of instructional focus to a particular set of objectives not necessarily more valuable than those pursued by the control group. Unfortunately, it is impossible to determine from reports of mastery learning studies the degree to which control teachers were focusing on the objectives assessed on the experimenter-made measures, yet understanding this is crucial to understanding the effects reported in these studies.

Evidence for the Extra-Time Claim

The problem of unequal time for experimental and control groups is a serious one in mastery learning research in general, but the inclusion criteria used in the present review have the effect of eliminating the studies in which time differences are extreme. Mastery learning studies in which experimental classes receive considerably more instructional time than control classes are always either very brief, rarely more than a week (e.g., Anderson, 1975, 1976; Arlin & Webster, 1983), or they involve individualized or self-paced rather than group-paced instruction (e.g., Jones, 1975; Wentling, 1973). In studies of group-paced instruction conducted over periods of at least 4 weeks, extra time for corrective instruction rarely amounts to more than 20–25% of original time. It might be argued that additional instructional time of this magnitude might be a practicable means of ensuring all students a reasonable level of achievement, and the costs of such an approach might not be far out of line with the costs of current compensatory or special education.

Table 4.3 summarizes the characteristics and outcomes of group-based mastery learning studies in which the mastery learning classes received extra time for corrective instruction. All four of the studies in this category took place at the secondary level, grades 7–10. Also, these studies are distinctly shorter (5–6 weeks) than were most of the studies listed in Tables 4.1 and 4.2.

Overall, the evidence for the "extra time" claim is unclear. The median effect size for the small number of unequal time studies summarized in Table 4.3, ES = +.31, is no more positive than were those reported for other studies using experimenter-made measures (Table 4.2), in which mastery learning classes did not receive additional time. In fact, both of the unequal time studies that assessed retention (Fagan, 1976; Long, Okey, & Yeany, 1978) found that any effects observed at post-test disappeared as soon as 4 weeks later. Substantial achievement effects of extra time for corrective instruction appear to depend on provisions of substantial amounts of extra time, well in excess of 20–25%. However, studies in which large amounts of additional time are provided to the

TABLE 4.3

Unequal-Time Studies Using Experimenter-Made Measures

Article	Grades	Location	Sample Size	Duration	Design	Treatments	Extra Time	Subjects	Effect Sizes by Group/Measure	Total	Retention
Secondary											
Long et al. (1978)	8	Georgia	6 cl.	5 wks.	Students randomly assigned to 3 trts. Tchrs. rotated across trts.	Tchr-Directed ML-Formative tests given every 2 days. Remedial work given as corr. inst. "If problem persists," indiv. tutoring given by tchr. Student-Directed ML-Same formative tests used, returned to students for self-correction. Control-Same inst. but no tests, correctives	Not Stated	Earth Sci.	Tchr Directed ML vs. Control: Posttest Retention (12 wks) Tchr Directed ML vs. Student-Corected ML: Posttest Retention (12 wks)	+.43 +.19	+.08 −.03
Fagan (1976)	7	Dallas, Texas 1 middle class sch., 1 lower class sch.	17 cl.	5 wks.	4 tchrs randomly assigned to ML, control	ML-Formative tests given every wk. Tchrs drilled students who failed to achieve 80% criterion, then gave 2nd formative test. Control-Used same mtls. & procedures as ML. Formative tests taken as quizzes.	22%	Transp. & Environ.	Posttest Retention (4 wks)	−.11 −.11	−.15

(Table 4.3 continued)

Article	Grades	Location	Sample Size	Duration	Design	Treatments	Extra Time	Subjects	Effect Sizes by Group/Measure Total	Retention
Secondary										
Hecht (1980)	8	Urban, Suburban Midwest	5 cl.	6 wks.	Students randomly assigned to ML, control classes. Two tchrs taught ML and control classes.	ML-Formative tests given every 2 wks., followed by "intensive remedial help" Control-Used same mtls & Procedures as ML including both 1st & 2nd formative tests, but no remedial help.	Not Stated	Geometry		+.31
Mevarech (1980)	9	Chicago, middle class sch.	8 cl.	6 wks.	Students randomly assigned in 2x2 design to "algorithmic strategy" vs. "heuristic strategy" and to ML vs. control.	ML-Formative tests given every 2 wks. Students had 3 chances to obtain 80% criterion. Corr. inst. included grp. inst., peer tutoring, adult tutoring outside of class. Control-Used same mtls & procedures, took formative tests as quizzes. While ML classes received corr. inst., control worked add't problems.	Not Stated	Alg. I	Algorithmic Strategy +.70 Heuristic Strategy +.83	+.77

mastery learning classes either involved continuous-progress forms of mastery learning or are extremely brief and artificial. What is needed are long-term evaluations of mastery learning models in which corrective instruction is given outside of class time, preferably using standardized measures and/or criterion-referenced measures that register all objectives covered by all classes.

DISCUSSION

The best evidence from evaluations of practical applications of group-based mastery learning indicates that effects of these methods are moderately positive on experimenter-made achievement measures closely tied to the objectives taught in the mastery learning classes, and are essentially nil on standardized achievement measures. These findings may be interpreted as supporting the "weak claim" that mastery learning can be an effective means of holding teachers and students to a specified set of instructional objectives, but do not support the "strong claim" that mastery learning is more effective than traditional instruction given equal time and achievement measures that assess coverage as well as mastery. Further, even this "curricular focus" claim is undermined by uncertainties about the degree to which control teachers were trying to achieve the same objectives as the mastery learning teachers and by a failure to show effects of mastery learning on retention measures.

These conclusions are radically different from those drawn by earlier reviewers and meta-analysts. Not only would a mean effect size across the 17 studies emphasized in this review come nowhere near the mean of around 1.0 claimed by Bloom (1984a, b), Guskey and Gates (1985), Lysakowski and Walberg (1982), or Walberg (1984), but *no single study* reached this level. Only 2 of the 17 studies (Mevarech, 1980, 1986) had mean effect sizes in excess of the 0.52 mean estimated by Kulik et al. (1986) for pre-college studies of mastery testing. How can this gross discrepancy be reconciled?

First, these different reviews focus on very different sets of studies. Almost all of the studies cited in this review would have qualified for inclusion in any of the meta-analyses, but the reverse is not true. For example, of 25 elementary and secondary studies cited by Guskey and Gates (1985), only 6 qualified for inclusion in the present review. Of 19 such studies cited by Kulik et al. (1986), only 4 qualified for inclusion in the present review.

As noted earlier, the principal reason that studies cited elsewhere were excluded in the present paper is that they did not meet the 4-week duration requirement. The rationale for this restriction is that this review focuses on the effects of mastery learning *in practice,* not in theory. It would be difficult to maintain that a 2- or 3-week study could produce information more relevant to classroom practice than a semester- or year-long study, partly because artificial arrangements possible in a brief study could not be maintained over a longer period.

There are several important theoretical and practical issues raised by the studies of group-based mastery learning reviewed here. These are discussed in the following sections.

Why Are Achievement Effects of Group-Based Mastery Learning So Modest? The most striking conclusion of the present review is that other than perhaps focusing teachers and students on a narrow set of objectives, group-based mastery learning has modest to non-existent effects on student achievement in studies of at least four weeks' duration. Given the compelling nature of the theory on which mastery learning is based, it is interesting to speculate on reasons for this.

One possible explanation is that in long-term, practical applications of mastery learning, the quality of training, followup, and/or materials used to support the mastery learning approach are inadequate. One important piece of evidence in support of this possibility comes from a recent study by Dolan and Kellam (1987), who compared an enhanced mastery learning program to the standard mastery learning program used in Baltimore City first grades. The enhanced model provided teachers with 32 hours of instruction in mastery learning principles and practices, monthly progress meetings, classroom visits, files of formative tests, corrective activities, and enrichment activities keyed to school district objectives, and special curriculum materials and other resources to help teachers achieve reading objectives. Teachers using the standard mastery learning procedures also used the teach–test–corrective instruction–test cycle to achieve essentially the same reading objectives, but did not have the additional training, resources, or assistance. A year-long experiment assigned schools and the teachers within schools to the two models, and found that the enhanced mastery learning classes gained significantly more on standardized reading tests (ES = +.39).

A particular emphasis of the Dolan and Kellam (1987) enhanced mastery learning model was on the quality of the materials used for corrective instruction. In a letter explaining the extraordinary effects obtained in her studies, Zemira Mevarech (personal communication, January 25, 1987) also emphasized that the quality of the corrective procedures was a key factor in the success of her programs, noting that "corrective activities should be creative, attractive, and designed explicitly to remediate the skills that have not been mastered."

Another possible explanation for the disappointing findings of studies of group-based mastery learning is that it is not only that the *quality* of corrective instruction is lacking, but also that the *amount* of corrective instruction is simply not enough to remediate the learning deficits of low achievers. In none of the studies emphasized in this review did corrective instruction occupy more than one period per week, or 20% of all instructional time. This may be enough to get students up to criterion on very narrowly defined skills, but not enough to identify and remediate serious deficits, particularly when corrective instruction is given in group settings or by peer tutors (as opposed to adult tutors). Studies of students' pace through individualized materials routinely find that the slowest students require 200–600% more time than the fastest students to complete the same amount of material (Arlin & Westbury 1976; Carroll, 1963; Suppes, 1964), far more than what schools using mastery learning are likely to be able to provide for corrective instruction (Arlin, 1982).

The amount of corrective instruction given in practical applications of group-based mastery learning may be not only too little, but also too late. It may be that even 1 or 2 weeks is too long to wait to correct students' learning errors, and many studies provided corrective instruction less frequently, every 3 to 4 weeks. If one day's learning is a prerequisite for the next day's lesson, then perhaps detection and remediation of failures to master individual skills needs to be done daily to be effective. Further, in most applications of mastery learning, students may have years of accumulated learning deficits that 1 day per week of corrective instruction is unlikely to remediate.

Time for corrective instruction in group-based mastery learning is purchased at a cost in terms of slowing instructional pace. If this time does not produce a substantial impact on the achievement of large numbers of students, then a widespread although small negative impact on the learning of the majority may balance a narrow positive impact on the learning of the few students whose learning problems are large enough to need corrective instruction but small enough to be correctable in one class period per week or less.

However, it may be that the feedback–corrective cycle evaluated in the studies reported here is simply insufficient in itself to produce a substantial improvement in student achievement. As Bloom (1980, 1984b) has noted, there are many variables other than feedback–correction that should go into an effective instructional program. Both the process of learning and the process of instruction are so complex that it may be unrealistic to expect large effects on broadly based achievement measures from any one factor; instructional quality, adaptation to individual needs, motivation, and instructional time may all have to be impacted at the same time to produce such effects (see chapter 1; Slavin, 1987b).

Is Mastery Learning a Robin Hood Approach to Instruction?   Several critics of mastery learning (e.g., Arlin, 1984a; Resnick, 1977) have wondered whether mastery learning simply shifts a constant amount of learning from high to low achievers. The evidence from the present review is not inconsistent with that view; in several studies positive effects were found for low achievers only. In fact, given that overall achievement means are not greatly improved by group-based mastery learning, the reductions in standard deviations routinely seen in studies of these methods and corresponding decreases in correlations between pre-tests and post-tests are simply statistical indicators of a shift in achievement from high to low achievers. However, it is probably more accurate to say that group-based mastery learning trades coverage for mastery. Because rapid coverage is likely to be of greatest benefit to high achievers while high mastery is of greatest benefit to low achievers, resolving the coverage–mastery dilemma as recommended by mastery learning theorists is likely to produce a ''Robin Hood'' effect as a byproduct.

The coverage versus mastery dilemma and the corresponding ''Robin Hood'' effect are problematic only within the context of group-based mastery learning, and (at least in theory) only when instruction time is held constant. In continuous-progress or individualized forms of mastery learning in which students can move through material more or less at their own rates, the coverage–mastery dilemma is much less of a concern (Arlin & Westbury, 1976). This does not imply that continuous-progress forms of mastery learning are necessarily more effective than group-based forms; individualization solves the instructional pace problem but creates new problems, such as the difficulty of providing adequate direct instruction to students performing at many levels (Slavin, 1984b). However, there are examples of continuous-progress mastery learning programs that have positive effects on standardized achievement tests (see, for example, Cohen, 1977; Cohen & Rodriquez, 1980; Slavin & Karweit, 1985; Slavin & Madden, in press; Slavin, Madden, & Leavey, 1984).

Importance of Frequent, Criterion-Referenced Feedback.   Even if we accept the ''weak claim'' that mastery learning is an effective means of holding teachers and students to a valuable set of instruction objectives, there is still some question of which elements of mastery learning account for its effects on experimenter-made, criterion-referenced measures. There is some evidence that much of this effect may be accounted for by frequent testing and feedback to students rather than the entire feedback–corrective cycle. Kulik et al. (1986) report that mastery learning studies that failed to control for frequency of testing produced mean effect sizes almost twice those associated with studies in which mastery learning and control classes were tested with equal frequency. Long et al. (1978) compared mastery learning to a condition with the same frequency of testing and found a much smaller effect than in a comparison with a control group that did not receive tests. Looking across other studies, the pattern is complicated by the fact that most which held testing frequency constant also held the control groups to a slower pace than they might otherwise have attained.

Practical Implications.   The findings of the present review should not necessarily be interpreted as justifying an abandonment of mastery learning, either as an instructional practice or as a focus of research. Several widely publicized school improvement programs based on mastery learning principles have apparently been successful (e.g., Abrams, 1983; Levine & Stark, 1982; Menahem & Weisman, 1985; Robb, 1985), and many effective non-mastery-learning instructional strategies incorporate certain elements of mastery learning—in particular, frequent assessment of student learning of well specified objectives and basing teaching decisions on the results of these assessments. Further, the idea that students' specific learning deficits should be remediated immediately instead of being allowed to accumulate into large and general deficiencies makes a great deal of sense. More positive results are obtained in continuous-progress forms of mastery learning, in which students work at their own levels and rates. Use of Chapter I, special education, or other resources to provide substantial amounts of instructional time to help lower-achieving students keep up with their classmates in critical basic skills may also increase student achievement (Slavin & Madden, in press). This review only concerns the achievement effects of the group-based form of mastery learning (Block & Anderson, 1975) most commonly used in elementary and secondary schools.

Clearly, much more research is needed to explore the issues raised in this review. More studies of practical, long-term applications of mastery learning assessing the effects of these programs on broadly based measures of achievement that register coverage as well as mastery are especially needed; ideosyncratic features of the seven studies that used standardized tests preclude any interpretation of those studies as evidence that group-based mastery learning is *not* effective. There is very little known about what would be required to make group-based mastery learning instructionally effective; the Mevarech (1980, 1986) and Dolan and Kellam (1987) studies provide some clues along these lines, but much more needs to be known. In addition, studies carefully examining instructional pace in mastery and non-mastery models are needed to shed light on the coverage–mastery dilemma discussed here. Mastery learning models in which Chapter I or other remedial teachers provide significant amounts of corrective instruction outside of regular class time might be developed and evaluated, as well as models providing daily, brief corrective instruction rather than waiting for learning deficits to accumulate over 1 or more weeks. The disappointing findings of the studies discussed in this review counsel not a retreat from this area of research but rather a redoubling and redirection of efforts to understand how the compelling theories underlying mastery learning can achieve their potential in practical application.

Mastery learning theory and research has made an important contribution to the study of instructional methods; however, to understand this contribution it is critical to fully understand the conditions under which mastery learning has been studied, the measures that have been used, and other study features that bear on the internal and external validity of the findings. This best-evidence synthesis has attempted to clarify what we have learned from research on mastery learning in the hope that this knowledge will enrich further research and development in this important area.

REFERENCES

Abrams, J. D. (1983). Overcoming racial stereotyping in Red Bank, New Jersey. *School Administrator, 40,* 5, 7.

Anderson, L. W. (1975, April). *Time to criterion: An experimental study.* Paper presented at the American Educational Research Association, Washington, D.C.

Anderson, L. W. (1976). An empirical investigation of individual differences in time to learn. *Journal of Educational Psychology, 68,* 226–233.

Anderson, L. W. (1985). A retrospective and prospective view of Bloom's "learning for mastery". In M. C. Wang & H. J. Walberg (Eds.), *Adapting instruction to individual differences.* (pp. 254–268) Berkeley, CA: McCutchan.

Anderson, L. W., Scott, C., & Hutlock, N. (1976, April). *The effects of a mastery learning program on selected cognitive, affective and ecological variables in grades 1 through 6.* Paper presented at the annual meeting of the American Educational Research Association, San Francisco.

Arlin, M. (1973). *Learning rate and learning rate variance under mastery learning conditions.* Unpublished doctoral dissertation, University of Chicago.

Arlin, M. (1982). Teacher responses to student time differences in mastery learning. *American Journal of Education, 90,* 334–352.

Arlin, M. (1984a). Time variability in mastery learning. *American Educational Research Journal, 21,* 103–120.

Arlin, M. (1984b). Time, equality, and mastery learning. *Review of Educational Research, 54,* 65–86.

Arlin, M., & Webster, J. (1983). Time costs of mastery learning. *Journal of Educational Psychology, 75,* 187–195.

Arlin, M., & Westbury, I. (1976). The leveling effect of teacher pacing on science content mastery. *Journal of Research on Science Teaching, 13,* 213–219.

Block, J. H. (1972). Student learning and the setting of mastery performance standards. *Educational Horizons, 50,* 183–191.

Block, J. H., & Anderson, L. W. (1975). *Mastery learning in classroom instruction.* New York: MacMillan.

Block, J. H., & Burns, R. B. (1976). Mastery learning. In L. S. Shulman (Ed.), *Review of research in education* (vol. 4). Itasca, IL: F. E. Peacock.

Bloom, B. S. (1968). Learning for mastery. (UCLA-CSEIP). *Evaluation Comment, 1,* 2.

Bloom, B. (1976). *Human characteristics and school learning.* New York: McGraw-Hill.

Bloom, B. S. (1980). The new direction in educational research: Alterable variables. *Phi Delta Kappan, 62,* 382–385.

Bloom, B. S. (1984a). The 2 sigma problem: The search for methods of instruction as effective as one-to-one tutoring. *Educational Researcher, 13,* 4–16.

Bloom, B. S. (1984b). The search for methods of group instruction as effective as one-to-one tutoring. *Educational Leadership, 41,* (8), 4–17.

Bloom, B. S., Hastings, J. T., & Madaus, G. F. (1971). *Handbook on formative and summative evaluation of student learning.* New York: McGraw-Hill.

Cabezon, E. (1984). *The effects of marked changes in student achievement pattern on the students, their teachers, and their parents: The Chilean case.* Unpublished doctoral dissertation, University of Chicago.

Carroll, J. B. (1963). A model for school learning. *Teachers College Record, 64,* 723–733.

Chance, C. E. (1980). *The effects of feedback/corrective procedures on reading achievement and retention.* Unpublished doctoral dissertaion, University of Chicago.

Cohen, S. A. (1977). Instructional systems in reading: A report on the effects of a curriculum design based on a systems model. *Reading World, 16,* 158–171.

Cohen, S. A., & Rodriquez, S. (1980). Experimental results that question the Ramirez-Castaneda model for teaching reading to first grade Mexican Americans. *The Reading Teacher, 34,* 12–18.

Cooley, W. W., & Leinhardt, G. (1980). The instruction dimensions study. *Educational Evaluation and Policy Analysis, 2,* 7–15.

Crotty, E. K. (1975). An experimental comparison of a mastery learning and lecture–discussion approach to the teaching of world history. *Dissertation Abstracts International, 36,* 7150A (University Microfilms No. 76-10610).

Dolan, L. J., & Kellam, S. G. (1987). *Preliminary report of mastery learning intervention during first grade with cohort I students.* Baltimore, MD: Johns Hopkins University, Department of Mental Hygiene, Prevention Center.

Dunkelberger, G. E., & Heikkinen, H. (1984). The influence of repeatable testing on retention in mastery learning. *School Science and Mathematics, 84,* 590–597.

Fagan, J. S. (1976). Mastery learning: The relationship of mastery procedures and aptitude to the achievement and retention of transportation-environmental concepts by seventh grade students. *Dissertation Abstracts International, 36,* 5981. (University Microfilms No. 76-6402)

Fitzpatrick, K. A. (1985, April). *Group-based mastery learning: A Robin Hood approach to instruction?* Paper presented at the annual convention of the American Educational Research Association, Chicago.

Fuchs, L. S., Tindal, F., & Fuchs, D. (1985). *A comparison of mastery learning procedures among high and low ability students.* Unpublished manuscript, Vanderbilt University, Nashville, TN ERIC No. ED 259 307.

Gettinger, M. (1985). Time allocated and time spent relative to time needed for learning for learning as determinants of achievement. *Journal of Educational Psychology, 77,* 3–11.

Glass, G., Cahen, L., Smith, M. L., & Filby, N. (1982). *School class size.* Beverly Hills, CA: Sage.

Glass, G., McGaw, B., & Smith, M. L. (1981). *Meta-analysis in social research.* Beverly Hills, CA: Sage.

Guskey, T. R., & Gates, S. L. (1985, April). *A synthesis of research on group-based mastery learning programs.* Paper presented at the annual convention of the American Educational Research Association, Chicago.

Guskey, T. R., & Gates, S. L. (1986). Synthesis of research on the effects of mastery learning in elementary and secondary classrooms. *Educational Leadership, 43* (8), 73–80.

Gutkin, J. (1985, March). *The effect of diagnostic inservice training on class reading achievement and the number of lessons covered.* Paper presented at the annual convention of the American Educational Research Association, Chicago.

Hecht, L. W. (1980, April). *Stalking mastery learning in its natural habitat.* Paper presented at the annual convention of the American Educational Research Association, Boston.

Hymel, G. M. (1982). *Mastery learning: A comprehensive bibliography.* New Orleans: Loyola University.

Jones, B. F., Monsaas, J. A., & Katims, M. (1979, April). *Improving reading comprehension: Embedding diverse learning strategies within a mastery learning instructional format.* Paper presented at the annual meeting of the American Educational Research Association, San Francisco.

Jones, F. G. (1975). The effects of mastery and aptitude on learning, retention, and time. *Dissertation Abstracts, 35,* 6547 (University Microfilms No. 75-8126).

Katims, M., & Jones, B. F. (1985). Chicago Mastery Learning Reading: Mastery learning instruction and assessment of inner-city schools. *Journal of Negro Education, 54,* 369–387.

Katims, M., Smith, J. K., Steele, C., & Wick, J. W. (1977, April). *The Chicago Mastery Learning Reading Program: An interim evaluation.* Paper presented at the annual convention of the American Educational Research Association, New York.

Keller, F. S. (1968). "Good-bye, teacher . . ." *Journal of Applied Behavior Analysis, 1,* 78–89.

Kersh, M. E. (1970). *A strategy for mastery learning in fifth grade arithmetic.* Unpublished doctoral dissertation, University of Chicago.

Kulik, C. L., Kulik, J. A., & Bangert-Drowns, R. L. (1986, April). *Effects of testing for mastery on student learning.* Paper presented at the annual convention of the American Educational Rsearch Association, San Francisco.

Kulik, J. A., Kulik, C. L., & Cohen, P. A. (1979). A. meta-analysis of outcome studies of Keller's Personalized System of Instruction. *American Psychologist, 34,* 307–318.

Levine, D. U. (Ed.). (1985). *Improving student achievement through mastery learning programs.* San Francisco: Jossey-Bass.

Levine, D. V., & Stark, J. (1982). Instructional and organizational arrangements that improve achievement in inner-city schools. *Educational Leadership, 39,* 41–46.

Leyton, F. S. (1983). *The extent to which group instruction supplemented by mastery of initial cognitive prerequisites approximates the learning effectiveness of one-to-one tutorial methods.* Unpublished doctoral dissertation, University of Chicago.

Long, J. C., Okey, J. R., & Yeany, R. H. (1978). The effects of diagnosis with teacher- or student-directed remediation on science achievement and attitudes. *Journal of Research in Science Teaching, 15,* 505–511.

Lueckemeyer, C. L., & Chiappetta, E. L. (1981). An investigation into the effects of a modified mastery learning strategy on achievement in a high school human physiology unit. *Journal of Research in Science Teaching, 18,* 269–273.

Lysakowski, R., & Walberg, H. (1982). Instructional effects of cues, participation, and corrective feedback: A quantiative synthesis. *American Educational Research Journal, 19,* 559–578.

Menahem, M., & Weisman, L. (1985). Improving reading ability through a mastery learning program: A case study. In D. Levine (Ed.), *Improving student achievement through mastery learning programs.* San Francisco: Jossey-Bass.

Mevarech, Z. R. (1980). *The role of teaching–learning strategies and feedback–corrective procedures in developing higher cognitive achievement.* Unpublished doctoral dissertation, University of Chicago.

Mevarech, Z. R. (1986). The role of a feedback corrective procedure in developing mathematics achievement and self-concept in desegregated classrooms. *Studies in Educational Evaluation, 12,* 197–203.

Mueller, D. J. (1976). Mastery learning: Partly boon, partly boondoggle. *Teachers College Record, 78,* 41–52.

Nordin, A. B. (1979). *The effects of different qualities of instruction on selected cognitive, affective, and time variables.* Unpublished doctoral dissertation, University of Chicago.

Resnick, L. B. (1977). Assuming that everyone can learn everything, will some learn less? *School Review, 85,* 445–452.

Robb, D. W. (1985). Strategies for implementing successful mastery learning programs: Case studies. In D. Levine (Ed.), *Improving student achievement through mastery learning programs.* San Francisco: Jossey-Bass.

Slavin, R. E. (1984a). Meta-analysis in education: How has it been used? *Educational Researcher, 13* (8), 6–15, 24–27.

Slavin, R. E. (1984b). Component building: A strategy for research-based instructional improvement. *Elementary School Journal, 84,* 225–269.

Slavin, R. E. (1986). Best-evidence synthesis: An alternative to meta-analysis and traditional reviews. *Educational Researcher, 15,* (9), 5–11.

Slavin, R. E. (1987a). Mastery learning reconsidered. *Review of Educational Research, 57,* 175–213.

Slavin, R. E. (1987b). A theory of school and classroom organization. *Educational Psychologist, 22,* 89–108.

Slavin, R. E., & Karweit, N. (1984). Mastery learning and student teams: A factorial experiment in urban general mathematics classes. *American Educational Research Journal, 21,* 725–736.

Slavin, R. E., & Karweit, N. L. (1985). Effects of whole-class, ability grouped and individualized instruction on mathematics achievement. *American Educational Research Journal, 22,* 351–367.

Slavin, R. E., & Madden, N. A. (in press). Effective classroom programs for students at risk. In R.

E. Slavin, N. L. Karweit, & N. A. Madden (Eds.), *Effective programs for students at risk.* Needham Heights, MA: Allyn and Bacon.

Slavin, R. E., Madden, N. A., & Leavey, M. (1984). Effects of Team Assisted Individualization on the mathematics achievement of academically handicapped and nonhandicapped students. *Journal of Educational Psychology, 76,* 813–819.

Smith, J. K. (1981, April). *Philosophical considerations of mastery learning theory.* Paper presented at the annual convention of the American Educational Research Association, Los Angeles.

Strasler, G. M., & Rochester, M. (1982, April). *A two-year evaluation of a competency-based secondary school project in a learning for mastery setting.* Paper presented at the annual convention of the American Educational Research Association, New York.

Suppes, P. (1964). Modern learning theory and the elementary school curriculum. *American Educational Research Journal, 2,* 79–93.

Walberg, H. J. (1984). Improving the productivity of America's schools, *Educational Leadership, 41* (8), 19–27.

Wentling, T. L. (1973). Mastery versus nonmastery instruction with varying test item feedback treatments. *Journal of Educational Psychology, 65,* 50–58.

Wyckoff, D. B. (1974). *A study of mastery learning and its effects on achievement of sixth grade social studies students.* Unpublished doctoral dissertation, Georgia State University.

5 Cooperative Learning and Student Achievement

Robert E. Slavin
Center for Research on Elementary and Middle Schools
John Hopkins University

The Background of Cooperative Learning

Cooperative learning is a form of classroom organization in which students work in small groups to help one another learn academic material. Of course, group work has existed in education for centuries, but there have been three major developments in the past 15 years that have added substantially to traditional group work paradigms. First, researchers have developed specific, practical methods in which group work plays a central role, often in combination with other types of activities. These methods are designed more for use as the primary organizing scheme in the classroom than for occasional use. Second, a substantial research tradition has developed to examine the overall effects of alternative forms of cooperative learning and to understand the critical elements and internal processes of cooperating groups. Third, use of cooperative learning methods at all levels of education has mushroomed in recent years. Teachers who make regular use of cooperative learning methods are still a small minority of all teachers, but they nevertheless number in the tens of thousands.

Research on cooperative learning has found positive effects of these strategies on such outcomes as intergroup relations (Slavin, 1985a), acceptance of mainstreamed academically handicapped students by their classmates (Johnson & Johnson, 1980; Madden & Slavin, 1983a; Slavin, 1984a; Slavin, Stevens, & Madden, in press), and such other outcomes as self-esteem, liking of class or subject, and general acceptance of others (Slavin, 1983a; Sharan, 1980).

However, the greatest controversy has emerged around the question of the achievement effects of cooperative learning. All reviewers of the achievement literature have concluded that, on average, achievement effects of cooperative learning are positive (see Davidson, 1985; Johnson, Maruyama, Johnson, Nelson, & Skon, 1981; Newmann & Thompson, 1987; Slavin, 1980a, 1983a, 1983b). However, reviewers have differed sharply on the *conditions* under which cooperative learning affects student achievement. For example, in a meta-analysis of 122 studies, Johnson et al. (1981) concluded that while all forms of cooperative learning were more effective than individualistic or competitive learning, cooperation without intergroup competition was more effective than cooperation with intergroup competition. This meta-analysis was criticized for ignoring critical interactions (Cotton & Cook, 1982; McGlynn, 1982), for including such "achievement" measures as block-stacking, card-playing, golf, and mazes, for including very brief and artificial experiments, and for including studies in which cooperative (but not individualistic or competitive) students were allowed to help one another on the test or task used as the dependent measure of achievement (Slavin, 1984b).

In contrast to the Johnson et al. (1981) meta-analysis, other reviewers have concluded that cooperative learning does not always enhance student achievement, but that positive achievement effects depend on the presence of two factors: *group goals* and *individual accountability*. Group goals refer to rewards given to groups depending on the performance of the group or of its members. For example, a group may receive certificates based on the sum of group members' performances, or may be graded or evaluated on the basis of a group product. Individual accountability means that the contribution of each group member is identifiable. This may mean that the group is rewarded based on the sum of individual quiz scores, or that a group task is broken into subtasks, with each group member responsible for a unique subtask. A comprehensive review by Slavin (1983b) concluded that both group goals and individual accountability were essential elements of cooperative learning for student achievement, and later reviews of cooperative learning in mathematics (Davidson, 1985) and in secondary schools (Newmann & Thompson, 1987) have reached similar conclusions.

This chapter summarizes the current state of the art in cooperative learning and student achievement. This is the first comprehensive review on this topic since the Slavin (1983b) article, and is the first since the much-criticized Johnson et al. (1981) meta-analysis to attempt to estimate the *magnitude* of cooperative learning effects on achievement. The review method used is an abbreviated form of best-evidence synthesis (Slavin, 1986a), a procedure that combines the use of effect size (proportion of a standard deviation separating experimental and control groups) as a standard metric of treatment effects with the discussion of individual studies and critical issues characteristic of traditional narrative reviews. In addition, best-evidence synthesis focuses on studies that meet a set of a priori standards relating to germaneness to the issue at hand and methodological characteristics.

COOPERATIVE LEARNING METHODS

There are now dozens of distinct cooperative learning methods, plus many variations (see, for example, Kagan, 1985). However, research on cooperative learning has focused on the products of four major centers of activity, each of which began work on cooperative learning in the early 1970s. These are the four Student Team Learning programs developed at The Johns Hopkins University by Robert Slavin, Nancy Madden, David DeVries, and their associates; methods developed by David and Roger Johnson and their associates at the University of Minnesota; Jigsaw Teaching, developed by Elliot Aronson at the University of California at Santa Cruz; and Group Investigation, developed by Shlomo and Yael Sharan and Rachel Hertz-Lazarowitz at the University of Tel Aviv, Israel.

In all seven of the most widely used cooperative learning methods, students work in heterogeneous learning groups of about four members. Group members are encouraged to help one another learn. However, in most other respects the methods vary considerably. Brief descriptions of the methods appear in the following sections.

Student Team Learning

Student Team Learning methods are cooperative learning techniques developed and researched at Johns Hopkins University. More than half of all studies of practical cooperative learning methods involve Student Team Learning methods.

All cooperative learning methods share the idea that students work together to learn and are responsible for one another's learning as well as their own. In addition to the idea of cooperative work, Student Team Learning methods emphasize the use of team goals and team success that can only be achieved if all members of the team learn the objectives being taught. That is, in Student Team Learning the students' tasks are not to *do* something as a team but to *learn* something as a team.

Three concepts are central to all Student Team Learning methods: *team rewards, individual accountability, and equal opportunities for success.* In these techniques, teams may earn certificates or other team rewards if they achieve above a designated criterion. *Individual accountability* means that the team's success depends on the individual learning of all team members. This focuses the activity of the team members on tutoring one another and making sure that everyone on the team is ready for a quiz or other assessment that students will take without teammate help. *Equal opportunities for success* means that students contribute to their teams by improving over their own past performance. This is intended to ensure that high, average, and low achievers are equally challenged to do their best, and that contributions of all team members will be valued (see Slavin, 1980b).

Student Teams—Achievement Divisions (STAD). In STAD (Slavin, 1978a, 1986b) students are assigned to four-member learning teams that are mixed in performance level, sex, and ethnicity. The teacher presents a lesson, and then students work within their teams to make sure that all team members have mastered the lesson. Finally, all students take individual quizzes on the material, at which time they may not help one another.

Students' quiz scores are compared to their own past averages, and points are awarded based on the degree to which students can meet or exceed their own earlier performance. These points are then summed to form team scores, and teams that meet certain criteria may earn certificates or other rewards. The whole cycle of activities, from teacher presentation to team practice to quiz, usually takes three to five class periods.

STAD has been used in most subjects, from mathematics to language arts to social studies, and has been used from grade 2 through college. It is most appropriate for teaching well defined objectives with single right answers, such as mathematical computations and applications, language usage and mechanics, geography and map skills, and science facts and concepts.

Teams-Games-Tournament (TGT). Teams-Games-Tournament (DeVries & Slavin, 1978; Slavin, 1986b) was the first of the Johns Hopkins cooperative learning methods. It uses the same teacher presentations and team work as in STAD, but replaces the quizzes with weekly tournaments, in which students compete with members of other teams to contribute points to their team scores. Students compete at three-person "tournament tables" against others with similar past records in mathematics. A "bumping" procedure keeps the competition fair. The winner at each tournament table brings six points to his or her team, regardless of which table it is; this means that low achievers (competing with other low achievers) and high achievers (competing with other high achievers) have equal opportunities for success. As in STAD, high-performing teams earn certificates or other forms of team rewards.

Team Assisted Individualization (TAI). Team Assisted Individualization (TAI; Slavin, Leavey, & Madden, 1986) shares with STAD and TGT the use of four-member mixed ability learning teams and certificates for high-performing teams. But where STAD and TGT use a single pace of instruction for the class, TAI combines cooperative learning with individualized instruction. Also, where STAD and TGT apply to most subjects and grade levels, TAI is specifically designed to teach mathematics to students in grades 3–6 (or older students not ready for a full algebra course).

In TAI, students enter an individualized sequence according to a placement test and then proceed at their own rates. In general, team members work on different units. Teammates check each others' work against answer sheets and help one another with any problems. Final unit tests are taken without teammate help and are scored by student monitors. Each week, teachers total the number of units completed by all team members and give certificates or other team rewards to teams that exceed a criterion score based on the number of final tests passed, with extra points for perfect papers and completed homework.

Because students take responsibility for checking each others' work and managing the flow of materials, the teacher can spend most class time presenting lessons to small groups of students drawn from the various teams who are working at the same point in the mathematics sequence. For example, the teacher might call up a decimals group, present a lesson on decimals, and then send the students back to their teams to work on decimal problems. Then the teacher might call the fractions group, and so on.

Unlike STAD and TGT, TAI depends on a specific set of instructional materials. These materials cover concepts from addition to an introduction to algebra. Although designed for use in grades 3–6, they have been used for primary instruction in grades 2–8 and as remedial instruction in high schools and community colleges.

Cooperative Integrated Reading and Composition (CIRC). The newest of the Student Team Learning methods is a comprehensive program for teaching reading and writing in the upper elementary grades called Cooperative Integrated Reading and Composition, or CIRC (Madden, Slavin, & Stevens, 1986). In CIRC, teachers use basal readers and reading groups, much as in traditional reading programs. However, students are assigned to teams composed of pairs of students from two different reading groups. While the teacher is working with one reading group, students in the other groups are working in their pairs on a series of cognitively engaging activities, including reading to one another, making predictions about how narrative stories will come out, summarizing stories to one another, writing responses to stories, and practicing spelling, decoding, and vocabulary. Students work in teams to master main idea and other comprehension skills. During language arts periods, students engage in writing drafts, revising and editing one another's work, and preparing for "publication" of team books.

In most CIRC activities, students follow a sequence of teacher instruction, team practice, team pre-assessments, and quiz. That is, students do not take the quiz until their teammates have determined that they are ready. Team rewards are certificates given to teams based on the average performance of all team members on all reading and writing activities.

Jigsaw

Jigsaw was originally designed by Elliot Aronson and his colleagues (Aronson, Blaney, Stephan, Sikes, & Snapp, 1978). In this method, students are assigned to six-member teams to work on academic material that has been broken down into sections. For example, a biography might be later divided into early life, first accomplishments, major setbacks, later life, and impact on history. Each team member reads his or her section. Next, members of different teams who have studied the same sections meet in "expert groups" to discuss their sections. Then the students return to their teams and take turns teaching their teammates about their sections. Because the only way students can learn other sections than their own is to listen carefully to their teammates, they are motivated to support and show interest in one another's work.

Slavin (1986b) developed a modification of Jigsaw at Johns Hopkins University and then incorporated it in the Student Team Learning program. In this method, called Jigsaw II, students work in four-or-five-member teams as in TGT and STAD. Instead of each student being assigned a unique section, all students read a common narrative, such as a book chapter, a short story, or a biography. However, each student receives a topic on which to become an expert. Students with the same topics meet in expert groups to discuss them, after which they return to their teams to teach what they have learned to their teammates. Then students take individual quizzes, which result in team scores based on the improvement score system of STAD. Teams that meet preset standards may earn certificates.

Learning Together

David and Roger Johnson at the University of Minnesota developed the Learning Together model of cooperative learning (Johnson & Johnson, 1975). The methods they have researched involve students working in four-or-five-member heterogeneous groups on assignment sheets. The groups hand in a single sheet, and receive praise and rewards based on the group product. In recent studies, the Johnsons have incorporated the use of individual accountability by giving students grades based on the average of all group members' individual quiz scores, making Learning Together similar to STAD.

Group Investigation

Group Investigation is a general classroom organization plan in which students work in small groups using cooperative inquiry, group discussion, and cooperative planning and projects (Sharan & Sharan, 1976). In this method, students form their own two- to six-member groups. After choosing subtopics from a unit being studied by the entire class, the groups further break their subtopics into individual tasks, and carry out the activities necessary to prepare group reports. Each group then makes a presentation or display to communicate its findings to the entire class.

A TYPOLOGY OF COOPERATIVE LEARNING

Cooperative learning methods differ in many ways, but they can be categorized according to six principal characteristics, described following. Table 5.1 summarizes the characteristics of the most widely researched methods.

1. *Group Goals.* Most cooperative learning methods use some form of group goals. In the Student Team Learning methods, these may be certificates or other recognition given to teams that meet a preset criterion; in the Johnsons' methods group grades are given.

2. *Individual Accountability.* Individual accountability is achieved in cooperative learning in two ways. One is to have group scores be the sum or average of individual quiz scores or other assessments, as in the Student Team Learning models. The other is task specialization, giving each student unique responsibility for a part of the group task (see #5.).

3. *Equal Opportunities for Success.* A characteristic unique to the Student Team Learning methods is the use of scoring methods that ensure all students an equal opportunity to contribute to their teams. This is done using improvement points in STAD, competition with equals in TGT, and adapting tasks to individual performance levels in TAI and CIRC.

4. *Team Competition.* Early studies of STAD and TGT used competition between teams as a means of motivating students to cooperate within teams.

5. *Task Specialization.* A key element of Jigsaw and Group Investigation is the assignment of unique subtasks to each group member.

6. *Adaptation to Individual Needs.* Most cooperative learning methods use group-paced instruction, but two—TAI and CIRC—adapt instruction to students' individual needs.

For a discussion of these characteristics and theories relating them to student achievement, see Slavin (1983a).

REVIEW METHODS

This review uses an abbreviated form of best-evidence synthesis (Slavin, 1986a). In particular, it uses almost exactly the same literature search procedures, statistical methods, and study inclusion criteria as were used in the review of research on group-based mastery learning presented in chapter 4 (also see Slavin, 1987a). The study inclusion criteria were slightly modified to adapt to the characteristics of the cooperative learning literature. They were as follows.

TABLE 5.1
Typology of Major Cooperative Learning Methods

Method	Group Goals	Individual Accountability	Equal Opportunities For Success	Team Competition	Specialization	Adaptation to Individuals
Student Team Learning Methods						
Student Teams-Achievement Divisions	yes	yes	yes (improvement points)	sometimes	no	no
Teams-Games-Tournaments	yes	yes	yes (tournament system)	yes	no	no
Team Assisted Individualization Math	yes	yes	yes (individualized)	no	no	yes
Cooperative Integrated Reading and Composition	yes	yes	yes (subgrouped)	no	no	yes
Learning Together	yes	sometimes	no	no	no	no
Jigsaw	no	yes (task spec.)	no	no	yes	no
Jigsaw II	yes	yes (task spec.)	yes (improvement points)	no	yes	no
Group Investigation	no	yes (task spec.)	no	no	yes	no
Traditional Group Work	no	no	no	no	no	no

Germaneness Criteria

To be included in this review, studies had to evaluate forms of cooperative learning in which small groups of elementary or secondary students worked together to learn. Studies of peer tutoring, in which one student teaches another, were excluded.

Methodological Criteria

1. Studies had to compare cooperative learning to control groups studying the same material. This excluded a few studies that used time-series designs (e.g., Hamblin, Hathaway, & Wodarski, 1971; Lew, Mesch, Johnson, & Johnson, 1986), and excluded a few comparisons within studies in which control groups were not studying the same materials as experimental groups (e.g., Vedder, 1985). In a few studies, cooperative learning students could help one another on the test used as the dependent measure whereas individualistic or competitive students could not (e.g., Johnson, Johnson, & Scott, 1978). Comparisons involving these "congruent tests" or "daily achievement" were excluded (see Slavin, 1984b, for more on this).

2. Evidence had to be given that experimental and control groups were initially equivalent. Studies had to either use random assignment of students to conditions or present evidence that classes were initially within 50% of a standard deviation of one another and use statistical controls for pre-test differences. This excluded a few studies with large pre-test differences. (Oishi, Slavin, & Madden, 1983; Okebukola, 1986c; Ziegler, 1981).

3. Study duration had to be at least 4 weeks (20 hours). As in the mastery learning review (Slavin, 1987a), this caused by far the largest number of exclusions. For example, of 17 achievement studies that used control groups at the elementary or secondary level cited by Johnson & Johnson (1985) in a review of their own work, only 1 just barely met the 4-week requirement. The median duration of all 17 studies was 10 days. Such brief studies are useful for theory-building, but are too short to serve as evidence of the likely achievement effects of cooperative learning as a principal mode of classroom instruction. Studies of such limited duration are often also quite artificial; in the case of the Johnsons' studies, none of the treatment groups received any instruction. This means that in the cooperative groups, students at least had a chance to receive explanations from group-mates, whereas students in the individualistic and competitive control groups were left to try to figure out worksheets on their own with limited teacher assistance.

4. In the Slavin (1987a) mastery learning review, there was a requirement that at least two experimental and two control classes be involved in the study, to reduce the impact of teacher effects. This criterion was not applied in the present

review, because it would have the effect of excluding most of the Johnsons' studies that did meet the duration requirement. However, studies with small samples of classes or teachers should be interpreted with caution, because they may confound teacher and treatment effects.

5. Achievement measures had to assess objectives taught in experimental as well as control classes. If experimental and control classes were not studying precisely the same materials, then standardized tests had to be used to assess objectives pursued by all classes.

Computation of Effect Sizes and Medians

Computations of effect sizes (proportion of a standard deviation separating experiment and control classes after adjustment for pretest differences) were the same as for the mastery learning (chapter 4; Slavin, 1987a) and ability grouping (chapter 6; Slavin, 1987c) reviews. Also, when median values are given, these are computed as in the earlier reviews.

Research on Achievement Effects of Cooperative Learning

Research on the achievement effects of cooperative learning methods is summarized in Tables 5.2–5.8. A total of 60 studies met the inclusion requirements. Because studies that compared multiple cooperative learning methods are listed more than once, the tables list 68 comparisons of cooperative learning and control methods. Effect sizes could be computed for 51 of the comparisons. Effects in the remaining 17 are characterized in the tables as significantly positive (+), no significant differences (0), or significantly negative (−).

Overall, the effects of cooperative learning on achievement are clearly positive; 49 of the 68 comparisons were positive (72%), whereas only 8 (15%) favored control groups. However, looking across Tables 5.2–5.8, it is also apparent that the different cooperative learning methods vary widely in achievement effects.

Table 5.9 summarizes the outcomes of cooperative learning studies according to several criteria. The first column lists the percent of effect sizes in each category of studies that were above the overall median of +.195. For this column, studies coded as (+) were counted as above the median, and those coded as (0) or (−) were counted as below the median. The second column lists the percentage of studies falling at or above the median (+.21) when only studies from which effect sizes could be computed are included. The third column lists the median effect size for these studies, and the median effect sizes on standardized achievement measures are listed in the fourth column.

Table 5.9 shows that the Student Team Learning methods, STAD, TGT, TAI, and CIRC, are consistently more effective for increasing student achievement

TABLE 5.3
Teams Games Tournament

Article	Grades	Location	Sample Size	Duration (Weeks)	Design	Subjects	Effect Size by Subgroup/Measure	ES Stdized	ES Total
DeVries & Mescon (1975)	3	Syracuse, NY	60 (2 cl.)	6	Students randomly assigned to TGT or control classes.	Lang Arts	Hoyum Sanders +.19 Exp-made test +.57	+.19	+.38
DeVries, Mescon, & Shackman (1975a)	3	Syracuse, NY	53 (2 cl.)	5	Students randomly assigned to TGT or control classes.	Verbal Analogies	Gates-McGinitie +.60 Exp-made tests +.85	+.60	+.73
DeVries, Mescon, & Shackman (1975b)	3	Syracuse, NY	54 (2 cl.)	6	Students randomly assigned to TGT or control classes.	Lang Arts	Hoyum-Sanders +.64 Exp-made tests +.80	+.64	+.72
Edwards, DeVries, & Snyder (1972)	7	Baltimore, MD	96 (4 cl.)	9	Classes randomly assigned to TGT or control, all taught by same tchr.	Math	Stanford: +.50 GE Exp-made tests: (+)	(+)	(+)
Edwards & DeVries (1972)	7	Baltimore, MD	117 (4 cl.)	4	Students randomly assigned to TGT or control classes.	Math			(0)
Edwards & DeVries (1974)	7	Baltimore, MD	128 (4 cl.)	12	Students randomly assigned to TGT or ctrl. classes.	Math (+) Social Studies (0)			(+)
DeVries, Edwards, & Wells (1974)	10-12	Suburban, FL	191 (6 cl.)	12	Classes randomly assigned to TGT, ctrl.	American History			+.29
Hulton & DeVries (1976)	7	Suburban MD	299	10	Classes randomly assigned to TGT, control.	Math	Stanford	+.33	+.33
DeVries, Lucasse, & Shackman (1980)	7-8	Grand Rapids, MI	1742	10	Teachers randomly assigned to TGT or individualized instruction.	Lang Arts	Hoyum-Sanders (0) Exp-made tests (+)	(0)	(+)
Slavin & Karweit (1981)	4-5	Hagerstown, MD	465 (17 cl.)	16	Coop learning classes used TGT in math, STAD in lang arts, Jigsaw in social studies. Compared to matched ctrls.	Math	CTBS: Math computations .00 -.05 Math concepts .10	-.05	-.05
Kagan et al. (1985)	2-6	Riverside, CA	600 (25 cl.)	6	Student teachers randomly assigned to STAD, TGT, control.	Spelling			(0)
Okebukola (1985)	8	Nigeria	359	6	Student teachers randomly assigned to TGT, STAD, Jigsaw, LT, comp., or ctrl.	Science	TGT vs ctrl +2.41 TGT vs comp +1.69	+2.05	+2.05

Key: (+) Significant effect favoring cooperative learning
(0) No significant difference

TABLE 5.2
Student Teams Achievement Divisions

Article	Grades	Location	Sample Size	Duration (Weeks)	Design	Subjects	Effect Size by Submeasure/Measure	ES Stdized	ES Total
Slavin (1980c)	4	Hagerstown, MD	424	12	STAD classes compared to matched controls.	Lang Arts	Hoyum-Sanders	+.18	+.18
Madden & Slavin (1983b)	3,4,6	Baltimore, MD	183	7	Tchrs taught 1 STAD, 1 focused instruction class, randomly assigned.	Math	Nonhandicapped +.12	+.13	+.13
Slavin & Karweit (1983)	4-5	Hagerstown, MD	456 (17 cl.)	16	Coop. lrng. classes used STAD in lang. arts, TGT in math, Jigsaw in social studies. Compared to matched controls.	Lang Arts	CTBS Lang Mech +.12 CTBS Lang Exp. +.12	+.12	+.12
Stevens, Slavin, Farnish, & Madden (1987)	3-4	Harrisburg, PA	30 cl.	4	Classes randomly assigned to STAD, ctrl.	Reading Comp.	Main Ideas +.24 Inferences +.11		+.18
Slavin (1978b)	7	Frederick, MD	205 (8 cl.)	10	Tchrs taught 1 STAD, 1 focused inst. class, randomly assigned.	Lang Arts			(0)
Slavin (1977)	7	Baltimore, MD	52 (2 cl.)	10	Tchrs taught 1 STAD, 1 focused inst. class, randomly assigned.	Lang Arts	Blacks + Whites 0 Hoyum-Sanders +.76 Exp. Made Test +.36	+.76	+.56
Slavin (1979)	7-8	Baltimore, MD	424	12	Tchrs taught 1 STAD, 1 focused inst. class, randomly assigned.	Lang Arts	Hoyum-Sanders	(0)	(0)
Slavin & Oickle (1981)	6-8	Rural MD	230	12	Tchrs taught 1 STAD, 1 focused inst. class, randomly assigned.	Lang Arts	Hoyum-Sanders: Blacks +.72 Whites +.14	+.33	+.33
Slavin & Karweit (1974)	9	Philadelphia, Low ach.	588	30	Tchrs randomly assigned to STAD, mastery learning, combined & control	Genl Math	CTBS: STAD vs. Ctrl +.19 +.21 STAD+ML vs Ctrl +.23	+.21	+.21
Tomblin & Davis (1985)	4-6	San Diego, CA	509 (8 cl.)	8	classes randomly assigned to STAD, untreated ctrl.	Spelling			+.07
Frantz (1979)	4-5	Rural VA	48	6	Classes randomly assigned to STAD, ctrl.	Reading			+.27

(continued...)

(Table 5.2 continued)

Article	Grades	Location	Sample Size	Duration (Weeks)	Design	Subjects	Effect Size by Submeasure/Measure	ES Stdized	ES Total
Kagan, Zahn, Widaman, Schwartwald, & Tyrrell (1985)	2-6	Riverside, CA	600 (25 cl.)	6	Student teachers randomly assigned to STAD, TGT, untreated control.	Spelling			(0)
Perrault (1982): Study 1	7	Suburban MD	88 (4 cl.)	6	Tchr taught 2 STAD, 2 ctrl classes, randomly assigned.	Drafting	Ach. Test +.28 Drawing +.81		+.55
Study 2	7	Suburban MD	48 (4 cl.)	6	Tchr taught 2 STAD, 2 ctrl classes, randomly assigned	Drafting	Ach. Test +.53 Drawing (0)		+.26
Sherman & Thomas (1986)	10	Ohio	38 (2 cl.)	5	Classes randomly assigned to STAD, individualistic.	Genl Math			+1.20
Allen & Van Sickle (1984)	9	Rural GA	51 (2 cl.)	6	Tchr taught 1 STAD, 1 ctrl class, randomly assigned.	Geography			+.94
Sharan et al. (1984)	7	Israel	Eng: 470 Lit: 538	16	Tchrs randomly assigned to STAD, Group Investigation or control.	Eng. as a sec. lang. English Literature	+.14 -.08		+.03
Mevarech (1985a)	5	Israel	134	15	Students randomly assigned to STAD, ML, combined, and control.	Math	STAD vs Ctrl +.19 STAD+ML vs Ctl +.28		+.24
Mevarech (1985b)	9	Israel	113	18	Students randomly assigned to combination of STAD and mastery learning or to mastery learning.	Consumer Math			+1.04
Okebukola (1985)	8	Nigeria	358	6	Student teachers randomly assigned to STAD, TGT, Jigsaw, LT, Comp., Ctrl.	Science	STAD vs ctrl +2.52 STAD vs comp +1.79		+2.15
Okebukola (1986a)	7	Nigeria	99	24	Students randomly assigned to STAD, LT, comp., ctrl, all taught by same teacher.	Science	STAD vs ctrl +5.14 STAD vs comp +2.72		+3.93

Key: (+) Significant effect favoring cooperative learning
(0) No significant difference

141

TABLE 5.4

Team Assisted Individualization and Cooperative Integrated Reading and Composition

Article	Grades	Location	Sample Size	Duration (Weeks)	Design	Subjects	Effect Size by Subgroup/Measure	ES Stdized	ES Total
Team Assisted Individualization									
Slavin, Leavey, & Madden (1984)									
Study 1	3-5	Suburban MD	506	8	Schools randomly assigned to TAI, control.	Math	CTBS Computations	+.09	+.09
Study 2	4-6	Suburban MD	320	10	TAI classes compared to matched control.	Math	CTBS Computations	+.11	+.11
Slavin, Madden, & Leavey (1984)									
	3-5	Suburban MD	1371	24	TAI classes compared to matched control.	Math	CTBS Comput. +.18 / CTBS Concepts +.10	+.14	+.14
Study 1	4-6	Wilmington, DE	212	18	Classes randomly assigned to TAI, control.	Math	CTBS Comput. +.77 / CTBS Concepts .00	+.39	+.39
Study 2	3-5	Hagerstown, MD	220	16	Classes randomly assigned to TAI, control.	Math	CTBS Comput. +.58 / CTBS Concepts +.04	+.31	+.31
Cooperative Integrated Reading and Composition									
Stevens, Madden, Slavin, & Farnish (1987)									
Study 1	3-4	Suburban MD	461	12	CIRC classes matched with control.	Reading / Language / Spelling / Writing	CAT Rdg. Comp. +.19 / CAT Rdg. Voc. +.18 / CAT Lang. Exp. +.24 / CAT Lang. Mech. +.12 / CAT Spelling +.29 / Wrting Samples +.25	+.20	+.21
Study 2	3-4	Suburban MD	450	24	CIRC classes matched with control.	Reading / Language / Writing	CAT Rdg. Comp. +.35 / CAT Rdg. Voc. +.12 / Durrell IRI's +.60 / CAT Lang. Exp. +.29 / CAT Lang. Mech. +.30 / Wrting Samples +.23	+.33	+.32

TABLE 5.5
Learning Together (Johnsons' Methods)

Article	Grades	Location	Sample Size	Duration (Weeks)	Design	Subjects	Effect Size by Subgroup/Measure	ES Total
Learning Together Models Lacking Individual Accountability								
Johnson, Johnson, & Scott (1978)	5-6	Minnesota Hi ach.	30	10	Students randomly assigned to LT or indiv. inst.	Math	Posttests -7.1, Retention -.81 (2 months)	-.71
Johnson, Johnson, Scott & Remolae (1985)	5-6	Suburban MN	154	4	Students randomly assigned to LT or individualistic. No teacher instr.	Science		.00
Robertson (1982)	2-3	Suburban NJ	166	6	Teachers randomly assigned to LT, indiv./comp., ctrl.	Math	LT vs. ind./comp. -.02, LT vs. control +.16	+.07
Okebukola (1985)	8	Nigeria	356	6	Student teachers randomly assigned to LT, STAD, TGT, Jigsaw, comp., ctrl.	Science	LT vs. control +.43, LT vs. comp. -.30	+.37
Okebukola (1986a)	7	Nigeria	97	24	Students randomly assigned to LT, STAD, comp., or control, all taught by same teacher	Science	LT vs. control +3.43, LT vs. comp. +1.20	+2.32
Okebukola (1984)	9	Nigeria	720	11	Student teachers randomly assigned to LT, comp., ctrl.	Biology	LT vs. control +.27, LT vs. comp. -.89	-.31
Okebukola (1986b)	9	Nigeria	493	6	Student teachers randomly assigned to LT or comp.	Biology	Prefer coop. +1.85, Prefer comp. -1.97	-.06
Learning Together Models with Individual Accountability								
Humphreys, Johnson, & Johnson (1982	9	Suburban MN	44	6	Compared LT, comp., ind., controlling for pretests. Grades in LT based on group averages. No teacher instruction.	Physical Science	Posttest (+), Retention (+) (1 week)	(+)
Yager, Johnson, Johnson, & Snider (1986)	3	Suburban MN	88	5	Students randomly assigned to LT or ind.; grades in LT based on group averages. No teacher instruction.	Transportation	Posttest (+), Retention (+)	(+)

Key: (+) Significant effect favoring cooperative learning.

TABLE 5.6
Jigsaw

Article	Grades	Location	Sample Size	Duration (Weeks)	Design	Subjects	Effect Size by Subgroup/Measure	ES Stdized	ES Total
Gonzales (1981)	3-4	Hollister, CA (bilingual)	99	20	Bilingual Jigsaw classes compared to matched ctrls.	Reading Lang. Arts Math	CAT Reading CAT Lang. CAT Math	(0) (0) (0)	(0)
Moskowitz et al. (1983)	5-6	Suburban CA	261	24	Schools randomly assigned to Jigsaw, control.	Reading Math	Stanford Reading Stanford Math	(0) (0)	(0)
Moskowitz et al. (1985)	5	Suburban CA	480	30	Jigsaw classes compared to matched controls.	Reading Math	Stanford Reading Stanford Math	(0) (-)	(-)
Tomblin & Davis (1985)	Jr. HI	San Diego, CA	90	8	Classes randomly assigned to Jigsaw, control.	English			-.51
Lazarowitz et al. (1985)	10-12	Suburban UT	113 (4 cl.)	6	Jigsaw classes compared to matched indiv. inst.	Biology			(0)
Hertz-Lazarowitz, Sapir, & Sharan (1981)	8	Israel	68	5	Same teacher taught matched Jigsaw, GI, control classes.	Arabic language & culture			+.22
Rich, Amir, & Slavin (1986)	7	Israel	339 (9 cl.)	12	Classes randomly assigned to Jigsaw, control.	Literature History	-.32 +.04		-.14
Okebukola (1985)	8	Nigeria	359	6	Student teachers randomly assigned to Jigsaw, STAD, TGT, LT, comp. ctrl.	Science	Jig. vs. ctrl. +.84 Jig. vs. comp. +1.41		+1.14

Key: (+) Significant effect favoring cooperative learning.
(0) No significant difference.
(-) Significant effect favoring control group.

TABLE 5.7
Group Investigation and Related Methods

Article	Grades	Location	Sample Size	Duration (Weeks)	Design	Subjects	Effect Size by Subgroup/Meas.	ES Stdized	ES Total
Sharan et al. (1984)	7	Israel	Eng: 504 Lit: 465	18	Teachers randomly assigned to GI, STAD, or control.	English as a second lang. Literature	+.10 +.14		+.12
Hertz-Lazaro-witz, Sapir, & Sharan (1981)	8	Israel	67	5	Same teachers taught matched Jigsaw, GI, control classes.	Arabic language and culture			.00
Sharan & Shachar (1986)	8	Israel (priv. sch.)	351 (11 cl.)	18	Classes randomly assigned to GI, control.	Geography +1.41 History +1.45			+1.43
Sherman & Zimmerman (1986)	10	Ohio	46 (2 cl.)	7	Compared GI and matched competitive class taught by same teacher.	Biology			-.15
Talmage, Pascarella, & Ford (1984)	2-6	Elgin, IL	493	1 yr.	Teachers using form of GI compared to matched controls.	Reading SAT Reading +.18 SAT Lang. Arts +.11	+.14		+.14

145

TABLE 5.8
Other Cooperative Learning Methods

Article	Grades	Location	Sample Size	Duration (Weeks)	Design	Subjects	Effect Size by Subgroup/Measure	ES Stdized	ES Total
Methods Lacking Group Goals and Individual Accountability									
L. Johnson (1985)	4-5	Suburban Houston, TX	859 (51 cl.)	27	Teachers trained in Marilyn Burns "Groups of Four" method compared to matched controls. No group goals or indiv. accountability.	Math	Romberg-Wearne: Comprehesnion -.08, Application +.01, Prob. Solving +.22	+.04	+.04
L. Johnson & Waxman (1985)	8	Houston, TX	150	1 yr.	Teachers trained in Marilyn Burns "Groups of Four" method compared to matched controls. No group goals or indiv. accountability.	Math	SAT Prob. Solv.: Hi Ach. (0), Mod Ach. (0), Lo Ach. (+)	(0)	(0)
Van Oudenhoven, Van Berkum, & Swen-Koopmans)1987)	3	Netherlands	218 (14 cl.)	12	Classes randomly assigned to pair learning with indiv. feedback, pair learning with shared feedback, or control.	Spelling	Pairs w/indiv. feedback: (+), Pairs w/shared feedback: (+)		(+)
Van Oudenhoven, Wiersma, & Van Yperen (1987)	3	Netherlands	261	15	Classes randomly assigned to pair learning, indiv. learning with feedback from classmate, or indiv. with no feedback. No group goal or indiv. accountability.	Spelling	Hi, Av. Ach. (0), Lo Ach. (+)		(+)
Vedder (1985)	4	Netherlands	191	4	Classes randomly assigned to pair learning or indiv. learning. No group goal or indiv. accountability.	Geometry	Posttests +.06, Followup +.05 (3 weeks)		+.06
Methods with Group Goals but no Individual Accountability									
Artzt (1983)	9-11	Suburban New York	304	20	Teachers taught exp and control classes. Cooperative groups in competition based on one group worksheet. Group goal, no indiv. accountability.	Math			+.13

Key: (+) Significant effect favoring cooperative learning.
(0) No significant difference.

146

TABLE 5.9
Breakdown of Effect Sizes by Characteristics of Methods

	Pct. at or Above median, All Studies	Pct. at or Above Median, ES Known	Median, ES Known	Median, Standardized Tests
All studies	50 (68)	50 (51)	+.21	
Student Team Learning Methods:				
STAD	57 (21)	67 (18)	+.265	+.21
TGT	75 (12)	86 (7)	+.38	+.33
TAI/CIRC	57 (7)	57 (7)	+.21	+.20
All STL	63 (40)	69 (32)	+.30	+.21
Learning Together	44 (9)	29 (7)	.00	
Jigsaw	25 (8)	50 (4)	+.04	
Group Investigation	20 (5)	20 (5)	+.12	
Other	33 (6)	0 (3)	+.06	
Group Goals & Indiv. Acct.	65 (43)	69 (32)	+.30	+.21
Group Goals Only	25 (8)	25 (8)	+.035	
Indiv. Acct. Only (Task Spec.)	23 (13)	33 (9)	+.12	
No Group Goals, Indiv. Acct.	25 (4)	0 (2)	+.05	

Note. Numbers in parentheses are total numbers of studies in each category.

than are other forms of cooperative learning. Using chi squares with above–below median and STL versus non-STL as factors, this difference is statistically significant using all studies ($\chi^2 = 9.1$, $p<.01$) or only using studies from which effect sizes could be computed ($\chi^2 = 7.0$, $p<.01$). Comparisons within studies generally support the same differences. In two studies done in Nigeria, Peter Okebukola compared alternative forms of cooperative learning in secondary science classes. In one (Okebukola, 1986a) a form of STAD was found to be significantly more effective than the Johnsons' Learning Together methods (ES = +1.28). In another, (Okebukola, 1985), TGT, STAD, Jigsaw, and Learning Together were compared to individual competition and control treatments. Both STAD (ES = +1.72) and TGT (ES = +1.60) were found to be substantially more effective than Learning Together, and, to a smaller degree, than Jigsaw (ES = +1.09, +.98, respectively). On the other hand, an Israeli study comparing Group Investigation and STAD in teaching literature and English as a second language found no significant differences (Sharan et. al., 1984).

One addition this review makes to earlier reviews of cooperative learning is a determination of the *size* of achievement effects found in methodologically adequate studies of at least 4 weeks duration. Here again, the effect sizes vary greatly by method. Overall, the Student Team Learning methods had a median effect size of +.30; on average, students experiencing these methods attained scores that would be at the 62nd percentile on the control group's distribution. On standardized tests, typically a much more stringent criterion of treatment effects because of their lack of overlap with any particular curriculum, the median effect size for all Student Team Learning methods was +.21.

The median effect sizes presented in Table 5.9 may underestimate the effects of a few of the cooperative learning methods. First, it is important to note that the studies of TAI and CIRC used *only* standardized tests, with the exception of the writing samples used in CIRC. Because standardized tests usually produce smaller effect size estimates than do criterion-referenced tests, this makes the effects for TAI and CIRC appear smaller than they are. As one indication of this, it is interesting to note that on computations measures, TAI students gained an average of twice as many grade equivalents as control students across all studies (see Slavin, 1985b), and CIRC gains had a similar ratio to control group gains in reading comprehension, reading vocabulary, language expression, language mechanics, and spelling (Stevens, Madden, Slavin, & Farnish, 1987).

The median effect size of .00 for Learning Together also requires explanation. This estimate is probably accurate for forms of Learning Together lacking individual accountability, in which students are "praised and rewarded" on the basis of a single group worksheet. However, the situation is quite different for forms of Learning Together that do incorporate group goals and individual accountability by grading students on the basis of the average of all group members' individual quiz scores. Two studies that used a reward structure of this kind found significantly positive effects on student achievement (Humphreys, Johnson, & Johnson, 1982; Yager, Johnson, Johnson, & Snider, 1986), and a third study of 18 days' duration (Yager, Johnson, & Johnson, 1985) found similar effects. Unfortunately, none of the three studies presented data from which effect sizes could be estimated. These three studies suggest that the Learning Together model can be instructionally effective if it uses group goals and individual accountability. On the other hand, it is important to note that these studies are highly artificial experiments. In all three, teachers did not present lessons to students, but only helped individuals with worksheets. This arrangement creates a possible bias against the individualistic and competitive control students, who have no resources other than their worksheets to help them learn.

Finally, the effect size estimate for Group Investigation may be too low. The Sharan & Shachar (in press) study, which found by far the largest achievement effects of Group Investigation, was very well designed and executed; even though it is only one study, its effects cannot be discounted.

Group Goals and Individual Accountability

One problem in the cooperative learning literature is that theoretically important *factors* are often confounded with particular *methods*. For example, two of the crucial factors identified in previous reviews as critical for positive achievement effects are use of group goals and individual accountability. Most of the studies that used specific group goals and individual accountability are Student Team Learning studies, and therefore also use equal opportunity scoring systems, prepared instructional materials, and, in the case of most of the TGT and STAD studies, team competition. However, in addition to the evidence supporting the instructional effectiveness of the Student Team Learning methods, other evidence also supports the importance of group goals and individual accountability. First, as noted earlier, the Learning Together studies that used group goals and individual accountability appear to have been markedly more successful that those that did not; setting aside the Nigerian studies, these are the only studies that found significantly positive achievement effects for Learning Together. Two of the Nigerian studies (Okebukola, 1985, 1986a) found effects favoring a form of Learning Together without individual accountability, but two others (Okebukola, 1984, 1986b) found an opposite trend.

A 3-week study in West Germany by Huber, Bogatzki, and Winter (1982) specifically compared a form of STAD to traditional group work lacking group rewards or individual accountability, and found the former to produce higher mathematics achievement (ES = +.23). In a study of TAI math, Cavanagh (1984) found that students who received group recognition based on the number of units accurately completed by all group members both learned more (ES = +.24) and completed more units (ES = +.25) than did students who received individual recognition only. On the other hand, a Dutch study of pair learning in spelling found no achievement differences between a condition in which students received individual feedback only and one in which they received shared feedback, which might be considered a group goal (van Oudenhoven, van Berkum, & Swen-Koopmans, 1987).

The failure to find significant achievement effects in year-long studies of such traditional groupwork methods as Marilyn Burns' (1981) "Groups of Four" program (Johnson, 1985; Johnson & Waxman, 1985) further suggests the necessity of group goals and individual accountability. Traditional group work, in which students are encouraged to work together but are given little structure and few incentives to do so, has been repeatedly found to have small or non-existent effects on student learning.

Table 5.9 breaks down the results of the cooperative learning studies according to their use of group goals and individual accountability. As the foregoing discussion suggests, studies of methods that incorporate group goals and individual accountability found considerably more positive instructional effects than did other studies. The reason for the importance of group goals and individual accountability is that there must be some incentive for students to help one another learn. In traditional group work, students are encouraged to work together but have no stake in one another's success. Under this condition, students may not provide one another the elaborated explanations that are essential for the achievement effects of cooperative learning (see Slavin, 1987b; Webb, 1985).

Similarly, when there are group goals but no individual accountability, as in most of the Learning Together studies, the group's goal is to complete a single worksheet or solve a single set of problems. In this circumstance, it may waste time and interfere with the group's success to stop and explain concepts to group members who are having problems; the students who are perceived to be the most able may simply do the work with little input from others.

Task Specialization

One interesting difference not shown in Table 5.9 involves the two major task specialization methods, Group Investigation, and Jigsaw. In both, students are given responsibility for one unique portion of the group's overall learning task. Yet in other respects the two methods are quite different. In the original form of Jigsaw, the principal team activity involves students taking turns making reports to one another on the topics they studied; in the absence of any sort of group goals, there is little incentive for students to help one another learn. In contrast, interaction among groupmates in Group Investigation is constant, and the group is working together to prepare a report of the rest of the class. Because the group report is evaluated by the teacher, Group Investigation could be considered to use a form of group goals and individual accountability.

With the exception of the Okebukola (1985) study, positive achievement effects of Jigsaw have not been found. In one particularly well designed study done in Israel, Jigsaw students learned significantly less than control students in literature (Rich, Amir, & Slavin, 1986). In contrast, the two longest and best designed studies of Group Investigation, by Sharan et al. (1984) and Sharan and Shachar (in press), both found significant positive effects, as did an earlier study of 3 weeks' duration (Sharan, Hertz-Lazarowitz, and Ackerman, 1980).

Other than comparisons among methods and across the factors of group goals and individual accountability, few other factors clearly differentiated more and less successful studies. There was a tendency for different methods to be differentially effective at different grade levels; STAD and TGT were the most successful methods at the secondary level, whereas TAI, CIRC, and TGT were most successful in elementary schools (TAI and CIRC are only used in elementary schools). There were no consistent patterns according to study duration, sample size, or experimental design.

Effect sizes were greatest for Student Team Learning methods in science, but this was entirely due to the Okebukola studies that tended to find extraordinarily large effects. Research examining effects separately for high, average, and low achievers has tended to find equal effects for all students (see Slavin, 1983a).

DISCUSSION

As was the case with earlier reviews by Slavin (1980a, 1983a, 1983b), Davidson (1985), and Newmann and Thompson (1987), the present review concludes that cooperative learning can be an effective means of increasing student achievement, but only if group goals and individual accountability are incorporated in the cooperative methods. This review updates the earlier reviews and provides estimates of the size of achievement effects characteristic of cooperative learning methods used over periods of at least 4 weeks in elementary and secondary schools. Among methods that use group goals and individual accountability (principally Student Team Learning methods), the median effect size is about +.30 for all measures and +.21 for standardized measures. These are moderate but important effects, particularily given the fact that they can be achieved in practice at very little cost and that cooperative learning also produces positive effects on such outcomes as race relations (Slavin, 1985b), acceptance of mainstreamed academically handicapped students (Johnson & Johnson, 1980; Madden & Slavin, 1983a), self concept, and other social variables (Slavin, 1983a).

Much research remains to be done to further understand the effects of cooperative learning and to apply cooperative learning principles to new objectives and settings, but the research reviewed in this chapter clearly shows that under certain well defined circumstances, cooperative learning can be an effective form of classroom organization for accelerating student achievement.

ACKNOWLEDGMENTS

This paper was written under a grant from the Office of Educational Research and Improvement (No. OERI-G-86-0006). However, any òpinions expressed are mine, and do not represent OERI policy.

REFERENCES

Allen, W. H., & Van Sickle, R. L. (1984). Learning teams and low achievers. *Social Education, 48*, 60–64.

Aronson, E., Blaney, N., Stephan, C., Sikes, J., & Snapp, M. (1978). *The jigsaw classroom.* Beverly Hills, CA: Sage.

Artzt, A. F. (1983). *The comparative effects of the student-team method of instruction and the traditional teacher-centered method of instruction upon student achievement, attitude, and social interaction in high school mathematics courses.* Unpublished doctoral dissertation, New York University.

Burns, M. (1981, September). Groups of four: Solving the management problem. *Learning, 46–51.*

Cavanagh, B. R. (1984). Effects of interdependent group contingencies on the achievement of elementary school children. *Dissertation Abstracts International, 46,* 1558.

Cotton, J., & Cook, M. (1982). Meta analyses and the effects of various systems: Some different conclusions from Johnson et al. *Psychological Bulletin, 92,* 176–183.

Davidson, N. (1985). Small-group learning and teaching in mathematics: A selective review of the research. In R. E. Slavin, S. Sharan, S. Kagan, R. Hertz-Lazarowitz, C. Webb, & R. Schmuck (Eds.), *Learning to cooperate, cooperating to learn (pp. 211–230).* New York: Plenum.

DeVries, D. L., Edwards, K. J., & Wells, E. H. (1974). *Teams–Games–Tournament in the social studies classroom: Effects on academic achievement, student attitudes, cognitive beliefs, and classroom climate.* (Report No. #173). Baltimore, MD; The Johns Hopkins University, Center for Social Organization of Schools.

DeVries, D. L., Lucasse, P. R., & Shackman, S. L. (1980). *Small group versus individualized instruction: A field test of relative effectiveness* (Report No. 293). Baltimore: The Johns Hopkins University, Center for Social Organization of Schools.

DeVries, D. L., & Mescon, I. T. (1975). *Teams–Games–Tournament: An effective task and reward structure in the elementary grades.* (Report No.189). Baltimore: The Johns Hopkins University, Center for Social Organization of Schools.

DeVries, D. L., Mescon, I. T., & Shackman, S. L. (1975a). *Teams–Games–Tournament (TGT) effects on reading skills in the elementary grades.* (Report No.200). Baltimore: The Johns Hopkins University, Center for Social Organization of Schools.

DeVries, D. L., & Slavin, R. E. (1978). Teams–Games–Tournament (TGT): Review of ten classroom experiments. *Journal of Research and Development in Education, 12,* 28–38.

Edwards, K. J., & DeVries, D. L. (1972). *Learning games and student teams: Their effects on student attitudes and achievement.* (Report No.147). Baltimore: The Johns Hopkins University, Center for Social Organization of Schools.

Edwards, K. J., & DeVries, C. L. (1974). *The effects of Teams–Games–Tournament and two structural variations on classroom process, student attitudes, and student achievement.* (Report No.172). Baltimore: The Johns Hopkins University, Center for Social Organization of Schools.

Edwards, K. J., DeVries, D. L., & Synder, J. P. (1972). Games and teams: A winning combination. *Simulation and Games, 3,* 247–269.

Frantz, L. J. (1979). *The effects of the student teams achievement approach in reading on peer attitudes.* Unpublished master's thesis, Old Dominion University, Richmond, VA.

Gonzales, A. (1981). *An approach to interdependent/cooperative bilingual education and measures related to social motives.* Unpublished manuscript, California State University at Fresno.

Hamblin, R. L., Hathaway, C., & Wodarski, J. S. (1971). Group contingencies, peer tutoring, and accelerating academic achievement. In E. Ramp & W. Hopkins (Eds.), *A new direction for education: Behavior analysis* (pp. 41-53). Lawrence, Kansas: The University of Kansas, Department of Human Development.

Hertz-Lazarowitz, R., Sapir, C., & Sharan, S. (1981). *Academic and social effects of two cooperative learning methods in desegregated classrooms.* Unpublished manuscript, Haifa University, Israel.

Huber, G. L., Bogatzki, W., & Winter, M. (1982). *Kooperation als Ziel schulischen Lehrens und Lehrens.* (Cooperation: Condition And Goal Of Teaching And Learning In Classrooms). Tubingen, West Germany: Arbeitsbereich Padagogische Psychologie der Universitat Tubingen.

Hulten, B. H., & DeVries, D. L. (1976). *Team competition and group practice: Effects on student achievement and attitudes.* (Report No. 212). Baltimore: The Johns Hopkins University, Center for Social Organization of Schools.

Humphreys, B., Johnson, R., & Johnson, D. W. (1982). Effects of cooperative, competitive, and individualistic learning on students' achievement in science class. *Journal of Research in Science Teaching, 19,* 351–356.

Johnson, D. W., & Johnson, R. T. (1975). *Learning together and alone.* New Jersey: Prentice-Hall.

Johnson, D. W., & Johnson, R. T. (1980). Integrating handicapped children into the mainstream. *Exceptional Children, 47,* 90–98.

Johnson, D. W., & Johnson, R. T. (1985). The internal dynamics of cooperative learning groups. In R. E. Slavin, S. Sharan, S. Kagan, R. Hertz-Lazarowitz, C. Webb, & R. Schmuck (Eds.), *Learning to cooperate, cooperating to learn.* New York: Plenum.

Johnson, D. W., Johnson, R. T., & Scott, L. (1978). The effects of cooperative and individualized instruction on student attitudes and achievement. *Journal of Social Psychology, 104,* 107–216.

Johnson, D.W., Maruyama, G., Johnson, R., Nelson, D., & Skon, L. (1981). Effects of cooperative, competitive, and individualistic goal structures on achievement: A meta-analysis. *Psychological Bulletin, 89,* 47–62.

Johnson, L. C. (1985). *The effects of the groups of four cooperative learning model on student problem-solving achievement in mathematics.* Unpublished doctoral dissertation, University of Houston.

Johnson, L. C., & Waxman, H. C. (1985, March). *Evaluating the effects of the "groups of four" program.* Paper presented at the annual convention of the American Educational Research Association, Chicago.

Johnson, R. T., Johnson, D. W., Scott, L. E., & Ramolae, B. A. (1985). Effects of single-sex and mixed-sex cooperative interaction on science achievement and attitudes and cross-handicap and cross-sex relationships. *Journal of Research in Science Teaching, 22,* 207–220.

Kagan, S. (1985). *Cooperative learning resources for teachers.* Riverside, CA: University of California at Riverside.

Kagan, S., Zahn, G. L., Widaman, K. F., Schwartzwald, J., & Tyrrell, G. (1985). Classroom structural bias: Impact of cooperative and competitive classroom structures on cooperative and competitive individuals and groups. In R. E. Slavin et al. (Eds.), *Learning to cooperate, cooperating to learn.* New York: Plenum.

Lazarowitz, R., Baird, J. H., Hertz-Lazarowitz, R., & Jenkins, J. (1985). The effects of modified Jigsaw on achievement, classroom social climate, and self-esteem in high-school science classes. In R. E. Slavin, S. Sharan, S. Kaga, R. Hertz-Lazarowitz, C. Webb, & R. Schmuck (Eds.), *Learning to cooperate, cooperating to learn.* New York: Plenum.

Lew, M., Mesch, D., Johnson, D. W., & Johnson, R. T. (1986). Positive interdependence, academic and collaborative-skills group contingencies, and isolated students. *American Educational Research Journal, 23,* 476–488.

Madden, N. A., & Slavin, R. E. (1983a). Mainstreaming students with mild academic handicaps: Academic and social outcomes. *Review of Educational Research, 53,* 519–569.

Madden, N. A., & Slavin, R. E. (1983b). Effects of cooperative learning on the social acceptance of mainstreamed academically handicapped students. *Journal of Special Education, 17,* 171–182.

Madden, N. A., Slavin, R. E., & Stevens, R. J. (1986). *Cooperative Integrated Reading and Comparison: Teacher's manual.* Baltimore, MD: The Johns Hopkins University, Center for Research on Elementary and Middle Schools.

McGlynn, R. (1982). A comment on the meta-analysis of goal structures. *Psychological Bulletin, 92,* 184–185.

Mevarech, Z. R. (1985a). The effects of cooperative mastery learning strategies on mathematics achievement. *Journal of Educational Research, 78* 372–377.

Mevarech, Z. (1985b, April). *Cooperative mastery learning strategies.* Paper presented at the annual convention of the American Educational Research Association, Chicago.

Moskowitz, J.M., Malvin, J. H., Schaeffer, G. A., & Schaps, E. (1983). Evaluation of a cooperative learning strategy. *American Educational Research Journal, 20,* 687–696.

Newmann, F. M., & Thompson, J. (1987). *Effects of cooperative learning on achievement in secondary schools: A summary of research.* Madison, WI: University of Wisconsin, National Center on Effective Secondary Schools.

Oishi, S., Slavin, R. E., & Madden, N. A. (1983, April). *Effects of student teams and individualized instruction on cross-race and cross-sex friendships.* Paper presented at the annual meeting of the American Educational Research Association, Montreal.

Okebukola, P. A. (1984). In search of a more effective interaction pattern in biology laboratories. *Journal of Biological Education, 18,* 305–308.

Okebukola, P. A. (1985). The relative effectiveness of cooperativeness and competitive interaction techniques in strengthening students' performance in science classes. *Science Education, 69,* 501–509.

Okebukola, P.A. (1986a). Impact of extended cooperative and competitive relationships on the performance of students in science. *Human Relations, 39,* 673–682.

Okebukola, P.A. (1986b). The influence of preferred learning styles on cooperative learning in science. *Science Education, 70,* 509–517.

Okebukola, P.A. (1986c). The problem of large classes in science: An experiment in co-operative learning. *European Journal of Science Education, 8,* 73–77.

Perrault, R. (1982). *An experimental comparison of cooperative learning to noncooperative learning and their effects on cognitive achievement in junior high industrial arts laboratories.* Unpublished doctoral dissertation, University of Maryland.

Rich, Y., Amir, Y., & Slavin, R. E. (1986). *Instructional strategies for improving children's cross-ethnic relations.* Ramat Gan, Israel: Bar Ilan University, Institute for the Advancement of Social Integration in the Schools.

Robertson, L. (1982). *Integrated goal structuring in the elementary school: Cognitive growth in mathematics.* Unpublished doctoral dissertation, Rutgers University.

Sharan, S. (1980). Cooperative learning in small groups: Recent methods and effects on achievement, attitudes, and ethnic relations. *Review of Educational Research, 50,* 241–271.

Sharan, S., Hertz-Lazarowitz, R., & Ackerman, Z. (1980). Academic achievement of elementary school children in small-group versus whole class instruction. *Journal of Experimental Education, 48,* 125–129.

Sharan, S., Kussell, P., Hertz-Lazarowitz, R., Bejarano, Y., Raviv, S., & Sharan, Y. (1984). *Cooperative learning in the classroom: Research in desegregated schools.* Hillsdale, NJ: Lawrence Erlbaum Associates.

Sharan, S., & Shachar, C. (in press). *Language and learning in the cooperative classroom.* New York: Springer.

Sharan, S., & Sharan, Y., (1976). *Small-group teaching.* New Jersey: Educational Technology Publications.

Sherman, L. W., & Thomas, M. (1986). Mathematics achievement in cooperative versus individualistic goal-structured high school classrooms. *Journal of Educational Research, 79,* 169–172.

Sherman, L. W., & Zimmerman, D. (1986, November). *Cooperative versus competitive reward-structured secondary science classroom achievement.* Paper presented at the annual convention of the School Science and Mathematics Association, Lexington, KY.

Slavin, R. E. (1977). *Student learning team techniques: Narrowing the achievement gap between the races* (Report No. 228). Baltimore: The Johns Hopkins University, Center for Social Organization of Schools.

Slavin, R. E. (1978a). Student teams and achievement divisions. *Journal of Research and Development in Education, 12,* 39–49.

Slavin, R. E. (1978b). Student teams and comparison among equals: Effects on academic performance and student attitudes. *Journal of Educational Psychology, 70,* 532–538.

Slavin, R. E. (1979). Effects of biracial learning teams on cross-racial friendships. *Journal of Educational Psychology, 71,* 381–387.

Slavin, R. E. (1980a). Cooperative learning. *Review of Educational Research, 50,* 315–342.

Slavin, R. E. (1980b). Effects of individual learning expectations on student achievement. *Journal of Educational Psychology, 72,* 520–524.

Slavin, R. E. (1980c). Effects of student teams and peer tutoring on academic achievement and time on-task. *Journal of Experimental Education, 48,* 252–257.

Slavin, R. E. (1983a). *Cooperative learning.* New York: Longman.

Slavin, R. E. (1983b). When does cooperative learning increase student achievement? *Psychological Bulletin, 94,* 429–445.

Slavin, R. E. (1984a). Team assisted individualization: Cooperative learning and individualized instruction in the mainstreamed classroom. *Remedial and Special Education, 5 (6),* 33–42.

Slavin, R. E. (1984b). Meta-analysis in education: How has it been used? *Educational Researcher, 13 (8),* 6–15, 24–27.

Slavin, R. E. (1985a). Cooperative learning: Applying contact theory in desegregated schools. *Journal of Social Issues, 41 (3),* 45–62.

Slavin, R. E. (1985b). Team-Assisted Individualization: Combining cooperative learning and individualized instruction in mathematics. In R. E. Slavin, S. Sharan, S. Kagan, R. Hertz-Lazarowitz, C. Webb, & R. Schmuck (Eds.), *Learning to cooperate, cooperating to learn.* 177–209. New York: Plenum.

Slavin, R. E. (1986a). Best-evidence synthesis: An alternative to meta-analytic and traditional reviews. *Educational Research, 15 (9),* 5–11.

Slavin, R. E. (1986b). *Using Student Team Learning.* (3rd ed.). Baltimore: Johns Hopkins University, Center for Research on Elementary and Middle Schools.

Slavin, R.E. (1987a). Mastery learning reconsidered. *Review of Educational Research, 57,* 175–213.

Slavin, R. E. (1987b). Cooperative learning: Where behavioral and humanistic approaches to classroom motivation meet. *Elementary School Journal, 88,* 29–37.

Slavin, R. E. (1987c). Ability grouping and student achievement in elementary schools: A best-evidence synthesis. *Review of Educational Research, 57,* 293–336.

Slavin, R. E., & Karweit, N. (1981). Cognitive and affective outcomes of an intensive student team learning experience. *Journal of Experimental Education 50,* 29–35.

Slavin, R. E., & Karweit, N. L. (1984). Mastery learning and student teams: A factorial experiment in urban general mathematics classes. *American Educational Research Journal, 21,* 725–736.

Slavin, R. E., & Karweit, N. L. (1985). Effects of whole-class, ability grouped, and individualized instruction on mathematics achievement. *American Educational Research Journal, 22,* 351–367.

Slavin, R. E., Leavey, M., & Madden, N. A. (1984). Combining cooperative learning and individualized instruction: Effects on student mathematics achievement, attitudes, and behaviors. *Elementary School Journal, 84,* 409–422.

Slavin, R. E., Leavey, M. B., & Madden, N. A. (1986). *Team Accelerated Instruction–Mathematics.* Watertown, MA: Mastery Education Corporation.

Slavin, R. E., Madden, N. A., & Leavey, M. (1984). Effects of Team Assisted Individualization on the mathematics achievement of academically handicapped students and nonhandicapped students. *Journal of Educational Psychology, 76,* 813–819.

Slavin, R. E., & Oickle, E. (1981). Effects of cooperative learning teams on student achievement and race relations: Treatment by race interactions. *Sociology of Education, 54,* 174–180.

Slavin, R. E., Stevens, R. J., & Madden, N. A. (in press). Accomodating student diversity in reading and writing instruction: A cooperative learning approach. *Remedial and Special Education.*

Stevens, R. J., Madden, N. A., Slavin, R. E., & Farnish, A. M. (1987). Cooperative Integrated Reading and Composition: Two field experiments. *Reading Research Quarterly, 22,* 433–454.

Stevens, R. J., Slavin, R. E., Farnish, A. M., & Madden, N. A. (1987). *Effects of cooperative learning and direct instruction in reading comprehension strategies on main idea and influence skills.* Baltimore, MD: The Johns Hopkins University, Center for Research on Elementary and Middle Schools.

Talmage, H., Pascarella, E. T., & Ford, S. (1984). The influence of cooperative learning strategies on teacher practices, student perceptions of the learning environment, and academic achievement. *American Educational Research Journal, 21,* 163–179.

Tomblin, E. A., & Davis, B. R. (1985). *Technical report of the evaluation of the race/human relations program: A study of cooperative learning environment strategies.* San Diego, CA: San Diego Public Schools.

Van Oudenhoven, J. P., Van Berkum, G., & Swen-Koopmans, T. (1987). Effect of cooperation and shared feedback on spelling achievement. *Journal of Educational Psychology, 79*, 92–94.

Van Oudenhoven, J. P., Wiersma, B., & Van Yperen, N. (1987) Effects of cooperation and feedback by fellow pupils on spelling achievement. *European Journal of Psychology of Education, 2*, 83–91.

Vedder, P.H. (1985). *Cooperative learning: A study on processes and effects of cooperation between primary school children.* The Hague, The Netherlands: Stichting Voor Onderzoek Van Het Onderwijs.

Webb, N. (1985). Student interaction and learning in small groups: A research summary. In R. E. Slavin, S. Sharan, S. Kagan, R. Hertz-Lazarowitz, C. Webb, & R. Schmuck (Eds.), *Learning to cooperate, cooperating to learn,* (pp. 147–172). New York: Plenum.

Yager, S., Johnson, D. W., & Johnson, R. T. (1985). Oral discussion, group-to-individual transfer, and achievement in cooperative learning groups. *Journal of Educational Psychology, 77*, 60–66.

Yager, S., Johnson, R. T., Johnson, D. W., & Snider, B. (1986). The impact of group processing on achievement in cooperative learning. *Journal of Social Psychology, 126*, 389–397.

Ziegler, S. (1981). The effectiveness of cooperative learning teams for increasing cross-ethnic friendship: Additional evidence. *Human Organization, 40*, 264–268.

IV SCHOOL ORGANIZATION

6 Grouping for Instruction in the Elementary School*

Robert E. Slavin
Center for Research on Elementary and Middle Schools
Johns Hopkins University

For as long as instruction has been delivered to class groups of students, teachers, administrators, and researchers have debated the question of how classes should be organized. Research on various grouping arrangements has been under way since the beginning of this century; yet still today, practitioners and policy makers agonize over how best to group students. Should students be assigned by ability? Is departmentalization a good idea? Should teachers group students within the class? Are different groupings appropriate for different subjects? In recent decades, such grouping arrangements as mastery learning and cooperative learning have appeared on the scene, increasing the range of grouping options available, but also further adding complexity to the problem.

Many grouping decisions are made on the basis of unsubstantiated opinion, perhaps on the assumption that research on grouping is equivocal, irrelevant, or lacking. For some forms of grouping, evidence is indeed lacking or inconclusive, but in many cases there is rather conclusive evidence concerning the achievement effects of particular grouping practices. This chapter summarizes the best available evidence concerning the achievement effects of common grouping arrangements in elementary schools (see chapter 7 for a discussion of research on grouping in secondary schools).

Why Group

Grouping of students for instruction is done for many reasons, but most grouping plans exist to deal with one central fact of mass education: that students differ in

---

*This chapter is adapted from an earlier article by Slavin (1987a).

knowledge, skills, developmental stage, and learning rate. If a teacher is to present a lesson to a class, then it seems intuitively obvious that the lesson should be neither too easy nor too difficult for the students. If the class is highly heterogeneous, then one lesson will of necessity be easier than would be optimal for some students, and more difficult than would be optimal for others. For the sake of instructional efficiency, it seems that students should be grouped so that they will all be able to profit from one lesson.

Yet virtually every means of grouping students by ability or performance level has its own drawbacks, which may be serious enough to offset any advantages. Grouping by age is so common now that we take it for granted, yet this was itself an innovation of the 19th century (Goodlad & Anderson, 1963). Age-grading certainly reduces heterogeneity in comparison to the one-room schoolhouse, but still leaves a great deal of heterogeneity within each grade and may deprive students of the opportunity to learn from older students. Various ability grouping plans may stigmatize low achievers and put them into classes or groups for which teachers have low expectations, or lead to the creation of academic elites (Oakes, 1985, 1987; Persell, 1977). Methods of dealing with student heterogeneity within the classroom such as use of reading or math groups, mastery learning, and cooperative learning, create problems in terms of management of multiple groups and reductions in direct instruction received by individual students.

Some forms of grouping for instruction have important goals other than accommodation of student heterogeneity. For example, the use of cooperative, heterogeneous learning groups (see chapter 5; Slavin, 1983a) is directed primarily at increasing student motivation and allowing students to help one another learn. Departmentalization is largely designed to let teachers specialize in subjects they are most able or willing to teach. Use of within-class reading or math groups may be done in part to reduce the size of instructional groups. Yet on balance it is likely that if all students entered school with the same skills and abilities and progressed at identical rates, grouping would not be a major issue in elementary education.

Types of Grouping

The principal types of grouping arrangements fall into two major categories: Between-class and within-class (see Table 6.1). Between-class plans are school-level arrangements by which students are assigned to classes. Several means of assigning students to classes by ability fall into this category, as does departmentalization. Within-class grouping arrangements may attempt to reduce the heterogeneity of instructional groups, as in the use of within-class ability grouping or mastery learning. Finally, cooperative learning is a within-class grouping strategy that uses heterogeneous rather than homogeneous subgroups.

The types of grouping listed in Table 6.1 are not exhaustive of all possible grouping arrangements, but they are the most widely used and/or most exten-

TABLE 6.1
Typology of Elementary School Grouping

Type of Grouping	Specific Grouping Plan
I. Between-Class Grouping	
A. Ability Grouping	
1. Class Assignment	
a. Comprehensive.....	Ability Grouped Class Assignment
b. Selective.........	Gifted Programs, Special Education
2. Selected Subjects	
a. Within Grade......	Regrouping for Reading, Math
b. Cross-Grade.......	Joplin, Nongraded Plans
B. Departmentalization.....	Departmental, Semi-departmental Plans
II. Within-Class Grouping	
A. Ability Grouping........	Reading, Math Groups
B. Mastery Learning........	Group-Based Mastery Learning
C. Cooperative Learning....	Cooperative Learning Methods

sively researched grouping plans at the elementary level. Also, it is important to note that these plans are not mutually exclusive, but can be used in combination. The following sections define the various grouping plans, and briefly present the research that has been done on each.

Between-Class Ability Grouping

Perhaps the most controversial form of grouping at the elementary level is assignment of students to groups according to ability or performance. Arguments about the desirability of between-class ability grouping have raged from the 1920s (e.g., Miller & Otto, 1930) to the present (e.g., Good & Marshall, 1984; Kulik & Kulik, 1982, 1984). Over this time period, the same essential arguments have been advanced on both sides (see, for example, Borg, 1965; Esposito, 1973; Good & Marshall, 1984; Persell, 1977). Proponents have argued that ability grouping lets high achievers move rapidly and gives low achievers attainable goals and extra help. Opponents have countered that ability grouping is unfair to low achievers, citing problems of poor peer models, low teacher expectations, and slow instructional pace.

Recently, Slavin (1987c) reviewed research on ability grouping in elementary schools. He noted that ability grouping is not a single practice, but has many fundamentally different forms, which have different educational as well as psychological effects. The most important forms of between-class ability grouping are discussed in the following sections.

Ability Grouped Class Assignment.   In many elementary schools, students are assigned to self-contained classes on the basis of a general achievement or ability measure. This might produce, for example, a high-achieving fourth grade class, an average achieving class, and a low-achieving class, with students assigned to classes according to some combination of a composite achievement measure, IQ scores, and/or teacher judgment. Students remain with the same ability-grouped classes for all academic subjects.

The achievement effects of ability grouped class assignment (in comparison to heterogeneous grouping) are essentially zero. Slavin (1987c) identified 14 methodologically adequate studies of this practice, and found the median effect size on standardized achievement measures to be approximately .00. There is some evidence that high achievers may gain from ability grouping at the expense of low achievers (e.g., Borg, 1965; Flair, 1965; Tobin, 1966), but most studies find no such trend (see, for example, Bremer, 1958; Hartill, 1936; Morganstern, 1963). Overall, the effects of ability grouping cluster closely around zero for students of all achievement levels.

One probable reason that ability grouped class assignment has little effect on student achievement is that this plan typically has only a limited impact on the heterogeneity of the class. For example, Goodlad (1960) estimated that dividing a group of elementary students into two ability groups on the basis of IQ reduced total variability in each class by only 7%. With three groups, heterogeneity was reduced by 17%, still not likely to be enough to have a measurable impact. Even though a student's performance in any one subject is correlated with performance in other subjects, this correlation is far from perfect. This means that grouping students on any one criterion is sure to leave substantial heterogeneity in any specific skill domain. On the other hand, assigning students to ''high'' and ''low'' ability classes may have a stigmatizing effect on low achievers and may evoke low expectation for student achievement and behavior even if the grouping has a minimal impact on class heterogeneity. Thus, ability grouped class assignment may be enough to produce psychological drawbacks but does not do enough to reap the potential educational benefits of reducing student heterogeneity in any particular skill.

Regrouping for Reading and/or Mathematics.   Another commonly used ability grouping arrangement involves having students remain in heterogeneous classes most of the day but regrouping for selected subjects. For example, three fourth grade classes in a school might have reading scheduled at the same time. At reading time, students might leave their heterogeneous homerooms and go to a class organized according to reading levels.

There are three important advantages of regrouping for selected subjects over ability grouped class assignment. First, students remain in a heterogeneous setting most of the day, so they are likely to identify with that group, reducing the labeling effect of all-day grouping. Second, students are grouped solely on the basis of their achievement in reading or mathematics, not general achievement or ability level, so a meaningful reduction in heterogeneity in the skill being taught is possible. Third, regrouping plans tend to be more flexible than ability grouped class assignment, because changing students between reading or mathematics classes is less disruptive than changing basic class assignments. For this reason, any errors in assignment can be easily remedied, and any changes in student performance level can be accommodated with a change in grouping.

Research on regrouping plans indicates that they can be instructionally effective if two conditions are fulfilled: Instructional level and pace must be completely adapted to student performance level, and the regrouping must be done for only one or two subjects so that students stay in heterogeneous placements most of the day (Slavin, 1987c). Studies that met these conditions have generally found positive effects on student achievement in reading (Berkun, Swanson, & Sawyer, 1966), mathematics (Provus, 1960), and reading and mathematics taken together (Balow & Ruddell, 1963; Morris, 1969). On the other hand, when regrouping has been done without adapting the pace or level of instruction (Davis & Tracy, 1963; Moses, 1966) or in more than two different subjects (Koontz, 1961), no benefits for regrouping have been found.

Joplin Plan. One interesting form of regrouping plan is the Joplin Plan (Floyd, 1954), in which students are regrouped for reading without regard for grade levels. That is, a reading class at the fourth grade, first semester level might contain some third, some fourth, and some fifth graders. One importance consequence of this grouping plan is that it allows for the reduction or elimination of within-class grouping for reading, as students in each reading class may all be at the same reading level. This allows teachers to spend more of the reading class time doing direct instruction, reducing the time during which students must do unsupervised followup seatwork.

Effects of the Joplin Plan and closely related forms of nongraded plans (see following subsection) have been quite positive overall. Slavin (1987c) estimated the median effect size for Joplin and Joplin-like nongraded plans at +.44 for reading achievement, and one study (Hart, 1962) found similar effects for mathematics. Two of these studies (Hillson, Jones, Moore & Van Devender, 1964; Morgan & Stucker, 1960) used random assignment of students and teachers to treatments, and most others were good-quality matched equivalent studies.

Nongraded Plans. Nongraded plans (Goodlad & Anderson, 1963) are grouping arrangements in which formal grade levels are abolished in favor of flexible cross-age groupings for different subjects. Many different forms of nongrading have been evaluated. In some cases (e.g., Hillson, et al., 1964; Ingram, 1960) where nongrading is done in reading or mathematics only, nongrading is essentially identical to the Joplin Plan. At the other extreme, nongraded plans may involve many subjects, constant and flexible regrouping within and between classes, extensive use of individualized instruction, team teaching, and other features more in line with forms of the open classroom than with the still quite traditional Joplin Plan (see, for example, Bowman, 1971; Ross, 1967).

Achievement effects of comprehensive nongraded plans were found by Slavin (1987a) to be inconsistent but generally positive. However, most of the studies that failed to find positive effects of nongraded plans either took place in laboratory schools (e.g., Otto, 1969; Ross, 1967) or found few implementation differences between nongraded and traditional programs (e.g., Carbone, 1961; Hopkins, Oldridge, & Williamson, 1965). Studies in regular classrooms in which the nongraded program was used conscientiously usually found positive effects on student achievement (e.g., Bowman, 1971; Machiele, 1965).

Gifted Programs. One form of between-class ability grouping that is increasingly seen at the elementary level in recent years is the provision of special classes for the gifted and talented. Gifted programs may be offered only in one subject (often mathematics), or separate classes for high achieving or otherwise exceptional students may be provided.

Most research on special programs for the gifted contains a serious, systematic bias. Much of this research (e.g., Simpson & Martison, 1961) compares students in gifted programs to students in the same schools who did not participate in the gifted program, matching on IQ or other measures. However, if there are two students with IQs of 130 and one was accepted for a gifted program whereas the other was rejected, then we can be sure that there were other factors, such as motivation, achievement, and so on, that also differentiate these students, all of which are likely to work to the advantage of the students accepted for the special program. Nonrandomized comparisons across schools with and without gifted programs (e.g., Baldauf, 1959; West & Sievers, 1960) are somewhat better, but also suffer from this systematic selection bias. Studies of acceleration (see J. A. Kulik & C.-L. Kulik, 1984), exposing gifted students to higher levels of information in some subjects or skipping them to higher grades, share the same problems of selection bias, with the additional problem that the accelerated students are exposed to material not seen by regular students, making comparisons difficult.

The literature on gifted programs at the elementary level is small, inconclusive, and methodologically inadequate for the reasons described previously and others. A few studies have reported achievement benefits of special programs for the gifted (e.g., Atkinson & O'Connor, 1963; Bell, 1957; West & Sievers, 1960) whereas others found no significant advantages (e.g., Baldauf, 1959; Becker, 1963).

Special Education. Assignment to full- or part-time special education programs for learning problems (e.g., learning disabilities, mental retardation) can also be seen as a form of between-class ability grouping. This form of grouping is discussed in chapter 8 (see also Leinhardt & Pallay, 1982; Madden & Slavin, 1983). Unfortunately, most research on the efficacy of special education has the same type of methodological flaws characteristic of studies of gifted programs. Matched comparisons between students assigned to special education and those remaining in regular classes are biased toward regular class assignment because of the likelihood of systematic differences between students of, for example, the same IQ assigned to regular or special classes (Madden & Slavin, 1983).

However, there are a few randomized studies of special education versus mainstreaming (regular class placement) for students with mild academic handicaps, such as learning disabilities and mild retardation. For example, Goldstein, Moss, and Jordan (1966) found that students randomly assigned to a high quality special education program learned no more than did students who remained in regular classes. Calhoun and Elliott (1977) found that mildly retarded and emotionally disturbed students randomly assigned to regular classes that used individualized instruction gained substantially more in achievement than did students who experienced the same individualized program with the same teachers in self-contained special education classes. Overall, evidence from studies of special education and mainstreaming supports the use of means of accommodating student differences within the regular classroom rather than separating students into special classes (Madden & Slavin, 1983).

Summary and Conclusions: Between-Class Ability Grouping. Evidence from studies of various forms of between-class ability grouping in elementary schools indicates that achievement effects depend on the types of programs evaluated. In general, ability grouping plans are beneficial for student achievement when they incorporate the following features (adapted from Slavin, 1987c):

1. Students remain in heterogeneous classes most of the day and are regrouped by performance level only in such subjects as reading and mathematics, in which reducing heterogeneity is particularly important.
2. The grouping plan reduces heterogeneity in the specific skill being taught.
3. Group assignments are flexible and are frequently reassessed.
4. Teachers adapt their level and pace of instruction in regrouped classes to accommodate students' levels of readiness and learning rates.

The between-class grouping plan that most completely incorporates the four principles in the preceding list is the Joplin Plan, in which students remain in heterogeneous classes except for reading, are grouped strictly according to reading level, and are constantly re-evaluated, and in which all achievement levels are accommodated. Evidence on the Joplin Plan strongly supports the effectiveness of this arrangement and of within-grade regrouping plans and nongraded plans that most resemble it. In contrast, ability grouped class assignment, special programs for the gifted, and special education for students with learning problems do not generally meet the four criteria. Typically, they segregate students all or most of the day, are based on general ability or achievement rather than skill in a specific subject, and tend to be highly inflexible. Teachers may or may not adjust their level and pace of instruction to adapt to students' needs in these plans. Evidence at the elementary level finds no benefits for ability grouped class assignment or special education assignment, and only inconsistent and flawed evidence in favor of special programs for the gifted.

Departmentalization

One between-class grouping plan often seen in elementary schools is some form of departmentalization, in which teachers teach one or a few (but not all) subjects to multiple class groups. Departmentalization in the elementary school can take many forms. Sometimes elementary schools (especially grades 4–6) are organized very much like secondary schools, with teachers teaching one subject to five or six different groups of students. Alternatively, there are departmentalized plans in which one teacher might see two classes for reading and language while another sees the same two classes for mathematics, social studies, and science. Semi-departmentalized plans may have all teachers teach a set of subjects to students in their homeroom groups in the morning, whereas other subjects are departmentalized in the afternoon.

The main advantage of departmentalization is that it allows teachers to specialize, teaching subjects they are most able and willing to teach. For example, some otherwise excellent elementary teachers just do not feel comfortable teaching mathematics, while others love to do so. However, departmentalization risks diffusing responsibility for individual children, making it difficult for a student to identify with a single caring adult. It may represent an unhealthy intrusion of the ''subject-centered'' secondary organization into the more typically ''child-centered'' elementary school.

Unfortunately, there is very little research on departmentalization in elementary schools. However, what does exist fails to support this practice. Ward (1970) found that students in grades 4–6 learned reading and science significantly better in self-contained classes than in departmentalized classes, and there were no differences in mathematics and social studies. Hosley (1954) also found that sixth graders' achievement was higher in self-contained K–6 schools than in semi-departmentalized junior high schools. No achievement differences were found between departmentalized and non-departmentalized plans at the elementary or junior high school levels in a study by Jackson (1953), and a study of seventh and eighth graders found that their achievement was higher in self-contained than in departmentalized settings (Spivak, 1956). Only one study, a dissertation by Case (1971), found an achievement benefit of departmentalization, comparing fifth graders in a new middle school to matched control students remaining in self-contained elementary classrooms.

Within-Class Ability Grouping

Within-class ability grouping is the practice of assigning students to homogeneous subgroups for instruction within the class. In general, each subgroup receives instruction at its own level and is allowed to progress at its own rate. Within-class ability grouping is virtually universal in elementary reading instruction and is common in elementary mathematics (Barr & Dreeben, 1983; Hallinan & Sorensen, 1983).

Within-class grouping plans generally conform to the four requirements for effective ability grouping proposed earlier. They involve only reading and/or mathematics, leaving students in relatively heterogeneous classes the rest of the school day. They group students in specific rather than general skills, and, at least in principle, within-class groupings are easy to change. Most teachers do adapt their level and pace of instruction to meet students' needs (Barr & Dreeben, 1983). However, within-class ability grouping introduces a problem not characteristic of between-class grouping plans. This is the problem of management of multiple groups. When the teacher is instructing one reading group, for example, the remaining students must work independently on seatwork activities, which may be of questionable value (see Anderson, Brubaker, Alleman-Brooks, & Duffy, 1985). Supervising multiple groups and transitions between them are major classroom management problems (Anderson, Evertson, & Brophy, 1979).

Methodologically adequate research on within-class ability grouping has unfortunately been limited to the study of mathematics grouping, perhaps because few teachers would be willing to participate in an experiment in which they had to teach heterogeneous classes without breaking students into reading groups. However, the research on within-class grouping in mathematics clearly supports this practice. Every one of eight studies of within-class ability grouping in mathematics identified by Slavin (1987c), including five randomized studies, favored the grouped treatment (median effect size = +.34). Effects of within-class grouping were somewhat higher for low achievers (median ES = +.65) than for average and high achievers. There was some trend for effects to be more positive when the number of ability groups was two or three rather than four.

Effects of within-class grouping on mathematics achievement cannot be assumed to hold for reading. In mathematics, there is a need for students to work problems independently, so there is an appropriate place for independent seatwork. A corresponding need for independent seatwork time is less compelling in reading. However, the universality of within-class grouping in reading provides at least some indication that this form of within-class ability grouping is also instructionally necessary.

Mastery Learning

Group-based mastery learning, a form of within-class grouping in which students are flexibly assigned to "masters" and "non-masters" groups at the end of each lesson, is discussed in chapter 4. Essentially, research on this strategy finds few positive effects on student achievement in methodologically adequate studies of at least 4-weeks' duration (also see Slavin, 1987b).

Cooperative Learning

Another form of within-class grouping, cooperative learning (Slavin 1983a, 1983b), differs from within-class ability grouping not only in that cooperative learning groups are small and heterogeneous, but also in that these groups are expected to engage in a great deal of task-focused interaction, such as studying together or completing group assignments.

Research on the achievement effects of cooperative learning, reviewed in chapter 5, has found that the effects of this grouping strategy depend on how it is organized. Instructionally effective cooperative learning methods provide group rewards based on the individual learning of all group members. In contrast, methodologically adequate studies of cooperative learning methods in which students complete a single group worksheet or other product (e.g., Johnson, Johnson, & Scott, 1978; Vedder, 1985) have not generally found positive achievement effects.

DISCUSSION

Research on grouping in elementary schools has generally been out of vogue in recent years. In particular, very few studies of the achievement effects of between- and within-class ability grouping, gifted programs, and special education/mainstreaming have appeared since the mid-1970s. Yet debate on the appropriateness of various grouping plans continues, and practices very widely. Grouping remains a critical topic, and understanding the effects of different grouping plans is still of great practical and theoretical importance.

Reviewers of the 1960s (e.g., Borg, 1965; NEA, 1968; Passow, 1962) generally concluded that research on ability grouping was a hopeless muddle. However, these and later reviewers (e.g., Begle, 1975; Esposito, 1973) often failed to make critical distinctions between different types of grouping plans, combining studies of programs for the gifted with comprehensive between-class ability grouping plans, regrouping for selected subjects, and within-class ability grouping. Yet when the research on these different plans is separated, the picture becomes relatively clear. Ability grouping plans, such as the Joplin Plan and certain forms of nongraded and regrouping plans, can be instructionally effective. They all meet a set of criteria proposed earlier in this text: They leave students in heterogeneous classes most of the school day, regroup only for reading and/or mathematics according to student performance in these skills, can flexibly change student placements, and tend to completely adapt the level and pace of instruction to the needs and preparedness of the regrouped classes. Within-class ability grouping in mathematics also meets these criteria, and has also been consistently found to increase student achievement. On the other hand, wholesale between-class grouping plans, such as ability grouped class assignment, special classes for the gifted, and self-contained special education, have not generally been found to be beneficial for student achievement. Considering evidence on all kinds of grouping plans, it can be concluded that ability grouping can be a useful tool in elementary school organization, but it is a tool that must be used sparingly, precisely, and planfully if it is to have a positive effect on student achievement.

Many elementary schools in recent years have introduced departmentalization to enable teachers to specialize in their strongest or favorite subjects. The advent of the middle school has also introduced departmentalization to students at earlier ages than was once the case. There is little research comparing departmentalized and self-contained arrangements for students in the upper elementary grades, but what does exist tends to recommend against early departmentalization.

In the past decade, some interest in grouping has shifted to two within-class grouping plans, mastery learning and cooperative learning. Given its widespread use, it is surprising how little methodologically adequate research exists on mastery learning at the elementary level and how little support for this practice the research has provided (see chapter 4; Slavin, 1987b). On the other hand, there is a great deal of research on cooperative learning methods, which involve students working in small, heterogeneous learning groups. This research has indicated that if the groups are rewarded on the basis of the individual learning of all group members, then cooperative learning can consistently increase student achievement in the elementary grades (see chapter 5).

Although there is much we can learn from past research on grouping plans in elementary schools, there is still much we have yet to learn. For example, basic questions about the effects of within-class ability grouping in reading, of mastery learning, and of various forms of departmentalization remain unanswered. The mechanisms by which different grouping plans may have their effects are not at all clear; in many cases there are plausible explanations for effects of ability grouping plans that have nothing to do with ability grouping per se. For example, within-class ability grouping may be effective not because it reduces student heterogeneity but because it reduces the size of instructional groups (see Eddleman, 1971). However, the evidence that exists now does suggest that the study of grouping arrangements in elementary school is likely to bear fruit. Some forms of grouping can have strong effects on student achievement, and research directed at discovering effective grouping models and understanding the mechanisms that underlie their effectiveness is likely to contribute a critical element to the science and practice of effective elementary school organization.

REFERENCES

Anderson, L. M., Brubaker, N. L., Alleman-Brooks, J., & Duffy, G. G. (1985). A qualitative study of seatwork in first grade classrooms. *Elementary School Journal, 86,* 123–140.

Anderson, L. M., Evertson, C., & Brophy, J. (1979). An experimental study of effective teaching in first-grade reading-groups. *Elementary School Journal, 79,* 193–223.

Atkinson, J. W., & O'Connor, P. (1963). *Effects of ability grouping in schools related to individual differences in achievement-related motivation.* Final Report, Cooperative Research Project No. OE-2-10-024. U.S. Department of Health, Education, and Welfare.

Baldauf, R. S. (1959). A comparison of the extent of educational growth of mentally advanced pupils in the Cedar Rapids experiment. *Journal of Educational Research, 52,* 181–183.

Balow, I. H., & Rudell, A. K. (1963). The effects of three types of grouping on achievement. *California Journal of Educational Research, 14,* 108–117.

Barr, R., & Dreeben, R. (1983). *How schools work.* Chicago: University of Chicago Press.

Becker, L. J. (1963). *An analysis of the science and mathematics achievement of gifted sixth grade children enrolled in segregated, partially segregated, and non-segregated classes.* Unpublished doctoral dissertation, Syracuse University.

Begle, E. G. (1975). *Ability grouping for mathematics instruction: A review of the empirical literature.* Stanford, CA: Stanford University, Stanford Mathematics Education Study Group. (ERIC Document Reproduction Service No. ED 116 938).

Bell, M. E. (1957). *A comparative study of mentally gifted children children heterogenously and homogeneousy grouped.* Unpublished doctoral dissertation, Indiana University.

Berkun, M. M., Swanson, L. W., & Sawyer, D. M. (1966). An experiment on homogeneous grouping for reading in elementary classes. *Journal of Educational Research, 59,* 413–414.

Borg, W. R. (1965). Ability grouping in the public schools: A field study. *Journal of Experimental Education, 34,* 1–97.

Bowman, B. L. (1971). A comparison of pupil achievement and attitude in a graded school with pupil achievement and attitude in a nongraded school 1968–69, 1969–70 school years. *Dissertation Abstracts International, 32,* 86-A. (University Microfilms No. 71-20, 958).

Calhoun, G., & Elliott, R. (1977). Self-concept and academic achievement of educable retarded and emotionally disturbed children. *Exceptional Children, 44,* 379–380.

Carbone, R. F. (1961). A comparison of graded and non-graded elementary schools. *Elementary School Journal, 62,* 82–88.

Case, D. A. (1971). A comparative study of fifth graders in a new middle school with fifth graders in elementary self contained classrooms. *Dissertation Abstracts International, 32,* 86-A. (University Microfilms No. 71-16,770)

Davis, O. L., & Tracy, N. H. (1963). Arithmetic achievement and instructional grouping. *Arithmetic Teacher, 10,* 12–17.

Eddleman, V. K. (1971). A comparison of the effectiveness of two methods of class organization for arithmetic instruction in grade five. *Dissertation Abstracts International, 32,* 1744A. (University Microfilms No. 71-25035)

Esposito, D., (1973). Homogeneous and heterogeneous ability grouping: Principal findings and implications for evaluating and designing more effective educational environments. *Review of Educational Research, 43,* 163–179.

Flair, M. D. (1965). The effect of grouping on achievement and attitudes toward learning of first grade pupils. *Dissertation Abstracts, 25,* 6430. (University Microfilms No. 65-03,259)

Floyd, C. (1954). Meeting children's reading needs in the middle grades: A preliminary report. *Elementary School Journal, 55,* 99–103.

Goldstein, H., Moss, J. & Jordan, J. (1966). *The efficacy of special class training on the development of mentally retarded children.* (Cooperative Research Project No. 619). Washington, D.C.: U.S. Office of Education.

Good, T., & Marshall, S. (1984). Do students learn more in heterogeneous or homogeneous groups? In P. Peterson & L. Cherry Wilkinson (Eds.), *Student diversity and the organization, process, and use of instructional groups in the classroom.* New York: Academic Press.

Goodlad, J. I. (1960). Classroom organization. In C. W. Harris (Ed.), *Encyclopedia of Educational Research* (3rd Ed., pp. 221–225). New York: MacMillan.

Goodlad, J. I., & Anderson, R. H. (1963). *The nongraded elementary school.* (Rev. Ed.). New York: Harcourt, Brace, & World.

Hart, R. H. (1962). The nongraded primary school and arithmetic. *The Arithmetic Teacher, 9,* 130–133.

Hillson, M., Jones, J. C., Moore, J. W., & Van Devender, F. (1964). A controlled experiment evaluating the effects of a nongraded organization on pupil achievement. *Journal of Educational Research, 57,* 548–550.

Hopkins, K. D., Oldridge, O. A., & Williamson, M. L. (1965). An empirical comparison of pupil achievement and other variables in graded and nongraded classes. *American Educational Research Journal, 2,* 207–215.

Hosley, C. T. (1954). Learning outcomes of sixth grade pupils under alternative grade organization patterns. *Dissertation Abstracts, 14,* 490–491. (University Microfilms No. 7484).

Ingram, V. (1960). Flint evaluates its primary cycle. *Elementary School Journal, 61,* 76–80.

Jackson, J. (1953). The effect of classroom organization and guidance practice upon the personality adjustment and academic growth of students. *Journal of General Psychology, 83,* 159–170.

Johnson, D. W., Johnson, R. T., & Scott, L. (1978). The effects of cooperative and individualized instruction on student attitudes and achievement. *Journal of Social Psychology, 104,* 207–216.

Koontz, W. F. (1961). A study of achievement as a function of homogeneous grouping. *Journal of Experimental Education, 30,* 249–253.

Kulik, C.-L., & Kulik, J. (1982). Effects of ability grouping on secondary school students: A meta-analysis of evaluation findings. *American Educational Research Journal, 19,* 415–428.

Kulik, C.-L., & Kulik, J. A. (1984, August). *Effects of ability grouping on elementary school pupils: A meta-analysis.* Paper presented at the annual convention of the American Psychological Association, Toronto.

Kulik, J. A. & Kulik, C.-L. (1984). Effects of accelerated instruction on students. *Review of Educational Research, 54,* 409–425.

Leinhardt, G., & Pallay, A. (1982). Restrictive educational settings: Exile or haven? *Review of Educational Research, 52,* 557–578.

Madden, N. A., & Slavin, R. E. (1983). Mainstreaming students with mild academic handicaps: Academic and social outcomes. *Review of Educational Research, 53,* 519–569.

Miller, W. S., & Otto, H. J. (1930). Analysis of experimental studies in homogeneous grouping. *Journal of Educational Research, 21,* 95–102.

Machiele, R. B. (1965). A preliminary evaluation of the non-graded primary at Leal School, Urbana. *Illinois School Review, 1,* 20–24.

Morgan, E. F., & Stucker, G. R. (1960). The Joplin Plan of reading versus a traditional method. *Journal of Educational Psychology, 51,* 69–73.

Morris, V. P. (1969). An evaluation of pupil achievement in a nongraded primary plan after three, and also five years of instruction. *Dissertation Abstracts, 29,* 3809-A. (University Microfilms No. 69-7352).

Moses, P. J. (1966). A study of inter-class ability grouping on achievement in reading. *Dissertation Abstracts, 26,* 4342.

National Education Association (1968). *Ability grouping research summary*. Washington, DC: National Education Association.

Oakes, J. (1985). *Keeping track: How schools structure inequality*. New Haven, CT: Yale University Press.

Oakes, J. (1987). Tracking in secondary schools: A contextual perspective. *Educational Psychologist, 22*, 129–153.

Otto, H. J. (1969). *Nongradedness: An elementary school evaluation*. Austin: University of Texas.

Passow, A. H. (1962). The maze of research on ability grouping. *Educational Forum, 26*, 281–288.

Persell, C. (1977). *Education and inequality: The roots and results of stratification in America's schools*. New York: Free Press.

Provus, M. M. (1960). Ability grouping in arithmetic. *Elementary School Journal, 60*, 391–398.

Ross, G. A. (1967). A comparative study of pupil progress in ungraded and graded primary programs. *Dissertation Abstracts, 28*, 2146-A. (University Microfilms No. 67-16,428)

Simpson, R. & Martison, R. (1961). *Educational programs for gifted pupils: A report to the California Legislature pursuant to Section 2 of Chapter 2385, Statutes of 1957*. (ERIC Document No. ED 100 072).

Slavin, R. E. (1983a). *Cooperative learning*. New York: Longman.

Slavin, R. E. (1983b). When does cooperative learning increase student achievement? *Psychological Bulletin, 94*, 429–445.

Slavin, R. E. (1987a). Grouping for instruction in the elementary school. *Educational Psychologist, 22*, 109–127.

Slavin, R. E. (1987b). Mastery learning reconsidered. *Review of Educational Research, 57*, 175–213.

Slavin, R. E. (1987c). Ability grouping and student achievement in elementary schools: A best evidence synthesis. *Review of Educational Research, 57*, 293–336.

Spivak, M. L. (1956). Effectiveness of departmental and self-contained seventh- and eighth-grade classrooms. *School Review, 64*, 391–396.

Tobin, J. F. (1966). An eight year study of classes grouped within grade levels on the basis of reading ability. *Dissertation Abstracts, 26*, (University Microfilms No. 66-345)

Vedder, P. H. (1985). *Cooperative learning: A study on processes and effects of cooperation between primary school students*. The Hague, The Netherlands: Stichting Voor Onderzoer Van Het Onderwijs.

Ward, P. E. (1970). A study of pupil achievement in departmentalized grades four, five, and six. *Dissertation Abstracts International, 30*, 4749a. (University Microfilms No. 70-1201).

West, J. & Sievers, C. (1960). Experiment in cross grouping. *Journal of Educational Research, 54*, 70–72.

7 Tracking in Secondary Schools: A Contextual Perspective

Jeannie Oakes
RAND Corporation

For at least sixty years, schools have practiced tracking and ability grouping, and researchers have attempted to determine whether it "works," that is, whether tracking enhances schools' ability to educate their diverse student populations. Researchers typically oppose tracking because the bulk of the empirical literature finds it to be generally ineffective (see, for example, reviews by Esposito, 1973; Noland, 1985; Persell, 1977; Rosenbaum, 1980a). Desegregation litigation has focused attention on the contribution of tracking to unequal schooling for poor and minority children (Oakes, 1983b); and several courts, ruling on the schooling rights of the educationally handicapped to "mainstreamed" education, have cited negative effects of tracking (see, for examples, Mills v. Board of Education, 1972, PARC v. Commonwealth of Pennsylvania, 1971; 1972). Several recent educational reform proposals and schooling reports have criticized the negative consequences of tracking (see, for example, Achievement Council, 1985; Goodlad, 1984; College Entrance Examination Board, 1985; National Commission on Excellence in Education, 1983; Powell, Farrar, and Cohen, 1985; some advocate abandoning the practice (Adler, 1981; Berman, 1985; Goodlad, 1984; Ravitch and Finn, 1987).

Despite empirical evidence, court decisions, and reform proposals, tracking remains a nearly universal practice in secondary schools. Usually, tracking is not seriously questioned by practitioners and policymakers; it is simply "how schools work." When the issue is raised, practitioners usually support tracking for its benefits to students, and because it seems to ease the instructional problems posed by individual differences. Their experience in managing schools and classrooms has apparently convinced practitioners that tracking is necessary.

Unfortunately, the tracking literature provides only limited understanding. Until quite recently, two questions have been of primary interest. The first, "Does tracking work?", has resulted in numerous studies of tracking's effects on students' cognitive and affective outcomes. The second question, "What determines track placement?", has promoted considerable inquiry into the influence of student characteristics such as race, class, and prior achievement on track assignments. Seldom has either of these questions led researchers to investigate tracking practices themselves, how tracking practices affect the distribution of learning experiences, or how, in turn, these features of tracking may contribute to student outcomes. Thus, while we have some compelling evidence that tracking works against many (often poor and minority students) and in favor of few (often privileged whites), we have little understanding of *how* tracking produces those outcomes. Moreover, the research provides little insight into why tracking remains entrenched in secondary schools despite the lack of empirical support for its effectiveness.

This paper explores tracking from a contextual perspective. It argues that two contexts in which tracking is embedded are particularly important for understanding how tracking works and why it persists. The first is the schooling context of tracking, that is, tracking's consequences for school and classroom practice. This schooling context, increasingly of interest to researchers, permits some understanding of *how* tracking's educational effects may occur. The second context is the societal context of tracking, that is, the beliefs, values, and circumstances that originally influenced the institution of tracking in comprehensive secondary schools and may continue to shape current practice. This societal context provides a broader understanding of why tracking, and not some other approach, was adopted as the means for managing student diversity. It also provides insight into how issues of race and class were historically confounded with tracking and may continue to be influential. Analyses of these schooling and societal contexts suggests that tracking profoundly influences the day-to-day conduct of secondary schools and both reflects and interacts with fundamental assumptions about how schools should respond to student diversity. This contextual view of tracking permits a fuller understanding of why tracking is not easily reconsidered or changed. Before considering tracking's contexts, however, a brief review of tracking practices, assumptions, and evidence of effects is in order.

What is Tracking?

Tracking places students who appear to have similar educational needs and abilities into separate classes and programs of instruction. Two forms of tracking predominate, although each is found in a variety of permutations. One form found at most senior high schools is *curriculum tracking*. Students are classified as in one or another track, and are expected to complete sequences of courses designed for college-preparatory students, vocational students, or general track students. Some schools do not have all three of these tracks, and others have more. For example, in California, differing college requirements encourage separate tracks for students preparing for entrance into the more selective University of California system and the somewhat less selective California State University system. Other schools have separate tracks for vocational students with a business emphasis and for those preparing for a trade.

A second form of tracking, widely used at junior highs and middle schools as well as at senior high schools, is *ability grouping,* that is, the division of academic subjects (typically English, mathematics, science, and social studies) into classes at different ''levels'' for students of different abilities. Like curriculum tracking, ability grouping also varies from school to school. At some schools all academic subjects are tracked; at others, some are not (most often social studies). Schools also differ in the number of ability groups they form, and within the same school some subjects may have more levels than others. Some schools schedule students at the same ability level to stay together for blocks of subjects. At these schools a single decision about a student's ability often governs his or her placement in several subjects. Other schools track students separately for each subject. At these schools the same student might be placed in a ''high ability'' English class and in an ''average'' math class.

In many senior high schools, curriculum tracking and ability grouping overlap. These schools have both separate college preparatory, general, and vocational programs, *and* ability grouping in academic subjects. So, for example, a college bound student might be taking an ''honors'' English class, but also be in a ''regular'' section of college preparatory math or science (Oakes, 1985). More likely than not, the student in the vocational *curriculum* track will be in one of the lower *ability* tracks, so the distinction between the two types of tracking becomes more difficult to assess.

But tracking is not likely to proceed as neatly as the preceding descriptions imply. The inflexibility and idiosyncrasies of developing the ''master schedule'' can create unplanned tracking, generate further variations among tracking systems, and may affect the courses taken by individual students as well. In some schools, for example, elective subjects like art and home economics become low-track classes because college-preparatory students rarely have time to take them. In other schools, certain required classes, like drivers' training, health, or physical education, intended to be heterogeneous, become tracked when students' other track requirements keep them together for most or all of the day (Oakes, 1985).

Despite these variations, tracking has common and predictable characteristics:

1. Students' academic performance is judged, and these judgments are the basis of group placements.

2. Classes and tracks are labeled in terms of the performance levels of the

students in them (e.g., advanced, average, remedial) or according to students' expected post-secondary destination (e.g., college-preparatory, vocational).

3. The groups that are formed are not merely a collection of different but equally valued instructional groups. They form a hierarchy in schools with the most academic or advanced tracks seen as the "top." For evidence, we have only to look at how teachers jockey for assignment to the top tracks (Findley, 1984).

4. The curriculum and instruction in various tracks is tailored to the perceived needs and abilities of the students assigned to them.

5. Based on their track assignments, students at various track levels experience school differently.

What Assumptions Underlie Tracking?

First, and clearly most important, school pracitioners generally assume that tracking promotes students' achievement, that is, that all students will learn best when they are grouped with other students of similar capabilities or prior levels of achievement. Fundamental views of human capabilities appear to underlie this assumption, including the belief that students' capacities to master school work are so disparate that they require different and separate schooling experiences. Grouping is seen as the only appropriate means to accommodate these differences. A second assumption underlying tracking is that slow or less capable students will suffer emotional as well as educational damage from daily contact with brighter peers. Lowered self concepts and negative attitudes toward learning are widely considered to be consequences of mixed-ability grouping for slower learners. Also widely held is the assumption that group placements can be made both accurately and fairly. Finally, most teachers and administrators contend that homogeneous grouping greatly eases the teaching task. This assumption stems from the view that when tracks or ability groups are formed, the range of student differences is narrowed sufficiently to permit whole-class instruction, that is, lessons organized around a common set of learning objectives, a single teaching strategy, common learning tasks, and universally applied criteria for success and rewards.

What is the Evidence?

Effects on Student Outcomes.   Tracking's effects on student outcomes have been widely investigated. Unfortunately, this body of work is plagued with studies of varying quality and conflicting conclusions. The bulk of the evidence, however, does *not* support widely held beliefs that tracking generally increases students' learning or that it enhances students' attitudes about themselves and schooling.

Taken together, the literature on tracking's effects on student outcomes appears to support the following more specific conclusions: First, *some* tracking systems appear to provide a cognitive advantage for students who are placed in the top tracks. Recent analyses of High School and Beyond data, for example, provide evidence that membership in the college preparatory track has a positive influence on student achievement, even when student background characteristics and prior ability are controlled (Gamoran, 1986; Lee, 1986; Rock, Ekstrom, Goertz, Hilton, & Pollack, 1985). Further, when students are placed in accelerated courses or special programs for the gifted and talented, they appear to benefit (see, for example, the review by Kulik & Kulik, 1982). But these positive cognitive effects on high-ability students are not universally found (see Noland, 1985, for a recent review). Further, when advantages to students in the high-ability tracks do accrue, they do not seem to be primarily related to the fact that these tracks are homogeneously grouped. For example, controlled studies of students taking similar subjects in heterogeneous and homogeneous groups show that high-ability students (like other students) rarely benefit from these tracked settings (see Esposito, 1973; Kulik & Kulik, 1982; Noland, 1985, among others). Moreover, studies of students learning in small, heterogeneous, cooperative classroom groups provide evidence that the achievement of high-ability students can be enhanced in heterogeneous settings (Slavin, 1983; Webb, 1982).

Second, tracking systems appear to consistently disadvantage those students *not* placed in the top groups. Tracking is most often found to work to the academic detriment of students who are placed in low-ability classes or non-college-preparatory groups (see, for example, reviews by Calfee & Brown, 1979; Esposito, 1973; Findlay & Bryan, 1970; Froman, 1981; Noland, 1985; Rosenbaum, 1980b). Further, students in vocational tracks do not even appear to be advantaged *vocationally* by their placements. Graduates of vocational programs may be less employable and earn lower wages than other high school graduates (Rubens, 1975; Grasso & Shea, 1979; Berg, 1971; Berryman, 1980; Stern, Hoachlander, Choy, & Benson, 1985). On the other hand, considerable support can be found for the positive effects on the least-able students of membership in heterogeneous classrooms (Esposito, 1973; Madden & Slavin, 1983; Noland, 1985; Persell, 1977; Rosenbaum, 1980b; Slavin, 1983).

Third, the bulk of the research does not appear to support the assumption that slow students will suffer emotional strains when enrolled in mixed-ability classes. In fact, the opposite has often been found to result. Rather than helping students to feel more comfortable about themselves, the tracking process seems to foster lowered self-esteem, lowered aspirations, and negative attitudes toward school (Alexander & McDill, 1976; Esposito, 1973; Noland, 1985; Rosenbaum, 1980a). Some studies have concluded that tracking leads these students to school misbehavior, and eventually to dropping out altogether (Schafer & Olexa, 1971).

Fourth, tracking's net effect is to widen the initial differences among students (Calfee & Brown, 1979; Esposito, 1973; Findlay & Bryan, 1970). Even students who are initially similar in background and aptitude exhibit increased differences resulting from their placements in higher and lower tracks. Tracking, therefore, can be seen to affect student outcomes *independent* of the characteristics that determined the track placement (Alexander & McDill, 1976; Alexander, Cook & McDill, 1978). The net effect appears to be cumulative, because studies investigating track mobility have found that students' track placements tend to be quite fixed and long-term. Students placed in low-ability groups in elementary school are likely to continue in these tracks in middle schools and junior highs; they typically are placed in non-college-preparatory tracks in senior high school. When mobility between track occurs, it is most often in a downward direction (Rosenbaum, 1980a, Oakes, 1985). Figure 7.1 illustrates this long-term tracking effect.

How Are Track Assignments Made?   The second topic of considerable investigation has been the determinants of track placements. To assign students to tracks, schools typically use standardized test scores, teacher and counselor recommendations, prior placements and grades, and (for some senior high school students) student choice. Considerable confusion exists in the research literature about which student characteristics contribute most to track placements. Studies can be found that conclude that tracking is a meritorious practice—based almost entirely on ability or prior achievement (Davis & Haller, 1980; Rehberg & Rosenthal, 1978). Others conclude the opposite, that race and class have substantial influence on placements (Alexander & McDill, 1976; Rosenbaum, 1980b; Jones, Vanfossen, & Spade, 1985). Some analysts suggest that the issues of class and merit cannot be disentangled. They argue that because race and class biases are embedded in measures of ability and prior achievement, by the time students reach secondary schools, track placement according to these measures cannot be seen as strictly meritorious (See, for example, Amato, 1980; Rosenbaum, 1980a). Other work suggests that students from different backgrounds are given different types of information, advice, and counselor attention, and that race and class-based placements are produced in the advising process (Cicourel & Kitsuse, 1963; Erickson, 1975; Heyns, 1974; Rosenbaum, 1976).

One finding about placements is undisputed, however: Disproportionate percentages of poor and minority youngsters (principally Black and Hispanic) are placed in tracks for low-ability or non-college-bound students (NCES, 1985b; Rosenbaum, 1980a; further, minority students are consistently underrepresented in programs for the gifted and talented (College Board, 1985). Other evidence indicates that additional race and class differentiation occurs within vocational tracks, with Blacks and Hispanics more frequently enrolled in programs that train for the lowest-level occupations (Oakes, 1983b; NCES, 1985b). These race and social class placement differences appear whether test scores, counselor and teacher recommendations, or student and parent choices are the basis for placement.

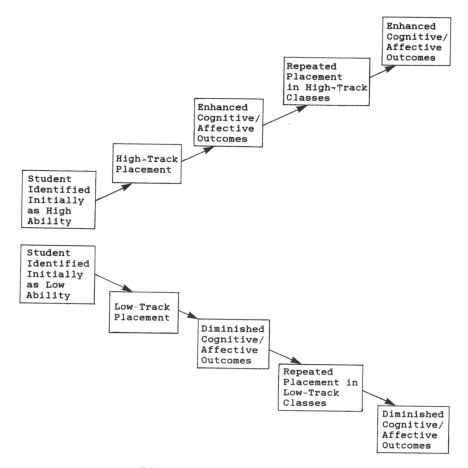

FIG. 7.1. Long-term tracking effects.

Is Tracking Required to Meet Individual Needs?

So far, I have argued that tracking is based in part on practitioners' beliefs both that individual differences matter in instruction and that separate classes are required to deal with these differences effectively. Clearly, students differ when they enter secondary schools. There is ample evidence that these differences influence learning. But separating students in order to accommodate the differences among them appears to be neither necessary nor appropriate.

The evidence cited previously indicates that tracking has proven to be generally ineffective. Almost 60% of students in American public high schools are not assigned to the top tracks at their schools (Lee, 1986), and these students appear to be educationally disadvantaged by tracking. The literature suggests that students at all ability levels can achieve at least as well in heterogeneous class-rooms, and those who are identified as of average or low-ability usually do better in mixed groups. Moreover, educational theory and research have yet to identify particular individual differences that seem to require specific and separate instructional treatments (Good & Stipek, 1983); neither have research attempts to match particular treatments to student differences in aptitudes been particularly successful (Cronbach, 1975). Further, a number of subject area experts argue that a common curricular experience provides the most promising approach to high-quality programs for all students (see for example, Romberg, 1983; Early, 1983).

The race and class consequences of tracking must be considered as well. Even if secondary school track placements are ostensibly "meritorious," that is, determined by prior school achievement, they usually represent judgments about supposedly fixed abilities. We could find appropriate the disproportionate placements of poor and minority students in low-track classes if these youngsters were, in fact, known to be innately less capable of learning than middle-and upper-middle class Whites. That is not the case. Or, we might think of these track placements as appropriate *if* being in the low-track served to remediate the obvious educational deficiencies that many poor and minority students exhibit. If the low track placements served to prepare disadvantaged students for success in higher tracks and lead them to future educational or post-secondary opportunities, we would not likely question the need for them; however, this rarely happens.

Further compounding the lack of evidence supporting tracking are compelling ethical arguments for exposing all students to a common curriculum, even if individual differences among them prevent students from benefitting equally. For example, Fenstermacher (1983) argues that "using individual differences in aptitude, ability, or interest as the basis for curricular variation denies students equal access to the knowledge and understanding available to humankind"; and "it is possible that some students may not benefit equally from unrestricted access to knowledge, but this fact does not entitle us to control access in ways that effectively prohibit all students from encountering what Dewey called, the 'funded capital of civilization' " (p. 3). This ethical concern takes on added significance given the links between track placements and student background characteristics. Because poor and ethnic minority students are disproportionately disadvantaged by the restricted access to knowledge that tracking creates, tracking appears to jeopardize equal educational opportunity.

In short, tracking's effects run counter to what school practitioners intend. While the literature on track placements and outcomes provides many clues, it offers little evidence as to why tracking has these effects or why it is difficult for schools to recognize and respond to these findings. For insight into these issues, we must consider tracking within its schooling and societal contexts.

The Schooling Context—School and Classroom Consequences of Tracking

The schooling context of tracking includes conditions and events in schools and classrooms that affect and are affected by tracking. This schooling context encompasses, first, the ways the tracking system influences schools' organization of curriculum and instruction generally, and, second, how membership in a particular track influences the experiences of students. Until quite recently, studies of tracking have not typically examined these contextual aspects of tracking as important in themselves; neither has research attempted to account for them in studies of tracking's effects on student outcomes. This "black box" approach to tracking has limited our understanding both of how tracking works and why it persists.

Recent quantitative and qualitative studies have begun to document the effects of tracking on such schooling events as students' coursetaking patterns, the presentation of particular curriculum content, the use of various instructional strategies, the creation of classroom environments, and the development of peer relationships. The differences uncovered show that the opportunities to learn that result from these track-related events are considerably greater for students enrolled in the top tracks. By placing these studies in a larger framework, we can speculate about how the schooling context itself plays a role in producing the pattern of tracking effects described earlier.

Figure 7.2 illustrates more specifically how an extensive set of conditions and events associated with tracking may contribute to student outcomes and the stability of student placements over time. The figure suggests complex relationships among several elements: students' background characteristics, the particular tracking system the school employs, students' track placements, their school and classroom experiences, their responses to those experiences, their cognitive and affective outcomes, and their subsequent track placements. An important caveat goes with the following initial discussion of Figure 7.2: The purpose here is to draw broadly some principal relationships among contextual elements diagramed in the figure. The challenge is to avoid seeing these relationships as a set of linear relationships or mechanical processes. Once these principal relationships are sketched, the *dynamics* of how they operate are suggested as an "iterative process" that is produced as teachers and students respond to circumstances in their schools.

The relationships depicted in the Fig. 7.2 highlight concerns quite different from those guiding the research discussed earlier. That work typically focused on how student characteristics directly affect track placements and how placements directly affect student outcomes. Figure 7.2 suggests several important school, teacher, and student factors that may mediate track placements and outcomes. It suggests that tracking placements and effects may be influenced by the interplay

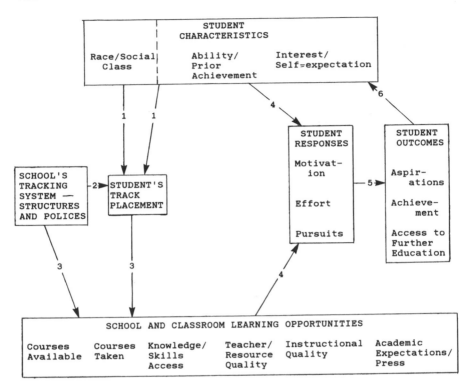

FIG. 7.2.   The schooling context of tracking.

of school and student characteristics *within the school context*. The sections that follow briefly review what a number of recent studies have learned about each of the relationships identified in the Fig. 7.2, offer some additional speculations about their contributions to tracking effects, and identify important gaps in our understanding.

Student Characteristics
and Track Placements (Arrows #1)

Beginning at the upper left of Fig. 7.2, the first set of relationships illustrates that students' characteristics determine track placements. Student characteristics are inputs to the tracking process to the extent that they influence how students *begin* the secondary schooling process. Clearly, student ability, prior achievement, self-expectations, and interests differ among students, and these differences influence students' initial skill level and shape the ease with which they learn. These and other characteristics—students' SES and race, particularly—also influence the school's initial response to students. Differences among students are thought to require separate and different instructional treatments, and students with similar educational strengths and limitations or post-secondary destinations are sorted together into tracks. This relationship is well documented in the studies of track placement determinants discussed earlier (e.g., student ability, aspirations, race, and class).

Track Systems and Track Placements (Arrow #2)

Track placements are influenced by more than just *students'* characteristics; they are influenced by school characteristics as well. Although secondary school tracking systems share a number of common properties, they also differ in some important ways: They can differ considerably in *extensiveness* (the number of subjects tracked); *specificity* (the number of track levels offered); *placement criteria;* and *flexibility* (whether students are placed separately subject-by-subject or whether a single decision about all subjects is made) (Oakes, 1985).

These variations among track structures and policies will influence how any particular student is classified and placed. Placement criteria (e.g., cut-off scores on standardized tests, prerequisite course requirements, and considerations of students' aspirations) are likely to differ from place to place. These differences are likely to result in the same student being placed differently at different schools. For example, recent studies contrasting tracking in public and Catholic senior high schools found that schools in the two sectors differ in their track placements. This work suggests that student background characteristics are less influential in Catholic than in public schools, and that Catholic school placement practices result in about 20% more students in the college preparatory track, even after student background characteristics are controlled (Kilgore, 1984; Lee, 1986). Other track policy variations like "block-scheduling" (students staying together at a particular level for classes in several subjects) can be expected to result in student assignments that are different from class-by-class placements. For example, a student who excels in math but is average in verbal skills might, under block scheduling, be placed in an average math class. Under a class-by-class system, that student might be enrolled in an more advanced math class.

Track Systems, Student Placements, and Learning Opportunities (Arrows #3)

Both the track system at a school and a student's placement within that system influence the learning opportunities that the student has available. First, the school's tracking structures and policies shape opportunities by influencing the courses offered. For example, schools that emphasize their vocational or general track are less likely to offer advanced courses in science, mathematics, and foreign language than schools with extensive college-preparatory programs (Rock et al., 1985). School policies also establish curriculum guidelines and norms about what learning experiences are most suitable for students in the courses that are offered at various track levels. These also influence the learning opportunities.

Students' learning opportunities are further prescribed by teachers' day-to-day decisions about what knowledge and classroom experiences will be appropriate. Track-specific learning opportunities are not simply created by teachers at various levels enacting a predetermined curriculum. Although track differences are established in curriculum guides that contain the knowledge, skills, and activities thought best suited for different tracks, they are also daily mediated within classrooms by teachers' global preconceptions about what types of lessons best "meet the needs" of various groups (Metz, 1978; Page, 1988).[1] Nevertheless, although teachers may have considerable autonomy in creating classroom experiences, there appears to be a striking regularity in the differences in learning opportunities experienced by students in different tracks.

Access to Knowledge.   Track placements affect students' access to various course offerings and shape the paths they take through the school curriculum. Lower-track students have fewer mathematics and science courses available to them, and they are nearly always required to take fewer academic courses (California State Department of Education, 1984; Gamoran, 1986; Guthrie & Leventhal, 1985; Vanfossen, Jones, & Spade, 1985). On the other hand, low-track students have greater access to elective courses in the arts and vocational subjects than most college-preparatory students, whose schedule of required courses allows little time for electives. The extent of differences varies among schools. For example, at Catholic senior high schools, students enrolled in non-academic tracks typically take more academic courses and fewer electives than do their counterparts in public schools (Lee, 1986).

Within academic subjects, additional differences are found. The emphasis in low-track classes is on low-level topics and skills, and the focus of high-track classes is on concepts, processes, and higher-order skills (California Department of Education, 1984; Davis, 1986; Hargreaves, 1967; Metz, 1978; Oakes, 1985; Powell, Farrar, & Cohen, 1985; Squires, 1966; Trimble & Sinclair, 1986). Beyond academic content is the socialization students receive in class. Some work has suggested that differences in classroom socialization among track levels parallels the anticipated adult work roles of high-, average-, and low-track students (Bowles & Gintis, 1976; Oakes, 1985; Rosenbaum, 1976; Shafer & Olexa, 1971).

Instructional Quality.   Findings on the classroom effects of tracking are consistent. There is a clear pattern of instructional inequalities for students

---

[1]Some related investigations of teachers responses' to student differences with instructional "prescriptions" for reading groups have taken place at the elementary level. See, for example, work of Borko, Shavelson, and Stern, 1981.

placed in low-ability groups or non-college-preparatory tracks (California Department of Education, 1984; Davis, 1986; Metz, 1978; Oakes, 1985; Trimble & Sinclair, 1986; Vanfossen, Jones, & Spade, 1985). Differences have been found in the allocation of time (both in class and for homework), in teaching strategies employed, and in classroom climate. High-track students have the most time to learn. Teachers in high-track classes are clearer, more enthusiastic, and use less strong criticism, and classroom learning tasks appear to be better organized and of greater variety. Further, teacher–student relationships in high-track classes are more often characterized by warmth and supportiveness. Classroom climate differences include greater student disruption, hostility, and alienation in low-track classes. Given these differences, is not surprising that teachers prefer high tracks and have more management problems in low-ability classes (Evertson, 1980).[2]

Academic Expectations and Press.   Teacher expectations influence student outcomes. Academic press can be thought of as a combination of expectations and the focus and energy used to consistently "press" students toward academic accomplishments. Of interest here is how press is affected by the tracking context. A number of studies have documented the expected influences of a student's track level, and "track label," on teacher expectations (see Persell, 1977, for a review of this literature). Thus, it is not surprising to find that the press for academic learning has been found to be distributed unequally within schools, and that, in the course of classroom interactions, students in higher tracks receive the bulk of it (Oakes, 1985, Page, 1988).

Track membership also influences students' peer associations in classes and in extracurricular activities; students' friendship choices (e.g., Alexander & McDill, 1976; Rehberg & Rosenthal, 1978; Rosenbaum, 1976); and the academic orientations of these friends (Vanfossen, Jones, & Spade, 1985). These associations influence academic press. For example, peer relationships are important for school effort and academic aspirations (see, for example, Coleman, 1961). When the peer-group is oriented toward academics, student achievement is positively affected (McDill & Rigsby, 1973; Persell, 1977). Further, because track placement is based on student attitude, behavior, and motivation, as well as ability, low tracks are particularly impoverished in peer dispositions toward achievement.

All of the school-specific experiences discussed here illustrate a distribution of knowledge, activities, and relationships to other students that is influenced by the tracking system at their schools and their placement in it. These differences,

---

[2]It is interesting to note that the perceived homogeneity of tracked classes appears to obscure the need to differentiate instruction *within* classes. Even though promising strategies do exist for dealing productively with heterogeneous student groups (See, for example, the work on cooperative, small groups learning, Slavin, 1983), little evidence exists that such techniques are being used widely in secondary schools (Sirotnik, 1983).

in turn, influence how students respond to their school experiences, to what they learn, and to which tracks they are assigned in the future.

Characteristics, Opportunities and Students' Responses to Schooling (Arrows #4)

Both students' characteristics and their opportunities to learn influence their responses to schooling, including their motivation for learning, the level of effort they put forth, and their actual classroom pursuits (e.g., what learning tasks they engage in). The knowledge and skills students are asked to learn, the classroom activities they engage in, their relationships with their classmates, and the quality of teaching they experience are all likely to influence attendance, time spent on homework, and attention in class—to name a few of the most easily observed indicators of motivation and effort. These responses, perhaps even more than background characteristics, further influence what teachers attempt to accomplish in class. Recent qualitative studies of low-track classrooms provide some evidence of how this interactive process occurs (Everhart, 1983; McNeil, 1981, 1986; Page, 1987; Willis, 1977). These studies show clearly that tracking is not merely a neutral or passive conduit through which students' characteristics "take their natural course" toward high, average, or low achievement outcomes, aspirations, and attitudes.

Responses, Outcomes, and Future Placements (Arrows #5 and #6)

Finally, Fig. 7.2 posits that students' responses to schooling mediate the effects of students' characteristics and track-determined learning opportunities on outcomes. This suggested relationship is consistent with recent studies supporting a chain of influence from student characteristics, through track-specific coursetaking patterns, to student outcomes (Gamoran, 1986; Lee, 1986). Figure 7.2, however, goes further and suggests that students' responses to their track experiences directly affect student attitudes, aspirations, achievement, and access to further education. Thus, as a result of these mutual influences, Fig. 7.2 depicts a cycle with student responses, an integral component of the schooling context, leading not only to outcomes but to future track placements as well. It is in the connection between these outcomes and completion of the cycle where the outcomes *become* next year's prior achievement, ability, and interest. This cycle is the context for understanding the evidence on tracking's effects.

An Iterative Process

Largely because it occupies two-dimensional space, the depiction of the schooling context in Fig. 7.2 creates an unfortunate linear impression. Understanding

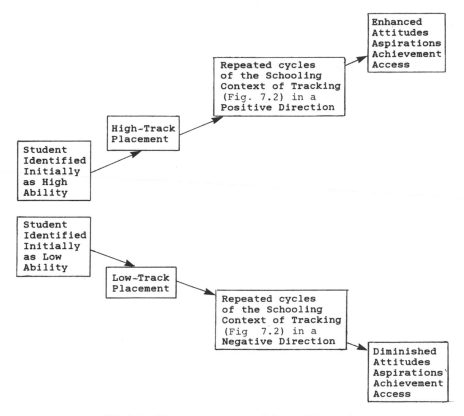

FIG. 7.3. The consequences of the tracking cycle.

tracking as a series of inputs, mediating variables, and outcomes is insufficient. Disentangling causes and effects over the long-term may prove impossible. Tracking as a contextual process is likely to spiral. At any point in time, a particular element (placement, student characteristics, classroom experiences, effort, achievement, etc.) may be an input, mediator, or outcome; a cause or an effect. Because track placements begin early (some suggest with first-grade reading group assignments), it is probable that the processes described in Fig. 7.2 cycle repeatedly during a student's schooling experience, not identically, but with each successive cycle building on the effects of the previous series of interactions and effects. Small differences at any one point in time very likely add up over time. The impact is likely to be cumulative, in a particular direction, and, metaphorically, gather momentum. When the evidence about tracking effects is placed in this cumulative contextual perspective, the hypotheses suggested in Fig. 7.3 can be raised. The cycle depicted here shows the how the schooling context structures tracking's long-term effects on student outcomes.

Figure 7.3 suggests that initial and relatively small aptitude differences among students (often due to social background differences) (Calfee, 1979) are exacerbated by ability group placement, resulting experiences, attendant attitudes, interests, and expectations, in elementary school. By middle school or junior high, track placement is more or less crystallized. The process cycles throughout secondary school, with the differences among students growing dramatically wider.

This framework helps account for the "blindness" to tracking's effects of some practitioners and other school observers. Decisions at any one moment—especially in earlier grades—may seem slight and even go undetected. Because differentiating decisions are made on the behalf of students, the supposed benefits of the moment (remediation, for example) help to obscure the possibility of longer-range negative effects. In later school years, the accumulated incremental effects of tracking are so consequential that the suggestion that students could benefit from a common curricular and instructional experience is difficult to comprehend and accept. Even the suggestion that the tracking structure itself has played a part in creating these differences (rather than simply biology, culture, or merit) is not compatible with observed "reality."

The Societal Context

So far, schools and their tracking systems have been considered in relative isolation, as if they were untouched by a larger societal context. This is not surprising, because tracking is most often studied as a technical pedagogical response to individual differences. Tracking, however, stems from and exists within a set of historical circumstances and values that provided the basis for its institution in American secondary schools.[3] Tracking also exists within a current social millieu that shares norms and expectations about what schools ought to accomplish. If academics and practitioners are to understand why tracking, and not some other approach developed in response to student diversity, and why it is so resistant to change, this context also requires scrutiny.

Understanding the societal context of tracking is useful because it raises the possibility that the persistence of tracking rests more on social and historical than on educational grounds.[4] It permits consideration of whether the continued use of tracking reflects some remaining, if unintended, influence of the events and assumptions that led to its adoption (Oakes, 1986)—whether, for example, the need to certify students as eligible for various post-high school opportunities

[3]Fortunately, this history has been richly documented in several excellent sources. See, for example, chapter 6 in Powell, Farrar, and Cohen's *The Shopping Mall High School* (1985). Other important sources include Callahan (1962); Cohen and Lazerson (1972); Goldman (1952); Gould (1981); Kliebard (1979); and Lazerson (1971), to name just a few.

[4]See Sirotnik and Oakes (1986), for a discussion of the possibilities and problems of context-based inquiry as an ongoing process in schools attempting to improve.

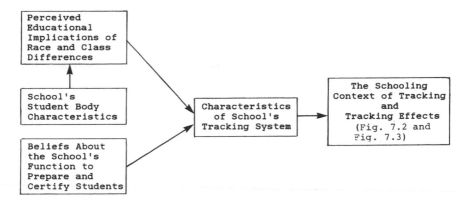

FIG. 7.4.   The societal context of tracking.

overrides the potential educational benefits of common curricular experiences. In short, this perspective might help clarify some enduring anomalies.

Figure 7.4 attempts to situate tracking into its larger societal context and to speculate how this context serves to influence current tracking practices. The process depicted in Fig. 7.4 suggests that a school's student body characteristics, the perceived educational implications of race and class differences, and prevailing beliefs about secondary schooling's purpose to prepare and certify students for their adult roles in the workplace interact to influence the particular kind of tracking system that is developed. This hypothesis is consistent with evidence showing that tracking systems vary among schools serving different types of students in characteristic ways. For example, the number, size, and substance of tracks have been found to differ with the composition of schools' student populations—the greater the percentage of minorities, the larger the low-track program; the poorer the students, the less rigorous the college preparatory program (Hanson, 1985; 1986). Further, High School and Beyond data show that schools serving predominantly poor and minority populations offer fewer advanced and more remedial courses in academic subjects, and that they have smaller academic tracks and larger vocational programs (NCES, 1985a; Rock et al., 1985). This work supports the hypothesis that schools design tracking structures that make sense to them, given their student populations and their beliefs about what programs are appropriate for them.

Of course, minority and low-SES students are, on the average, lower in achievement by the time they reach secondary school, and schools respond to those differences with programs they see as educationally appropriate. But, what is of particular interest here is that the prevailing view of approriate schooling for these students—lower-track and vocational programs—is, in fact, detrimental. Placement in these programs, as has been argued here, continues a cycle of restricted opportunities, diminished outcomes, and exacerbated differences between low-track students and their counterparts in higher tracks. These placements do not appear to either overcome students' academic deficiencies or to provide them access to high-quality learning opportunities. Despite this evidence, tracking persists. School practitioners appear to be impeded in their attempts to achieve *educational* ends by *socially influenced definitions* of students' differences and *socially influenced prescriptions* for educational practice to accomodate them.[5]

Implications of a Contextual Perspective

School practitioners support tracking because they are convinced that, considering the trade-offs, it is best for students. Because tracking enables schools to provide differentiated curriculum and instruction, practitioners are persuaded that if students are placed in the "right track" they will have the best opportunity for school success. Because the empirical evidence suggests a substantial gap between these intentions and the effects of tracking, the dilemma is that well-intentioned, hard-working people appear locked into a school structure that is contradictory to the expressed goals of schooling. This is surely a testimony to the power and complexity of the both the schooling and societal contexts of tracking.

The schooling and societal contexts hlep to explain *why* practitioners respond to empirical findings on tracking with ambivalence. First, practitioners almost universally recognize and lament the negative consequences of tracking on students in low-track classes; most teachers and administrators have had discouragingly unsuccessful experiences trying to make these programs work. Many suspect that when a group of the lowest achieving and most poorly behaved students are together in classrooms, the individuals in the class perform far below what they might under other circumstances. But practitioners' concerns about protecting the educational opportunities of the top-track students are even more salient. Research conclusions that able students are likely to continue to do well even if they are placed in heterogeneous groups are dissonant with practitioners' experiences. The schooling context of tracking offers clear school advantages to students in the top tracks, and findings that high-achieving students can learn equally well in mixed classes simply don't account for noticeable, concrete advantages practitioners, students, and parents can see in schools.

Much practical concern centers on the perceived near-impossibility of teaching classes with a wide range of student ability. Maintaining current curriculum and instructional practices under conditions of classroom heterogeneity is a mind-boggling proposition to practitioners already struggling with too many students and ever-increasing expectations for improved achievement. Instruction

---

[5]See Popkewitz (1983) for an insightful essay on the social and political bases for the definitions of individual differences and their pedagogical implications.

in secondary classrooms (regardless of track level) is grounded in the presumption of student homogeneity. It is characterized by competitive whole-group instruction; lecturing as the prevailing teaching strategy; common assignments, due dates, and tests for all students; and a single set of standards of competence and criteria for grades. Although diversity among students *within* tracks is evident, it is not thought to be of a magnitude to require multiple learning experiences. It is not so much that practitioners have had extended or deliberate experiences trying to teach hetergeneous groups at the secondary level; few have. It is more that they cannot imagine mixing what they believe to be two or three distinctly different groups of students and maintaining the high quality of instruction they see high-ability groups now receiving.

Moreover, schools do not operate in a vacuum. Definitions of "individual differences" and of what different students "need" are social as well as educational. Students who are identified as *less able* are more often those who have less socially and economically. These kids are often seen as more disposed to working with their "hands" rather than their "heads." What they "need" is not seen to be the same abstract knowledge and skills that are suited to their more able peers. What they need is more often thought to be functional literacy skills and good deportment that will provide them entry into the lower levels of workforce. Given these *socially influenced* definitions, practitioners are not easily persuaded that a largely common curriculum taught mostly in heterogeneous groups is a promising approach to educating diverse groups of students. Further, alterations in school practice must pass "social" as well as "educational" tests. Certifying some for entrance into colleges and universities and preparing others with functional skills and acceptable workplace behaviors are what society expects from its schools. Even if practitioners were convinced of the educational value of "detracking" schools, the tracked curriculum is well suited to certifying students for different futures.

Throughout this paper, I have raised set of hypotheses to account for tracking's effects and its persistence as school practice. These hypotheses focus on the importance of both the schooling and societal contexts of tracking. First, I have posited that the schooling context of tracking consists of a complex set of relationships among structures and events within schools, and that this schooling context has long-term consequences for students' cognitive and affective outcomes. Second, I have suggested that the societal context of tracking—specifically, historically-grounded assumptions and shared norms about how schools should respond to student diversity—shapes the content and processes of school tracking. Third, I have argued that these contextual considerations can explain tracking's persistence in schools despite empirical evidence against its effectiveness.

These hypotheses imply that asking practitioners to rethink tracking is asking them to reconceptualize fundamental secondary school processes and purposes. Serious consideration of altering tracking practices in ways that might interrupt the now predictable cycle of student background differences, track placements, and student outcomes requires an understanding of both its centrality and its complexity. The societal context of tracking must be examined for its relevance to schooling assumptions and events. The schooling context of day-to-day practices must be considered as integral to tracking outcomes. These contextual considerations can extend the frustrating "Does it work?" question to include the issues of "How?", "For whom", and "Toward what ends?". For researchers to fully understand tracking and practitioners to make informed decisions about it, these questions must be addressed.

REFERENCES

Achievement Council. (1985). *Excellence for whom?* San Francisco: The Achievement Council.

Adler, M. (1981). *The paiedia proposal: An educational manifesto.* New York: Macmillan.

Alexander, K. A., Cook, M., & McDill, E. L. (1978). Curriculum tracking and educational stratification: Some further evidence. *American Sociological Review, 43,* 47–66.

Alexander, K. A., & McDill, E. L. (1976). Selection and allocation within schools: Some causes and consequences of curriculum placement. *American Sociological Review, 41,* 969–980.

Amato, J.A. (1980, April). *Social class discrimination in the schooling process: Myth and reality.* Paper presented at the annual meeting of the American Educational Research Association, Boston.

Berg, I. (1971). *Education and jobs: The great training robbery.* Boston: Beacon Press.

Berman, P. (1985). The next step: The Minnesota plan. *Kappan, 67,* 188–193.

Berryman, S. E. (1980). *Vocational education and the work establishment of youth: Equity and effectiveness issues.* Santa Monica, Ca: The Rand Corporation.

Borko, H., Shavelson, R. J., & Stern, P. (1981). Teachers' decisions in the planning of reading instruction. *Reading Research Quarterly, 16,* 449–466.

Bowles, S., & Gintis, H. (1976). *Schooling in capitalist America.* New York: Basic Books.

Calfee, R. C. (1979). *Human diversity: Implications for schools.* Unpublished manuscript, Stanford University, Stanford, CA.

Calfee, R. C., & Brown, R. (1979). Grouping students for instruction. In D. L. Duke (Ed.), *Classroom Management* Seventy-eighth yearbook of the National Society for the Study of Education. Chicago: University of Chicago Press.

California State Department of Education. (1984). *California high school curriculum study: Paths through high school.* Sacramento, Ca: California State Department of Education.

Callahan, R. E. (1962). *Education and the cult of efficiency.* Chicago: University of Chicago Press.

Cicourel, A. V., & Kitsuse, J. I. (1963). *The educational decisionmakers.* Indianapolis: Bobbs-Merrill.

Cohen, D. A., & Lazerson, M. K. (1972). Education and the corporate order. *Socialist Revolution, 2,* 53.

Coleman, J. S. (1961). *The adolescent society.* New York: The Free Press.

College Entrance Examination Board. (1985). *Equality and excellence: The educational status of Black Americans.* New York: College Entrance Examination Board.

Cronbach, L. J. (1975). Beyond the two disciplines of scientific inquiry. *American Psychologist, 30,* 116–127.

Davis, D. G. (1986, April). *A pilot study to assess equity in selected curricular offerings across three diverse schools in a large urban school district: A search for methodology.* Paper presented at the Annual Meeting of the American Educational Research Association, San Francisco.

Davis, S. A., & Haller, E. J. (1980, April). *Determinants of eighth graders' placement in high school tracks*. Paper presented at the annual meeting of the American Educational Research Association, Boston.

Early, M. (1983). A common curriculum in language and literature. In G.D. Fenstermacher & J. I. Goodlad (Eds.), *Individual differences and the common curriculum*, eighty-second yearbook of the National Society for the Study of Education. Chicago: University of Chicago Press.

Erickson, F. (1975). Gatekeeping the melting pot. *Harvard Educational Review, 45*, 44–70.

Esposito, D. (1973). Homogeneous and heterogeneous ability grouping: Principal findings and implications for evaluating and designing more effective educational environments. *Review of Educational Research, 43*, 163–179.

Everhart, R. B. (1983). *Reading, writing, and resistance: Adolesence and labor in a junior high school*. London: Routledge & Kegan Paul.

Evertson, C. M. (1980). *Differences in instructional activities in high and low achieving junior high classes*. Austin, Tx: University of Texas, Research and Development Center for Teacher Education.

Fenstermacher, G. D. (1983). Introduction. In G. D. Fenstermacher & J. I. Goodlad (Eds.), *Individual differences and the common curriculum*, eighty-second yearbook of the National Society for the Study of Education. Chicago: University of Chicago Press.

Findlay, W. G., & Bryan, M. M. (1970). *Ability grouping: 1970 status, impact, and alternatives*. Athens, Ga: University of Georgia, Center for Educational Improvement.

Froman, R. D. (1981, April). *Ability grouping: Why do we persist and should we*. Paper presented at the annual meeting of the American Educational Research Association, Los Angeles.

Gamoran, A. (1986, April). *The stratification of high school learning opportunities*. Paper presented at the annual meeting of the American Educational Research Association, San Francisco.

Goldman, E. (1952). *Rendezvous with destiny*. New York: Random House

Good, T. L., & Stipek, D. J. (1983). Individual differences in the classroom: A psychological perspective. In G. D. Fenstermacher & J. I. Goodlad (Eds.), *Individual differences and the common curriculum*, eighty-second yearbook of the National Society for the Study of Education. Chicago: University of Chicago Press.

Goodlad, J. I. (1984). *A place called school: Prospects for the future*. New York: McGraw-Hill.

Gould, S. J. (1981). *The mismeasure of man*. New York: W. W. Norton.

Grasso, J., & Shea, J. (1979). *Vocational education and training: Impact on Youth*. Berkeley, Ca: Carnegie Council on Policy Studies in Higher Education.

Guthrie, L. F.,& Leventhal, C. (1985, April). *Opportunities for scientific literacy for high school students*. Paper presented at the annual meeting of the American Educational Research Association, Chicago.

Hanson, S. (1985, April). *The college preparatory curriculum at two high schools in one school district*. Paper presented at the annual meeting of the American Educational Research Association, Chicago.

Hanson, S. (1986, April). *The college preparatory curriculum across schools: Access to similar types of knowledge?* Paper presented at the annual meeting of the American Educational Research Association, San Francisco.

Hargreaves, D. H. (1967). *Social relations in a secondary school*. London: Routledge & Kegan Paul.

Heyns, B. (1974). Social selection and stratification within schools. *American Journal of Sociology, 79*, 1434–1451.

Jones, J. D., Vanfossen, B., & Spade, J. (1985, April). *Curriculum placement: Individual and school effects using the High School and Beyond data*. Paper presented to the annual meeting of the American Sociological Association, Chicago.

Kilgore, S. (1984). Schooling effects: Reply to Alexander and Pallas. *Scoiology of Education, 57*, 59–61.

Kliebard, H. M. (1979). The drive for curriculum change in the United States, 1890–1958. *Curriculum Studies, 11,* 191–202.

Kulik, C. C., & Kulik, J. A. (1982). Effects of ability grouping on secondary school students: A meta-analysis of evaluation findings. *American Educational Research Journal, 19,* 415–428.

Lazerson, M. (1971). *The origins of the urban school.* Cambridge, MA; Harvard University Press.

Lee, V. E. (1986, April). *The effect of curriculum tracking on the social distribution of achievement in Catholic and public secondary schools.* Paper presented at the annual meeting of the American Educational Research Association, San Francisco.

Madden, N., & Slavin, R. E. (1983). Mainstreaming students with mild handicaps: Academic and social outcomes. *Review of Educational Research, 53,* 519–569.

McDill, E. A., & Rigsby, L. C. (1973). *The structure and process in secondary schools: The academic impact of educational climates.* Baltimore: Johns Hopkins University Press.

McNeil, L. M. (1981). Negotiating classroom knowledge: Beyond achievement and socialization. *Journal of Curriculum Studies, 13,* 313–328.

McNeil, L. M. (in press). *Contradictions and control: School structure and school knowledge.* London: Routledge & Kegan Paul.

Metz, M. H. (1978). *Classrooms and corridors: The crisis of authority in desegregated secondary schools.* Berkeley, CA: University of California Press.

Mills v. Board of Education, 348 F. Supp 866 (1972).

National Center for Educational Statistics. (1985a). *Analysis of course offerings and enrollments as related to school characteristics.* Washington, D.C.: U.S. Government Printing Office.

National Center for Educational Statistics. (1985b). *High School and beyond: An analysis of course-taking patterns in secondary schools as related to student characteristics.* Washington, DC: U.S. Government Printing Office.

National Commission on Excellence in Education. (1983). *A nation at risk.* Washington, D.C: U.S. Government Printing Office.

Noland, T. K. (1985). *The effects of ability grouping: A meta-analysis of research findings.* Unpublished doctoral dissertation, University of Colorado, Boulder.

Oakes, J. (1983a). Limiting opportunity: Student race and cirricular differences in vocational education. *American Journal of Educaiton, 91,* 801–820.

Oakes, J. (1983b). Tracking and ability grouping in American schools: Some constitutional questions. *Teachers College Record. 84,* 801–819.

Oakes, J. (1985). *Keeping Track: How schools structure inequality.* New Haven CT: Yale University Press.

Oakes, J. (1986). Tracking, inequality, and the rhetoric of reform: Why schools don't change. *Journal of Education, 168,* 161–181.

Page, R. (1988). Lower-track classes at a college-preparatory high school: Caricatures of educational encounters. In G. Spindler & L. Spindler (Eds.) *Interpretive ethnography of education at home and abroad.* Hillsdale, NJ: Lawrence Erlbaum Associates.

Pennsylvania Association of Retarded Children v. Commonwealth of Pennsylvania (PARC), 334 F. Supp. (1971) and 343 F. Supp. 279 (1972).

Persell, C. J. (1977). *Education and inequality: The roots and results of stratification in America's schools.* New York: The Free Press.

Popkewitz, T. S. (1983). The sociological bases for individual differences: The relation of solitude to the crowd. In G. D. Fenstermacher & J. I. Goodlad (Eds.), *Individual differences and the common curriculum,* eighty-second yearbook of the National Society for the Study of Education. Chicago: University of Chicago Press.

Powell, A. G., Farrar, E., & Cohen, D. K. (1985). *The shopping mall high school: Winners and losers in the educational marketplace.* Boston: Houghton Mifflin Company.

Ravitch, D., & Finn, C. (1987). *What Do Our Seventeen-year olds know? The first national assessment of what American students know about history and literature*. New York: Harper and Row.

Rehberg, R. A., & Rosenthal, E. R. (1978). *Class and merit in the American high school*. New York: Longman.

Rock, D. A., Ekstrom, R. B., Goertz, M. E., Hitton, T. L., & Pollack, J. (1985). *Study of excellence in high school education: Longitudinal study, 1980–82. Final report*. Princeton, N.J: Educational Testing Service.

Romberg, T. A. (1983). A common curriculum for mathematics. In G. D. Fenstermacher & J. I. Goodlad (Eds.), *Individual differences and the common curriculum*, eighty-second yearbook of the National Society for the Study of Education. Chicago: University of Chicago Press.

Rosenbaum, J. E. (1976). *Making inequality: The hidden curriculum of high school tracking*. New York: Wiley.

Rosenbaum, J. E. (1980a). Social implications of educational grouping. In D. C. Berliner (Ed.), *Review of research in education, 8*, 361–401. Washington, D.C.: American Educational Research Association.

Rosenbaum, J. E. (1980b). Track misperceptions and frustrated college plans: An analysis of the effects of tracks and track perceptions in the national longitudingal study. *Sociology of Education, 53*, 74–88.

Rubens, B. (1975). Vocational education for all in high school? In J. O'Toole (Ed.), *Work and the quality of life*. Cambridge, Mass: MIT Press.

Schafer, W. E., & Olexa, C. (1971). *Tracking and opportunity*. Scranton, Pa: Chandler.

Sirotnik, K. A. (1983). What you see is what you get: Consistency, persistency, and mediorcrity in classrooms. *Harvard Educational Review, 53*, 16–31.

Sirotnik, K. A., & Oakes, J. (1981). A contextual appraisal system for schools: Medicine or madness? *Educational Leadership, 39*, 165–173.

Sirotnik, K. A., & Oakes, J. (1986). Critical inquiry for school renewal: Liberating theory and practice. In K. A. Sirotnik & J. Oakes (Eds.), *Critical perspectives on the organization and improvement of schooling*. Hingham, MA: Kluwer-Nijhoff Publishing.

Slavin. R. E. (1983). *Cooperative learning*. New York: Longman.

Squires, J. R. (1966). National study of high school English programs: A school for all reasons. *English Journal, 55*, 282–290.

Stern, D., Hoachlander, E. G., Choy, S., & Benson, C. (1985). *One million hours a day: Vocational education in California public secondary schools*. Report to the California Policy Seminar. Berkeley, Ca: University of California School of Education.

Trimble, K., & Sinclair, R. L. (1986, April). *Ability grouping and differing conditions for learning: An analysis of content and instruction in ability-grouped classes*. Paper presented at the annual meeting of the American Educational Research Association, San Francisco, CA.

Vanfossen, B. E., Jones, J. D., & Spade, J. Z. (1985, April). *Curriculum tracking: Causes and consequences*. Paper presented at the annual meeting of the American Educational Research Association, Chicago.

Webb, N. M. (1982). Group composition and group interaction and achievement in small groups. *Journal of Educational Psychology, 74*, 475–484.

Willis, P. E. (1977). *Learning to labour: How working class kids get working class jobs*. Lexington, Mass: Lexington Books.

8 Instruction's the Thing Wherein to Catch the Mind that Falls Behind

Gaea Leinhardt
William Bickel
Learning Research and Development Center
University of Pittsburgh

This chapter was written at a time when the press for educational excellence had reached immense proportions. *Educational excellence* has many different meanings, but certainly among them are the notions that the overall standard of education should be improved, and that expectations should be raised above notions of minimum competency toward an ideal of creative, analytical thinking. How could such goals be achieved? We could add a fixed amount of knowledge to the entire range of the student population. We could select the best and the brightest and move them ahead, thus raising the mean, but further separating the top from the bottom. We could select those most at risk of losing out and move them closer to the overall mean, thus redefining excellence to mean fewer students who fail. Of these three, the easiest solution (and to these authors an unsatisfactory solution) is the second option. It would be technically easier to expand the number of children receiving an elite education (Resnick, 1987) than to change either the overall content of general education sufficiently to improve everyone's scores, or to reduce the distance between the lower-performing students and the top-performing students. However, to choose this second option alone is to abandon the ideal of equal educational opportunity, and to risk undercutting successes of recent reform efforts designed to enhance basic skills achievement for all students.

This chapter takes the position that in the past two decades the combination of educational reform and research has produced some exciting results. The results suggest that we can have reasonable educational progress without abandoning the students for whom academic learning is a struggle rather than an easy developmental process. We now have techniques for improving the achievement of all students, including those with the greatest needs. This chapter reviews a number of the large–scale programs that have been the backbone of educational reform over the last two decades and also the research, both large-scale and more fine grained, that has helped us learn which aspects of those reforms were particularly effective. The outcome of this selective review is a discussion of instructional features or dimensions along which we can gauge both current and new efforts. A basic assumption in our review is that although past reforms basically have occurred in two separate areas (compensatory and special education), this distinction is unnecessary and artificial when considering effective remediation of student performance in basic skills. Our goal in this chapter is to identify effective instructional practices, not to point to one "program" or another as the "best," and to discuss briefly their implications for educational research, policy, and practice.

In 1985, billions of federal dollars were spent on the education of American school children (Grant & Snyder, 1985–86); of that, a significant percentage was designated for improving the learning chances of students who are felt to be in need of some type of extraordinary educational help. The laws and guidelines for programs to assist children who do not learn easily under normal conditions in school are massive and they come from all levels of government: federal, state, and local. Although there are literally hundreds of specific programs available, the two national umbrella programs for assisting children in academic need are compensatory education and special education. (A third major program, bilingual education, is not considered in this review.) These two categories can be thought of as subsystems within the educational environment that have been designed to allocate instructional and social resources to students who for a variety of reasons are not (or are not expected to be) progressing adequately in school. Under the auspices of these programs, children are identified, evaluated, and provided with a range of educational and other treatments. These treatments are all designed to improve education in the U.S. by reducing the level of failure.

Both special and compensatory education classify children who are already doing poorly or who are at risk of doing so. In the case of compensatory education, program participation is based on a combination of the economic status of the population served by the school and some measure of achievement for the collection of students actually involved. In the case of special education, the assignment of a label is based on an individual student's academic, or in some cases, social performance characteristics. The purpose in both cases is to somehow identify students who actually need or are likely to need additional resources. Elsewhere, we and others have argued that even though there exist strong historical reasons for the separate development of these programs, there is no compelling evidence for the educational efficacy of separate treatment based on classification. Rather, the position has been taken that it would be more reasonable to target treatments based on the type of educational support needed, thereby labeling instruction, not children (Bickel, 1982; Leinhardt, Bickel, &

Pallay, 1982; Myers & Hammil, 1973; Reynolds & Lakin, in press). One might in fact envision a coordinated, unified educational program that made provisions for students to access extra help whenever it was needed.

Both special education and compensatory education programs have achieved some measure of success. The success tends not to be so much at the large-scale programmatic level, but instead at the instructional-feature level. That is, specific clusters of instructional treatments seem to be effective for most children who are having mild to serious difficulty in school (in terms of basic skills achievement) regardless of the reason or program setting.

This chapter is organized into three major sections. The first briefly reviews the historical background and current status of the compensatory and special education programs; the second discusses the nature and extent of available treatments and their purported levels of success; and the third discusses implications of effective instruction research for future research, reform policies, and current educational practices. Several points should be made at the outset. First, in our examination of special education, attention is concentrated on programs for students labeled as mildly mentally handicapped and serviced in educable-mentally retarded (EMR) and learning disabilities (LD) programs. Second, in our review of instructional processes and outcomes, we emphasize those related to basic skills achievement as opposed to attitudinal issues. Third, this chapter builds directly from, and can be thought of as a continuation of, work done by us previously. In Leinhardt et al. (1982) and in this chapter we make the fundamental assumption that program labels are of little use in evaluating instructional success, but that specific features of instructional design and practice *are* useful (Bickel & Bickel, 1986; Epps & Tindal, in press; Leinhardt, 1980a; Reynolds, 1984; Strain & Kerr, 1981).

ORIGINS AND STRUCTURE
OF COMPENSATORY EDUCATION

During the two decades immediately following World War II, the American educational system grew closer to the goal of universal basic education. However, with this good news came a gradual recognition that providing equal educational opportunity was a complex educational *and* social goal, the implications of which went beyond the attempt to provide similar instructional resources in every school and classroom. By the early 1960s, significant segments of the educational and political communities were increasingly concerned about the educational prospects of children who came from poor families and who were performing significantly below the rest of American students. It was felt that children who began school performing behind their peers would fall continuously further behind. These students were likely to drop out of school at a point when they were still unable, like their parents before them, to compete successfully in society. Poor school performance that led to lack of success in the workplace was identified as the vicious cycle of poverty.

President Johnson's initiative to combat poverty on many fronts, popularly referred to as the "War on Poverty", saw the schools as a useful arena in which to attack this cycle. The students from impoverished backgrounds were to receive an enriched education by means of specially trained teachers and innovative techniques, before school, during school, and after school. The central ideas that influenced and still influence attitudes and treatments in compensatory education programs are (a) children from low-income families are more likely to do poorly in school than children from average- or high-income families; (b) their poor performance is due to social and economic conditions in their homes and communities rather than being due to organic deficits; and (c) even without treating these environmental conditions, progress can be made in treating the children's academic difficulties, which in turn will help to free these children from a future of poverty.

Federally supported compensatory education has its functional bases in two legislative acts, the Economic Opportunity Act (EOA) passed in 1964 (and amendments to it), and the Elementary and Secondary Education Act (ESEA) passed in 1965. EOA established Head Start; ESEA established Title I and Follow Through programs. With the passage of the Education Consolidation and Improvement Act (ECIA) in 1981, the programs provided by the ESEA Title I were transferred to Chapter 1 of the new legislation.

Head Start

Head Start, first implemented in 1965, was originally designed to be a broad social service program targeted at low-income preschool-age children. The fundamental goals of the program included guaranteeing the children's physical wellbeing; aiding their social-emotional development; improving their mental processes and skills; establishing patterns of success; improving family relationships; developing their social responsibility; and increasing their sense of worth and dignity (Richmond, Stipek, & Zigler, 1979; Zigler & Anderson, 1979). Head Start refers to the label of the program, not to any particular instructional process.

The target population of Head Start is children from age 3 to school entry. If the family meets low-income requirements, and if the community has a Head Start program available, then a child can gain access to Head Start. Head Start has maintained its base of financial support over the years with a current annual budget of approximately one billion dollars (ECIA, 1981; Human Services Authorization Act, HSAA, 1984; Schweinhart & Weikart, 1985).

Over time, evaluations of the effectiveness of Head Start have been mixed because the specific instructional (and other) treatments in these classrooms varied considerably across sites. There have been examples of unproductive efforts (Wolff & Stein, 1966), as well as successes in Head Start programs. An example of one of the most notable and well-documented successes is the Perry Preschool Program (Barnett, 1985; Berrueta-Clement, Schweinhart, Barnett, Epstein, & Weikart, 1985; Schweinhart & Weikart, 1980, 1985). This program was started in the early 1960s, before Head Start began, and later received funds from it.

Although the educational characteristics of the Perry Program were diffuse by the behaviorist standards of that time, the goals were clear: to stimulate and involve disadvantaged children cognitively, and to have them experience academic success rather than failure. There were many programs of that type within the general framework of Head Start. A unique feature of the Perry Program was that it included an ambitious and, in retrospect, marvelous experimental evaluation.

The main problem with many of the Head Start programs has been that when the participating students were tested in kindergarten and first grade, they showed few, if any, lasting academic gains (McKey, Condelli, Ganson, Barrett, McConkey, & Plantz, 1985). However, the initial Head Start goals also had included medical and social features that have sometimes been lost in the storms surrounding the apparent academic "failure." The Perry study documents that it was precisely those medical and social goals that were met, and that when they were met they had a powerful impact on life chances. A series of studies has followed Perry preschool children through kindergarten to age 15 and age 19 and has compared them to a control group. Assignment to these groups was random. The contrast has shown a clear advantage for the Perry group. By age 19, those who attended the program were more likely to have finished high school and gone on, were dramatically less likely to have committed a crime, were less likely to be on welfare, and were earning more money (Barnett, 1985). An enriched early experience appears to have been most beneficial for these children. There have been both personal (in terms of the recipients) and societal benefits from a relatively low cost investment (Barnett, 1985). Convergent findings have resulted from the research of Lazar and Darlington (1982) in their estimates of the reductions in special education assignment that are attributable to participation in Head Start programs. It is important to realize that individual programs under Head Start have been successful even if the total collection of initiatives demonstrates mixed results.

Follow Through

In 1967, President Lyndon Johnson, partly in response to an early and negative evaluation of the Head Start program (Wolff & Stein, 1966), recommended the establishment of a "follow through program" that would extend the Head Start efforts to kindergarten through third grade. The Wolff and Stein (1966) Head

Start evaluation had found that the program was successful based essentially on claims of parents and staff, but that its positive academic effects faded in elementary school. This was blamed on a presumed non-supportive educational environment in the nation's public schools.

Follow Through, like Head Start, was intended as a broad service-oriented program. It was designed specifically to support Head Start students as they began to progress through the first four years of elementary education. Follow Through never realized this initial intent. Caught in Congressional controversy over Johnson's "War on Poverty" and affected by growing budget constraints due in part to the Vietnam War, the initial Presidential recommendation of 200 million dollars for Follow Through in 1967 was slashed to 15 million. With such a drastic cut, it was impossible for Follow Through to be designed and implemented in a way that meshed with and built on Head Start efforts.

A new conception of Follow Through surfaced in response to the Congressional cuts. This was the so-called *planned variation approach* (Haney, 1977). In effect, Follow Through dollars would not be used to extend services to former Head Start students but rather would be used to develop demonstration projects around the country designed to identify promising instructional treatments. Most recently, as Follow Through funds have been cut even further, new sites with almost complete freedom in program design have been added. The preliminary self-reports are very disappointing, showing a repetition of mistakes made in the late 1960s and early 1970s (Abraham & Campbell, 1984; Detroit Public Schools, 1984; Riley & Nachtigal, 1984; Stallings & Robbins, 1985).

Follow Through planned variation meant that several types of educational approaches were implemented with accompanying evaluations focused on instruction. Evaluations were essentially of two types: (a) very large-scale national evaluations such as the controversial but often insightful studies conducted by Abt Associates (Stebbins, St. Pierre, Proper, Anderson, & Cerva, 1977) and (b) smaller project-level studies that focused on implementation evaluation and the impact of program features (Becker & Gersten, 1982; Bereiter & Kurland, 1981–1982; Gersten, 1984; Gersten, Carnine, Zoref, & Cronin, 1986; Leinhardt, 1976, 1977). Although recognizing that many important methodological and policy issues were raised by these studies, in sum it seems the findings point in similar directions. They tend to suggest that of the models available, the most effective were behaviorally focused, emphasized learning of math and reading, had systems for monitoring student progress and provided performance-based feedback, and had mechanisms that insured reasonable levels of implementation. The individual studies carried out by the program designers and developers or by their evaluation staffs found similar results. Students learned more in those classrooms in which much of the available time was spent on highly directed learning of basic skills, the progress of individuals or groups of students was monitored, and some type of reinforcement was available (Stebbins et al., 1977).

A serendipitous outcome of these studies and of those conducted to help evaluate Title I was that the research community learned that program membership made little difference in children's learning. For example, studies that contrast Follow Through with non-Follow Through students show little advantage for program participation because, like Head Start, the Follow Through programs were quite different across sites, and the membership differences were extreme. However, the Follow Through programs that engaged in elaborate programmatic descriptions and data collection were valuable in developing our understanding of what worked and why (Gersten, Carnine, & White, 1984).

Title I/Chapter 1

Title I was launched in the summer of 1965 as part of the Elementary and Secondary Education Act (ESEA). Like Head Start, Title I was a manifestation of the Johnson administration's conviction that education could be a powerful tool in breaking the cycle of poverty. Title I began as a massive program providing support to school districts that were heavily impacted by high numbers of disadvantaged and low-achieving students. In the initial enactment, maximum flexibility was given to local educational agencies. No specific educational treatments were mandated, although provision for some local evaluation was eventually included in the law. The ESEA was much more of a resource distribution bill than an educational bill. The law simply specified that "in recognition of the special needs of children of low-income families and the impact that concentrations of low-income families have on the ability of local educational agencies to support adequate educational programs . . . the United States . . . [should] provide financial assistance" (Bailey & Mosher, 1968, p. 235). Like those of the Head Start program, Title I goals reflected more clearly the political climate of the time rather than any specific educational theories or goals.

The target population of Title I was essentially defined by income and achievement measures. Grants were distributed to states and then to districts on the basis of the income levels of families. Within districts, schools were also identified on the basis of poverty indices. Within an eligible school, groups of students received services if the majority were performing below grade level as determined by a standardized measure of achievement or by the principal of the school. Often non-eligible (either by income or performance) students were in the group that received help (Carter, 1984).

A modification of Title I in 1981 occurred through the enactment of the Education Consolidation and Improvement Act (ECIA, 1981) under President Reagan. The ECIA Chapter 1 affected a number of important features in the way the former Title I resources were distributed and monitored. For example, the role of Parent Advisory Committees has tended to be reduced over the past several years as a result of the elimination of the 1970s federal requirement that each district have such a committee (Children's Defense Fund, 1984). However, for our purposes here, the 1981 ECIA modifications did not change the basic "educational" goal of Title I, which was to provide support for states and districts heavily populated with low-income and low-achieving students.

> As under Title I, Chapter 1-funded services in eligible schools must be targeted on the specific children with the greatest level of educational deprivation. To be eligible to receive Chapter 1 funds, school districts must identify these children, determine in which grades and subject areas Chapter 1 services are most needed, and develop programs to help educationally deprived children catch up with their peers. Unless certain restrictive conditions hold, Chapter 1-funded services cannot be offered to the general student population, but only to those children identified as educationally deprived. Children in the program have to receive more intensive educational services than children not in the program, and federal dollars can pay only for the incremental cost of the additional services. Schools and children participating in the program have to receive their fair share of state and local educational dollars (Dougherty, 1985).

Although the basic educational objectives have remained the same, funding for Chapter 1 programs has been reduced over the last 6 years, going from approximately 2.77 billion dollars in 1979–80 to 2.22 billion in 1984–85 in terms of constant 1979 dollars. Even with the reduction in funding, Title I/Chapter 1 is one of the longest-lived and largest federal compensatory education programs, serving approximately 4.7 million children in 1982–83 (Dougherty, 1985, p.17).

Like Head Start and Follow Through, Chapter 1 programs vary considerably from site to site in terms of their instructional content. The congressionally mandated evaluation data that is collected each year is not particularly helpful in understanding effective practice because little information is provided on the actual instructional processes inside the classroom. More useful Chapter 1-related data come from studies of particular instructional strategies that were implemented in Chapter 1 and other classrooms (Carter, 1984; Cooley & Leinhardt, 1980; Fisher et al., 1978). These are the studies that are relied on in our discussions of effective practices at a later point in this chapter.

ORIGINS AND STRUCTURE
OF SPECIAL EDUCATION

Compensatory education was designed as an educational treatment of a social problem, the cycle of poverty. In contrast, special education arose as an educational response to perceived mental handicaps in individuals. Before the turn of the century, such conditions were largely ignored by public educational institutions. A handicapped child was seen as an individual and private family concern, not as a societal responsibility (Lazerson, 1983). Early in the twentieth century, this view of mental handicaps as a family matter began to change. The change was parallel with a general societal shift in which compulsory education and child labor laws combined to push a much wider range of students into the highly visible arena of the public school. At the same time, social progressivists were pressing a variety of public institutions, including schools, for reform. With the means for reform and with a wider range of student talent and deficiency now present and visible, two concerns influenced the growth of special classes: (a) the potential harm that "deviant" or "incompetent" students might impose on more normal students and, (b) a humanitarian concern as to how best to serve these less able children (Lazerson, 1983).

A central feature of special education has been its use of a medical type of model to conceptualize the nature of mental handicaps. Handicapping conditions are viewed as residing inside the individual. Furthermore, it is assumed that different causes suggest different treatments. Ideally, special education students should be carefully diagnosed and then classified according to the presumed cause of their condition. This classification process implies that treatments are then tailored to the "illness" that has been diagnosed. These treatments are administered by professionals who have technical knowledge about the causes and cures of the problem. This model is consistent with the separate classification and organization of treatment of the Learning Disabled (LD), Socially and Emotionally Disturbed (SED), and Educable Mentally Retarded (EMR) that has evolved over this century, as well as with the separate treatment of special and compensatory education students. Theoretically, the problems of each group are thought to be unique and therefore, the two groups ought to be differentially treated. It should be noted, however, that many of the features of the medical model of special education have come under attack in recent years (Mercer, 1973).

The medical model of special education contrasts sharply with the compensatory education conceptualization of poor school performance, which emphasizes the social origins of the child's difficulties. The school problems of the compensatory education student are not seen as arising from a personal disability but rather from a deprivation of school relevant experience. The compensatory education teacher is seen not as a therapist curing or ameliorating a personal illness but as a teacher/social reformer who is providing extra educational resources to compensate for the lack of such resources in the child's home and community.

Table 8.1 provides some data on recent growth in the numbers of children classified as EMR, SED, and LD. One must interpret the numbers with considerable caution because of the variety of ambiguities built into the classification and placement of children into these programs. The numbers do give a sense of the overall rates of growth. The most interesting points concern the relative explosion of LD placements and the trailing off of EMR classifications.

TABLE 8.1
Enrollment in Special Education Classes Provided by Local Public School Systems in the U.S.

Area of Exceptionality	1916[1]	1932[2]	1948[3]	1963[4]	1968[5]	1972[6]	1980-81[7]
EMR	16,524	75,099	82,471	361,000	648,800	785,000	562,357
SED	--	14,354	15,340	30,871	99,400	156,486	200,841
LD	nil	nil	nil	nil	120,000	166,534	1,285,387

[1] Foster (1925)
[2] Foster (1933)
[3] Machie (1969)
[4] Grant & Lind (1975)
[5] Secretary's Committee on Mental Retardation (1970)
[6] U.S. Office of Education (1971)
[7] Plisko (1983) (Based on estimated percentages, 1980 times estimated public school population, 1981.)

The dominant goal of all special education classes is similar to that of mainstream education. This goal is to provide an educational program that allows each student to reach his or her fullest potential (Dunn, 1973). The differences between regular and special education often lie in the *levels* of goals set for special students. This is particularly the case in EMR classes. Students in need of special education are often judged as having reduced potential. Because of this, the specific skill and knowledge targets for special needs children are often lowered in comparison to those for children in regular classes. It is also true that, both historically and at present, there tends to be a greater emphasis on vocational and social skills in special rather than in regular class settings (Larry P. v. Riles, 1972; MacMillan, 1977).

Within special education programs, goals vary. LD classes tend to mirror mainstream education more closely probably because the LD handicaps are perceived as being milder than those of EMR labeled children. Further, the LD student is expected to compensate for a specific weakness by drawing on strengths in other areas. In contrast, EMR students are thought to have a generally depressed academic performance profile. For them, more time seems to be devoted to vocational and social training, with a reduced academic load as they progress through school.

In comparing the broad program goals of special and compensatory education, there are important differences. Compensatory education is aimed at breaking the cycle of poverty by boosting the education of poor, low achieving populations. Special education, however, is directed at specific children in need; the goal—as is common to all education—is the maximum realization of individual potential. Given the differences in focus, it is important to remember that, in actual practice, both programs spend a great deal of their time and money on instructional efforts designed to increase the academic and, to a lesser extent, social skills of students who have not done well in school.

Access to special education remains a complex matter across districts and states despite, or perhaps because of, a plethora of state and federal guidelines to regulate the process. A child is referred for evaluation by a teacher (or occasionally a parent) who makes the referral based on the child's poor academic and/or behavioral performance. Then, a school official (usually either the principal, regular education supervisor, or guidance counselor) initiates an evaluation. This evaluation is conducted by a team, usually made up of a school psychologist along with other school administrative and support personnel. Data collected from new tests and from past performance are reviewed, and a recommendation for placement is made. This means that a student is labeled EMR, or LD if they fall within the range of "mildly mentally handicapped" and meet the specifications extant in that locale. If the recommendation is accepted by the parent, then it becomes the basis for the development of a more detailed individual education plan (IEP). With some modifications in numbers of school personnel involved, sequence, and range of data collected, this description reflects how individuals typically gain access to special education classrooms. It is important to note that this complex process varies considerably by locale, as does the incidence of referral. Who is referred and who is left in the regular classroom differs considerably within districts and states, as well as between states (Bickel, 1982).

In comparison to special education, there are several important differences in the way children gain access to compensatory education that should be underscored. A student qualifies for compensatory education on the basis of the economic status of one's home, school, and district, and by one's own academic status. However, being qualified does not guarantee service under the law. In contrast, once a child is defined as handicapped, current federal legislation ostensibly guarantees access. We say "ostensibly" because in point of fact, actual access still seems to be heavily dependent on the coincidence of available programming in one's relatively immediate locale (Ysseldyke, Algozzine, Shinn, & McGue, 1979).

Compensatory and special education programs emerged as separate systems most fundamentally because of their different social and historical origins. They continue as separate systems partly because of specific political, professional, and educational rationales that work to maintain the current organization. We discuss these rationales elsewhere (Leinhardt et al., 1982). We are convinced, however, that there is growing evidence that the educational rationale for separate systems does not hold true. That is, specific instructional treatments tend not to vary across settings, and particular strategies found to be effective are effective in both compensatory and special education contexts.

We believe the presence of effective instructional practices that do not seem to be relegated to specific settings to be a powerful argument that challenges at least the instructional rationale for separate systems. Elsewhere (Leinhardt et al., 1982) we go on to make a case for merging social and educational programming for students with poor academic performance. In effect, our position is that it would be more reasonable to target treatments based on the type of educational support needed, thereby labeling instruction and not children. At least in the context of special education, the emphasis on specific treatment over categorical labels seems to be gaining some support in recent years (Heller, Holtzman, & Messick, 1982). For our purposes here, we now turn to what is the evidence for saying that there are effective instructional practices that help to move the lower quartile of students closer to the mean, that are not setting bound, and that do not seem to harm the more able students.

EFFECTIVE INSTRUCTION

It is important to remember that research on effective instruction comes from rather different sources. First, there are very global (200 classrooms and up) evaluations of policy in compensatory education programs. Then there are smaller studies, often part of the so-called fugitive literature (named because they either remain unpublished, or are published by institutions or in obscure journals). Such fugitive studies are typically carried out by program designers and developers and they focus on key programmatic features and their effects on a narrow population. There are mid-range studies that cross over one or more instructional treatments and ask questions of setting such as "pull out" versus "non pull out," mainstreaming versus self-contained, or self-contained versus resource room. Finally, there are meta analyses of research on specific practices.

There is some danger in extracting critical features of successful instruction from such a diverse pool of studies. However, we try to be cautious and point to those findings for which unequivocal results concur. For findings about which there is some debate, we make as clear as possible the lines of the debate and limitations of the success.

Some Background on Instructional Settings

Services to compensatory education students and the mildly handicapped students are delivered in quite different ways. Mildly handicapped students receive their education in one of three settings: (a) self-contained classrooms, from which they are mainstreamed to some extent, usually for non-academic classes; (b) resource rooms, in which they receive special help for reading and/or math and to which they go during some other content area instruction (thus, they may receive two math classes and no science, or they may go instead to regular math); or (c) regular room placement with a resource teacher who helps occasionally or daily to see that the targeted student is keeping pace. Clearly, the latter procedure is easiest if the mainstream classroom has extensive subgrouping or is individualized. In self-contained classes, there are between 12 and 15 students with one specially certified teacher and, depending on the disability, one aide. Approximately 70% of the school day is devoted to reading, and almost no time is spent on social studies or science (Leinhardt, Zigmond, & Cooley, 1981; Norman & Zigmond, 1980). In resource rooms, there are usually 6 to 12 students who go there for one or two periods a day (less than 30%). Both settings tend to emphasize behaviorist approaches to instruction and assessment. That is, specific narrow objectives are set and students use worksheets to master limited and subsequently tested skills. Global, vague, integrative work is eschewed.

Compensatory education students are either in classes with a teacher and an aide or a teacher and a part-time specialist teacher, or they attend pull-out classes, working with a specialist teacher. Approximately 85% of the reading instruction and 50% of the math instruction is given in pull-out rooms. Class size for pull-out rooms is variable, ranging from 10 to 35 students. As with special education, the most successful and predominant style of instruction is behaviorally based and tends not to be linked with the regular instructional activities.

In the next section, we describe and comment on the instructional practices that individually or in combination have been shown to be especially effective, regardless of setting. In describing these effective practices we are focusing on a small set of instructionally related features that seem to have a positive impact on student learning. Sometimes a feature is one that is implementable across a variety of possible programs—altering class size, for example. Other times, a feature is more associated with one type of program than another but can still be thought of as separable—mastery learning is one such feature. The point here is to think of an array of features that represent a positive configuration for learning. At present, these features are structural and *not* associated with success of just one type of student, grade, or subject. Recent work in cognitive psychology and education suggests that the next wave of improvement must be associated with a closer analysis of the subject matter than are these current findings (Shulman, 1986).

Class Size

Basically, class size is a feature that influences two major areas within the instructional environment: the opportunity a child has to use the resource of the teacher, and the cost of providing the student with instruction. The former aspect is fairly straightforward. If there are fewer children in any given unit, each student would then compete with fewer students for the finite instructional and attentional resources of the teacher than if the same student were in a larger class. The issue of cost is a little more complex: as the cost per pupil for teachers goes up, the ability to spend money on other valuable educational resources, such as supplemental texts or special teachers, is reduced.

One of the easiest ways to reduce educational costs is to increase class size. Such an increase reduces the number of total teachers needed—fewer teachers mean fewer supervisory personnel, and in some cases it also means that fewer school buildings are needed. Considering the fact that the single largest expenditure for most school districts is personnel and that plant costs are usually second, reducing those parts of the budget is always valued. Thus, there is a natural economic pressure to increase class size. On the other hand, there is also strong pressure to reduce class size. Teachers claim, although with little empirical support, that reduced class size improves the quality of education. It clearly makes the experience of teaching more pleasant, easier, and more personal. It probably makes the experience of being a student more pleasant also. The objective data unfortunately are quite mixed.

One way to test whether class size makes a difference would be to create the following situation: a set of many classes of heterogenous ability students ranging in size from 8 students per class to 50 students per class. Then select multiple program types, each to be implemented across the range of class sizes and control for the appropriate covariates. Only then could we tell if class size mattered. This natural experiment is not occurring in the U.S. at this time; however, we do have many naturally occurring differences in class size. Classes ranging in size from 8 to 12 are reserved for SED and LD students (in either self-contained or resource rooms). Classes of 15 to 20 with an instructional aide and a teacher typically are reserved for EMR students. Classes of 16 to 33 are reserved for normal students, and if an aide is present, it means that there are probably a preponderance of Chapter 1 students. In the cases where class size exceeds 33, it is often in a multi-graded rural school. In the rare cases where class size is smaller than 16, it is probably a short-term phenomenon where either the classes or the schools will soon be merged. Given this context, interpreting the results of the meta-analysis conducted by Glass, Cahen, Smith, and Filby (1982) is difficult.

In Glass et al. (1982) and in the earlier study by Glass and Smith (1978), class size was shown to matter if one went below 15 or above 40. In such cases, being in smaller classes meant that students learned more, received more of the teacher's instructional focus and time, and had to wait less for queries to be answered and for feedback (Smith & Glass, 1979). However, in re-analyzing the Glass data, Slavin (1984) and Walberg (1984) both show a minimal effect. There is some limited evidence that suggests that having an instructional aide in the classroom is generally associated with lower success in achievement (Scheutz, 1980). Therefore, it seems as if the rule should be to have as small a class as is practical, so long as it can be staffed with a fully qualified teacher. Plans that rely on large block groupings that are later subdivided tend to overlook the advantage of one competent adult knowing about the entire range of experiences of a particular child. However, we need to remember that over the normal range of observed class size (18–33), we see little or no empirical support for favoring small classes from an instructional standpoint, even though they may be nicer places to be for both teachers and students (Cooley & Leinhardt, 1980; Leinhardt, 1980a). Class size is closely related to issues of instructional grouping, which we turn to next.

Grouping

Grouping as a mechanism for improving students' learning is the topic of an entire chapter in this book (Chapter 6); therefore, we briefly cover the points that are critical for instruction. Grouping per se, like class size, is more of a social treatment than an instructional one. It tells us little about what knowledge or skill is being transmitted or how transmission occurs. However, it is a critical social and motivational variable, as well as a policy one. It is not likely that one particular grouping pattern is universally optimal; however, it is likely that within a given context (the U.S.), some patterns are much more likely than others to optimize conditions for learning.

All children are grouped for instruction. The issue is mainly the size of the group and whether or not the housing unit and the instructional unit are identical. At one extreme, the housing unit (classroom membership), which is usually determined by age and sometimes by a global ability level, forms the instructional unit for "whole class" instruction. Subjects such as social studies, science, gym, art, music, spelling, and math are most often taught to the entire class at one time.

Whole class lessons have a particular rhythm and flow to them (Stodolsky, 1983). The teacher starts with some type of transitional behavior and goal setting, then moves into a presentation of some type, and then has the students rehearse or practice. During the early stages of these rehearsals, the expert teacher gives a good deal of corrective feedback. Whole group instruction works very well if the teacher gives clear presentations or explanations, constructs an elegant tryout and has ways of tutoring both the faster and slower students. (See the detailed description of Leinhardt & Greeno, 1986, for an example.) It works very poorly if the teacher allows for no tryout or no feedback, gives a confusing presentation, and/or makes no adjustments for individuals. The distinct advantage of whole group instruction is its efficiency. If everyone is more or less paying attention and the lesson is good, then the majority of class time can be spent supporting those that need extra help while still maintaining a reasonable pace for all. This is done by expert teachers by carefully pacing the guided practice portion of a lesson so students in need are quickly identified and given brief tutorials. Teachers can have a maximal focus on content and constructing examples. Further, in whole-class instruction, each child not only has the teacher but also the rest of the class as helpers and models (Good, Grouws, & Ebmeier, 1983; Leinhardt & Greeno, 1986; Leinhardt & Pallay, 1982).

The second most common instructional unit is the small group. Almost all reading instruction is done in small groups whose membership is determined by some assessment of reading level. Small group lessons also have their own particular flow: a small presentation; discussion; supported task performance; then unsupervised, independent work. The major difficulty with small groups is the severe reduction of time available for direct teacher contact, the lowering of expectations for groups that lack high achievers, and a general lack of flexibility in group placement. However, grouping permits more focused attention on the needs of a smaller number of students. Small group instruction seems to be especially effective when (a) group size is determined by who fits rather than by some arbitrarily convenient number; (b) there are different groups formed for different subjects; (c) membership changes as often as necessary; (d) groups are based on specific skills within the subject; (e) membership is determined by instructionally based assessment, not standardized tests; and (f) small-group and whole-group instruction is interspersed (MacKenzie, 1983).

Anderson, Evertson, and Brophy (1979) have provided some evidence that under specific conditions, small groups are a particularly good instructional approach for reading instruction. However, small groups are dangerous when they form rigid subtracks and when the lower group gets decidedly less instruction (quantity and quality) than the higher group (Allington, 1977, 1980, 1983; Glaser, 1982).

Recent cognitive research on effective mathematics teachers (Lampert, 1986; Leinhardt & Greeno, 1986; Leinhardt & Smith, 1985) has shown that whole group instruction in math uses most of the time for teaching and learning, and does not generally have the 20–30 minute *unsupervised* seatwork. In these case studies of effective teachers, the "seatwork" time is divided into more or less public practice segments and roving tutorials. As Good and Grouws (1977) and Brophy and Good (1986) have pointed out, small group arrangements in math are often problematic because of the long stretches of unsupervised seatwork that it often entails.

The smallest "group" possible is, of course, the single individual; and so-called individualized instruction has been proposed for over 25 years as the true answer to many of the problems of education. Individualization has been considered especially appropriate for compensatory and special education. In individualized instruction the students move through either a fixed or flexible prepackaged curriculum at their own speed and master units of material before proceeding. In general, the teacher tutors only on demand and does not give lessons. For a number of reasons, individualized instruction is controversial. Some meta-analyses and reviews of effectiveness show positive results under some circumstances (Herrick, 1973a; Wang & Walberg, 1985), whereas other studies that assess the process alone tend to show no effects (Cooley & Leinhardt, 1980) or negative effects (Stallings, 1980).

Individualization seems to work when it is carefully combined with other educational procedures, such as well-programmed instruction, careful student monitoring, whole group lessons for major concepts, and small group interpersonal support. (See, for example, the programs described by Slavin, 1983a, 1983b, 1985.) In fact, under these conditions, individualization may be "the best" grouping arrangement (Slavin, 1985). Individualization is not effective when teachers are primarily managers, when high off-task rates are common, when busywork, dittos, or computer drill replace teacher instruction and when a student working alone is the only or major mechanism for learning and teaching (Stallings, Coury, Fairweather, & Needles, 1977).

It is as yet unknown whether complex, highly verbal and integrative content can be taught well under a "best-of-circumstances" individualized procedure for young students, although a university system, the English tutorial, combines the very individualized instruction of a tutor with whole-group instruction in a lecture. Proponents of individualized instruction see it as an opportunity to provide a setting in which children with special needs can be mainstreamed (Stainback & Stainback, 1984; Wang & Birch, 1984). Without a focused and concerted effort such as that provided by Team Assisted Individualization (TAI), it is unlikely that either the instructional or social needs of special children will be met (Slavin, 1983a, 1983b, 1985). Several features must be built into an individualized system to counteract the inherent problems. These include methods for having shared group intellectual experiences; providing peer models for complex performance; motivating students to move rapidly and deeply through the material (to think and say when queried, "I'm studying fractions" or "measurement in geometry" or "reading *King of the Wind*," instead of "I'm in level 6a" or "I'm ahead of Jenny" or "I'm in Reading 12"); and making certain that teachers really teach in solid and useful ways, not just manage or make meaningless subject matter comments.

Time

The time available for learning material is highly correlated with the degree to which the material is learned. However, time has come to mean so many different things that it is often quite difficult to sort out its so-called effects. Initial studies of time-on-task conducted by Bloom and his colleagues (Bloom, 1974) indicated that increases in time-on-task were strongly associated with increases in learning. This association was due to several features that tended to be overlooked in later attempts to replicate these early findings. The Bloom studies were of short duration (several months), controlled for variation in allocated time or time available for the subject, and controlled for the content covered. Given a fixed curriculum and a fixed boundary on time allocated, those students who were on-task more of the time than others learned more. In replications of this work, allocated time and content were often uncontrolled, as was absenteeism; and time-on-task became a surrogate for other instructional variables, such as effective management (Anderson, 1985; Carroll, 1985; Karweit, 1985; Stallings, 1980).

Elsewhere we have argued that time is best thought of not as a variable but as a convenient metric for expressing other more relevant variables (Leinhardt, 1985). Clearly, programs that manipulate conditions so that students have more time available to learn important material will allow them to learn more of that material. However, more important than time available are considerations of what is taught, how it is taught, what the students are required to do, and so on. Unfortunately, time is such an easily altered policy variable (by legislating 10 more minutes per day or even an extra month per year) that its importance has often been exaggerated. Interestingly, at the same time that policy makers are demanding that more school time become available, they are recommending programs such as pull-out and bussing that have large time-erosion features built into them. The importance, then, of time in assessing an innovative program is to see that allocation is at a reasonable level, that key features do not erode time, and that on-task behavior can be maintained.

Overlap

Another area of instructional manipulation that is of considerable importance to the quantity and quality of student learning is instructional overlap (Leinhardt & Seewald, 1981). Overlap refers to the fit between a criterion of learning—either test performance or some desired competency—and the instruction that a student receives that is supposed to teach that content. At the extremes, the point is so obvious that it seems almost trivial. If the goal is to have someone learn to speak German, then recitation of multiplication tables in English will be unlikely to produce the desired results. However, as one moves closer to realistic educational practice, the situation becomes a little more ambiguous. If a valued outcome is to have students read reasonably complex prose with a good level of understanding, then what should instruction look like? Many educators, especially teachers of disabled or compensatory students, have advocated a somewhat indirect approach using games or drills of word components and worksheets with missing words or phrases to be filled in as the main vehicles for teaching reading. A similar but less complex situation also exists for math (Leinhardt et al., 1981).

The results of many pieces of research clearly suggest that care should be taken to teach children the content one wants them to learn. That is, children learn more when they are spending their time working on the material to be learned rather than on activities designed to teach them in a more indirect way (Carter, 1984; Cooley & Leinhardt, 1980; Gersten, 1984; Leinhardt & Seewald, 1981; Leinhardt et al., 1981; Lloyd, in press; Rosenshine, 1978).

The danger in this finding is that what has been learned about insuring that a child benefits from instruction may be forgotten. It is important that we do not go overboard in either direction. When we discover that sudents in some LD classes are spending three times as much time in reading but getting less than half of the actual reading done than is regularly accomplished in a mainstream classroom, then there is too much indirect unfocused reading going on (Leinhardt, 1982). On the other hand, having a child attempt to read a full-length book when he or she cannot get through the first paragraph without help does not make much sense either.

In sum, when students spend their time and energy learning content that is directly related to the goals of instruction, they learn it. Evidence that supports this comes from the research on Follow Through (Stebbins et al., 1977), from the Beginning Teacher Evaluation Study (BTES) (Fisher et al., 1978), from the Instructional Dimensions Study (IDS) (Cooley & Leinhardt, 1980), from the Sustaining Effects Study (SES) (Carter, 1984), and from studies of special education (Leinhardt et al., 1981). It is true for both special education and for compensatory education. The limits of this focus on overlap must be remembered, however, when one wants students to learn a skill that is not assessed on standardized tests. For example, if one wants students to learn how to build logical arguments, then one must ensure the availability of focused and direct opportunities to learn such competencies.

Pacing

Pacing is an area of instruction that is related to time and overlap. If time is held constant, then the more material that is covered within a time unit, the more students will learn. However, pacing is a double-edged sword: the pace needs to be slow enough so that students can grasp the lesson content and fast enough so that time is not wasted on unnecessary repetitions. The relationship between what is needed and what is allowed has been quantified by Karweit (1985), and this quantification takes into account the effects that students' different levels of prior knowledge have on pacing. Interestingly, students do not seem to be able to pace themselves efficiently; they either race or dawdle (Anderson, Evertson, & Brophy, 1979; Gump, 1969; Leinhardt, 1977; Rosenshine, 1978). The best situation for students is when the pace is set fast enough to challenge them but not so fast that it overwhelms them (Barr & Dreeben, 1983; Leinhardt et al., 1981). The issue of pacing is particularly important for students in special education and compensatory education because teachers tend to lower the pace expectation for these children (Allington, 1983; Leinhardt, 1980b).

Pace can be lowered for a number of reasons. The fact that it takes more time to teach and learn under certain circumstances is not necessarily the correct explanation for slower pace. The pace of a lesson is often slowed down by weak management. In a nice bit of serendipity, Anderson et al. (1979) reported an inverse relationship between the time taken for a reading group to get settled before actually starting a lesson and their reading achievement. Thus, the longer students take to settle, the lower their reading achievement. Cooley and Leinhardt (1980) found a similar result for the beginning of the school day and Follow Through classrooms. With the lower reading groups, actual lesson time is often substantially shorter than with higher ones (Allington, 1980). This may be because the pace is slower, allowing much more time for getting settled. If less material is expected to be covered, then it does not seem to matter whether or not the lesson starts immediately (Barr & Dreeben, 1985; Fisher & Berliner, 1985; Karweit, 1985; Marliave & Filby, 1985).

Mastery Learning

Mastery learning refers to the practice of partitioning a block of instructional material, arranging those blocks sequentially, and teaching one block until each student reaches a specified level of performance before moving on (Bloom, 1985; Levine & Associates, 1985). Mastery learning takes as a premise that instruction is best when it is focused and that students are in the best position to learn new material when they have completely mastered prior related material. Claims of early success in mastery approaches have been substantial (Bloom, 1976). Most special education programs and many compensatory education programs incorporate many of the features of mastery learning: focused instruction, diagnostic assessment, post-testing, and criterion performance. As with programmed instruction and direct instruction, the focusing may gain instructional time. However, the focusing also causes a certain narrowness and can be easily abused (Doyle, 1986; Stallings & Stipek, 1986). It is also the case that increasing the time by waiting for students to "catch up" may be costly in terms of pacing. Block and Burns (1976) estimate that for the slowest students to reach mastery may require 50% more time to achieve. Nationally, the New Jersey Schools have used this approach and have reported impressive gains not only in the targeted subjects but in ancillary subjects (such as social studies), in which there is some reliance on a targeted skill like reading. However, the Chicago City Schools report poor results where teaching for the test becomes the only goal of the education, the curriculum becomes fragmented (Goodman, 1985), and it is not adequate (Olson, 1985).

It seems clear that focusing instruction and being certain that students learn one piece of instructional material before proceeding to the next is a good idea. However, complex reasoning, analytic thinking, a working knowledge of history, reading good literature and speaking articulately about it, and recognizing the difference between science and popular mythology are very relevant aspects of learning that may reach beyond the limitations of mastery learning approaches as they are currently understood. Further, Arlin (1984) has argued that initial claims for mastery learning, especially those associated with reducing variance among learners, are not justified because of the narrowing of curriculum and high costs of time needed.

Motivation

Motivation is an attribute of an individual towards performing a particular task. When someone is highly motivated to do a task, he or she will persist in trying to accomplish it despite internal or external obstacles. A classroom is considered motivating when a student persists in trying to learn something even though it may be somewhat difficult. Studies of motivation have a somewhat tautological flavor: if students behave diligently and work hard, we say they are motivated. Thus, any educational setting that gets students to work, or one in which they work spontaneously, is definitely motivating. From a different perspective, we can, however, view motivation on a continuum of intensity rather than duration. A student may become more profoundly involved in a task under some circumstances than under others. This increases time and overlap for the individual student. Candies, special prizes, and free time are tangible rewards that may produce greater effort, but the most powerful motivator seems to be social involvement and teacher and peer approval (MacKenzie, 1983; Slavin, 1984; Slavin & Karweit, 1985).

This discussion has omitted the issue of intrinsic versus extrinsic motivation. As soon as educators do something to alter the probability that a student will work, we are talking about external motivation. There has been some research that suggests that extrinsic rewards undermine intrinsic motivation (Blocker & Edwards, 1982). The concern that an individual somehow becomes contaminated by the use of extrinsic motivational devices seems somewhat misplaced. Extrinsic motivators are useful when individuals would not normally or spontaneously engage in a desired activity.

One of the best examples of the use of social motivation to improve the intensity of student effort, and therefore student learning, is Team Assisted Individualization (TAI) (Slavin, 1985). The evidence for the effectiveness of this strategy is quite strong and is present in multiple studies. The advantage is that social motivation can be gained by students across a rather wide band of abilities and personal characteristics. At present, there seem to be few disadvantages, although the approach has not yet been as successful with complex, intricate material as it has been with more straightforward material.

One of the most important premises of the early behaviorist research was the necessity of immediate feedback to the students about the correctness of their performance. Feedback itself is a kind of motivator. Only an individual tutor, programmed workbook, or the computer could really give feedback at the rate that was believed to be needed. The necessity of such immediate feedback for students in the classroom has not been supported; however, it is quite clear that when an instructional program includes some systematic way of providing reasonable, rapid feedback to the students about their performance, then learning is improved (Brophy & Good, 1986; Gersten, et al., 1984).

Feedback can be managed in a variety of ways, including having students self-correct, having other students correct, having teachers correct and analyze errors, or even having machines correct. It seems that, according to Slavin (1985), having students correct each others' work frees the teachers for more instructional time and also is motivating.

Links

A critical feature of any educational improvement effort is the need to integrate supplemental services with instruction provided in the mainstream. Responsibility for this coordination varies. Special educators are generally in the position of initiating and establishing links as the students in special education programs are mainstreamed. In contrast, compensatory education teachers are usually on the receiving end of shifts of pull-out students. Regardless of which position the teacher is in, both categories consider solid substantive and scheduling links between remedial and regular instruction to be important (Glavin, Quay, Annesly, & Nerry, 1971). The disturbing descriptions of some students' days in which they are on a roller coaster of "special" assignments provide evidence for one of the possible consequences of failing to provide for these links.

This linkage issue is only part of one that both special education and compensatory education teachers have stressed, namely, the importance of integrating "special" children with "normal" children (Herrick, 1973b). This emphasis has occasional support in the research literature (Leinhardt, 1980b; Leinhardt & Pallay, 1982) and in the literature on mainstreaming (Glavin et al., 1971). There are two important points. First, it is socially and morally desirable for children to be educated in integrated environments. This desirability constitutes an end in itself and does not require justification in terms of academic improvement. Second, it is also desirable for each child to be given the type of education necessary for his or her maximum growth. Although an appropriate education *may* entail some degree of segregation, that segregation should be absolutely minimized.

CONCLUSIONS

In this chapter we outlined the features of effective instruction. It is effective in the sense that if these features are present at least partially, then the learning behaviors and consequently the learning of poorly performing students is markedly improved. We emphasize that the "discovery" of these features has taken place over a very brief period of time—only 20 years. In this concluding section, we briefly comment on the implication that this work has for future educational research, for contemporary educational reform policy, and for current educational practice.

Future Research. It should be noted that the design of effective instructional programs has taken place in a unique context. In the United States, because of the value placed on local autonomy and decision making, we have tremendous variation in educational features that does not exist in other countries. This has meant that, at first glance, some of the findings may seem trivial or obvious.

Students learn what they spend time learning. However, 20 years ago there was a great deal of faith in "transfer" of skills from one subject matter to another and in more indirect approaches to learning. For example, one studied Latin to learn to think logically. We now know that if one is to learn to think logically or analytically, one needs to have direct practice doing that, probably in a variety of contexts. As we develop enthusiasm for computer literacy, we may want to remember these lessons. The study of Latin is not sufficient for teaching logical thinking, rather it is an enhancement. The study of computer programming should be justified because it is a useful skill, not because it develops some extraordinary logical problem-solving ability.

Building on the platform of global instructional results, we can turn to the more fine-grained issues of content instruction. If we want to go to the next level of improving the education and general knowledge level of students, then we must begin to become seriously engaged in the content of instruction and in the strategies associated with the mastery of that material (Palinscar & Brown, 1984). We must, for example, not only be willing to say that we want students to study a certain number of units of history, but be willing to engage in the discussions that will sketch out the scope and content of such courses. We will have to examine what kind of mathematics we want students to learn at which points in the curriculum, and how deep an understanding we want students to have of the basic subject matter principles in that discipline. Programs will have to be assessed not only on how well they manage the structural features of the instruction, but on how carefully explanations are built and on the types of models and representations that students are taught. (In math, for example, do they learn to reason from number lines and from geometric figures and from Diennes blocks, or just from one of these types of representations?) The expertise for asking and answering this next wave of questions is just beginning to develop. The expertise resides in part in curriculum experts who are raising new concerns and in recent work by cognitive psychologists (e.g., Beck, McKeown, & Gromoll, 1986; Palinscar & Brown, 1984; Resnick, 1987; Schoenfeld, 1983).

Contemporary Reform Policy.   We have learned a good deal about improving the overall knowledge levels in our society by improving the performance levels of those students who were furthest behind. Now, the interest seems to be shifting towards improving knowledge levels by pressing the top segment of our student population for excellence. This press should, and no doubt will, include a close examination of the depth and breadth of content to which students are exposed and an increase in the demands for performance placed on students. It is critical at this juncture of education reform policy that we do not lose sight of what has been accomplished with students who had fallen behind *and* what more needs to be accomplished with such students.

This is the second important implication to be drawn from our review of effective instructional practices. It would be the height of irony if, in the presence of powerful knowledge about how to organize effective instruction in basic skills for students in need of extraordinary assistance, we set loose a reform dynamic that de-emphasizes the importance of such efforts in the name of excellence. Yet, there are several important factors that could work toward such an unfortunate shift in priorities. It is not at all clear that practices that are effective for the achievement of basic skills are also necessarily effective for the encouragement of higher-order skills such as critical thinking. It may well be that an effective instructional program aimed at excellence will work quite differently, demanding different resources, instructional strategies and attitudes on the part of school personnel. Such new demands place a strain on existing human and emotional resources. Further, they risk the exacerbation of tracking systems that are already extant in such programs offered to advance placement and gifted students.

Our point here is to recognize that both equity and excellence are admirable goals. These goals are not *necessarily* complementary. They can be if students in need of assistance are included in the press for excellence; and if that press carefully builds on existing knowledge about basic skills achievement, working to integrate this knowledge into new instructional efforts where feasible, and where it is not, constructing bridges between instructional paths.

Contemporary Educational Practice.   A third implication to be drawn from a review of effective instructional practices concerns the current structures for delivering extraordinary services to students in need. It has been noted at several points in this review that we take the position that the *educational rationale* for separate compensatory and special education systems disappears in the presence of instructional practices that are effective in both types of settings and that they should be merged. We develop this position at some length elsewhere (Leinhardt et al., 1982).

Let it suffice to briefly review several of our central recommendations. We believe that there is a strong case to be made for merging special (LD, EMR) and compensatory educational systems, at least at the point of actual delivery. At the very least, we feel that the evidence of effective instruction is strong enough to shift the burden of proof onto those who would argue for separate systems. A merged instructional delivery system would seek to identify particular content deficits and link these to powerful instructional treatments. Thus, the labeling process would focus on the instructional need, not the student.

Access to extraordinary educational services would be based ultimately on instructional need. With important due process safeguards assumed, contact with such services would be fluid, based upon what skill deficits are presented. The walls that separate such services from the "mainstream" may range from very thin to non-existent, depending on the needs presented.

We realize calling for a merged system that focuses more certainly on identifying specific instructional needs, treatments, and outcomes does not answer issues related to political and professional rationales. These also work to support the current separateness of compensatory and special education structures. There are serious questions concerning resource generation, teacher training, and other issues that must be carefully considered. However, these notwithstanding, we believe that an important implication of effective instructional practices that work in both compensatory and special education settings is that the educational rationale for separate systems disappears. And further, we believe that a merged system focused on content to be taught, rather than labels to be certified, could be a powerful tool for eduational reformers concerned with both equity and excellence.

ACKNOWLEDGMENTS

The authors gratefully acknowledge the assistance of Mary Kay Stein in preparing this chapter.

Funding for the writing of this chapter was provided by the Center for the Study of Learning at the Learning Research and Development Center, University of Pittsburgh, supported in part by funds from the Office of Educational Research and Improvement (OERI), United States Department of Education. The opinions expressed do not necessarily reflect the position or policy of OERI, and no official endorsement should be inferred.

REFERENCES

Abraham, S. Y., & Campbell, C. (1984). *Peer teachers as mirrors and monitors: A qualitative analysis of teacher responses to project interventions.* Michigan: Wayne State University.

Allington, R. L. (1977, October). If they don't read much, how they ever gonna get good? *Journal of Reading, 2*(1), 57–61.

Allington, R. L. (1980). Teaching reading in compensatory classes: A descriptive summary. *The Reading Teacher, 57*(8), 178–183.

Allington, R. L. (1983). *Designing effective compensatory reading instruction: A review.* New York: State University of New York at Albany.

Anderson, L. W. (1985). Time and learning. In C. W. Fisher & D. C. Berliner (Eds.), *Perspectives on instructional time.* New York: Longman.

Anderson, L., Evertson, C., & Brophy, J. (1979). An experimental study of effective teaching in first-grade reading groups. *Elementary School Journal, 79,* 193–223.

Arlin, M. (1984). Time, equality, and mastery learning. *Review of Educational Research, 54*(1), 65–86.

Bailey, S. K., & Mosher, E. K. (1968). *ESEA, The Office of Education administers a law.* Syracuse, NY: Syracuse University Press.

Barnett, W. S. (1985). Benefit-cost analysis of the Perry Preschool Program and its policy implications. *Educational Evaluation and Policy Analysis, 7*(4), 333–342.

Barr, R., & Dreeben, R. (1983). *How schools work.* Chicago: University of Chicago Press.

Barr, R., & Dreeben, R. (1985). A sociological perspective on school time. In C. W. Fisher & D. C. Berliner (Eds.), *Perspectives on instructional time* (pp. 109–117). New York: Longman.

Beck, I. L., McKeown, M. G., & Gromoll, E. W. (1986). *Issues concerning content and structure of expository text for young readers.* Unpublished manuscript, University of Pittsburgh.

Becker, W. C., & Gersten, R. (1982). A follow-up of Follow Through: The later effects of the direct instruction model on children in fifth and sixth grades. *American Educational Research Journal, 19*(1), 75–92.

Bereiter, C., & Kurland, M. (1981–82). A constructive look at Follow Through results. *Interchange, 12*(1), 1–21.

Berrueta-Clement, J. R., Schweinhart, L. J., Barnett, W. S., Epstein, A. S., & Weikart, D. P. (1984). *Changed lives: The effects of the Perry Preschool Program on youths through age 19.* Ypsilanti, MI: The High/Scope Press.

Bickel, D. D., & Bickel, W. E. (1986). Effective schools, classrooms and instruction: Implications for special education. *Exceptional Children, 52*(6), 489–500.

Bickel, W. (1982). Classifying mentally retarded students: A review of placement practices in special education. In K. A. Heller, W. H. Holtzman, & S. Messick (Eds.), *Placing children in special education: A strategy for equity* (pp. 182–229). Washington, DC: National Academy Press.

Block, J., & Burns, R. (1976). Mastery learning. In L. S. Shulman (Ed.), *Review of research in education.* (Vol. 4). Itasca, IL: F. E. Peacock.

Blocker, R. A., & Edwards, R. P. (1982). The effects of extrinsic reinforcement on intrinsic motivation. *Psychology in the Schools, 19*(2), 260–268.

Bloom, B. S. (1974). Time and learning. *American Psychologist, 29*(2), 682–688.

Bloom, B. S. (1976). *Human characteristics and school learning.* New York: McGraw-Hill.

Bloom, B. S. (1985). Learning for mastery. In C. W. Fisher & D. C. Berliner (Eds.), *Perspectives on instructional time.* (pp. 73–93). New York: Longman.

Brophy, J. E., & Good, T. L. (1986). Teacher behavior and student achievement. In M. C. Wittrock (Ed.), *Handbook of research on teaching* (3rd ed.) (pp. 327–375). New York: Macmillan.

Carroll, J. B. (1985). A model of school learning. In C. W. Fisher & D. C. Berliner (Eds.), *Perspectives on instructional time.* (pp. 29–54). New York: Longman.

Carter, L. F. (1984). The Sustaining Effects Study of compensatory and elementary education. *Educational Researcher, 13*(7), 4–13.

Children's Defense Fund. (1984). *An interim report on the implementation of Chapter 1.* Washington, DC: Children's Defense Fund.

Cooley, W. W., & Leinhardt, G. (1980). The Instructional Dimensions Study. *Educational Leadership, 2*(1), 7–25.

Detroit Public Schools (1984). *Peer teachers as mirrors and monitors: First year evaluation report.* Detroit: Author.

Dougherty, J. C. IV (1985). *Report on changes under Chapter 1 of the Education Consolidation and Improvement Act.* Washington, DC: U.S. Government Printing Office.

Doyle, W. (1986). Classroom organization and management. In M. C. Wittrock (Ed.), *Handbook of research on teaching* (3rd ed.) (pp. 392–431). New York: Macmillan.

Dunn, L. M. (Ed.). (1973). *Exceptional children in the schools: Special education in transition* (2nd ed.). New York: Holt, Rinehart and Winston.

Economic Opportunity Act of 1964, P. L. 88–452, 78 Stat. 508, August 20, 1964.

Education Consolidation and Improvement Act of 1981, P. L. 97–35, 95 Stat. 367, August 31, 1981.

Elementary and Secondary Education Act of 1965, P. L. 89–10, 79 Stat. 27, April 11, 1965.

Epps, S., & Tindal, G. (in press). The effectiveness of differential programming in serving mildly handicapped students: Placement options and instructional programming. In M. C. Wang, M. C. Reynolds, & H. J. Walberg (Eds.), *Handbook of special education: Research and practice.* (Vol. 1). New York: Pergamon Press.

Fisher, C. W., & Berliner, D. C. (1985). *Perspectives on instructional time.* New York: Longman.

Fisher, C. W., Filby, N., Marliave, R., Cahen, L. S., Dishaw, M., Moore, J., & Berliner, D. (1978). *Teaching behaviors, academic learning time, and student achievement: Final report of Phase III-B, Beginning Teacher Evaluation Study.* (Tech. Rep. No. U-1). San Francisco, CA: Far West Laboratory for Educational Research & Development.

Foster, E. (1925). Schools and classes for feeble-minded and subnormal children. In *Biennial survey of education: 1920–1922* (Vol. 2), (Chapter XI, pp. 707–728). Washington, DC: U.S. Government Printing Office.

Foster, E. (1933). The education of exceptional children. In *Biennial survey of education: 1930–1932* (chapter 6, p. 12). Washington, DC: U.S. Government Printing Office.

Gersten, R. (1984). Follow Through revisited: Reflections on the site variability issue. *Educational Evaluation and Policy Analysis, 6*(4), 411–423.

Gersten, R., Carnine, D., & White, W. A. T. (1984). The pursuit of clarity: Direct instruction and applied behavior analysis. In W. L. Heward, T. E. Heron, D. S. Hill, & J. Trap-Porter (Eds.), *Focus on behavior analysis in education* (pp. 38–57). Columbus, OH: Merrill.

Gersten, R., Carnine, D., Zoref, L., & Cronin, D. (1986). A multifaceted study of change in seven inner-city schools. *The Elementary School Journal, 86*(3), 1–20.

Glaser, R. (Ed.). (1982). *Advances in instructional psychology.* (Vol. 2). Hillsdale, NJ: Lawrence Erlbaum Associates.

Glass, G. V., Cahen, L. S., Smith, M. L., & Filby, N. N. (1982). *School class size: Research and policy.* Beverly Hills, CA: Sage Publications, Inc.

Glass, G. V., & Smith, M. L. (1978). *Meta-analysis of research on the relationship of class size and achievement.* San Francisco, CA: Far West Laboratory for Educational Research and Development.

Glavin, J., Quay, H., Annesly, F., & Nerry, J. (1971). An experimental resource room for behavior problem children. *Exceptional Children, 38*(2), 131–137.

Good, T. L., & Grouws, D. A. (1977). Teaching effects: A process–product study in fourth grade mathematics classrooms. *Journal of Teacher Education, 28,* 49–54.

Good, T. L., Grouws, D. A., & Ebmeier, H. (1983). *Active mathematics teaching.* New York: Longman.

Goodman, K. S. (1985, October 9). Chicago mastery learning reading: A program with three left feet. *Education Week, 5*(6), p. 20.

Grant, W. V., & Lind, C. G. (1975). *Digest of educational statistics: 1974 edition.* Washington, DC: U.S. Office of Education.

Grant, W. V., & Snyder, T. (1985–86). *Digest of education statistics.* Washington, DC: U.S. Government Printing Office.

Gump, P. V. (1969). Intra-setting analysis: The third grade classroom as a special but instructive case. In E. Williams & H. Rausch (Eds.), *Naturalistic viewpoints in psychological research.* New York: Holt, Rhinehardt & Winston.

Haney, W. (1977). *The Follow-Through planned variation experiments.* (Vol. 5). Cambridge, MA: The Huron Institute.

Heller, K. A., Holtzman, W. H., & Messick, S. (Eds.). (1982). *Placing children in special education: A strategy for equity.* Washington, DC: National Academy Press.

Herrick, M. (1973a). Developing individualized instruction is the difference. *The Journal of Special Education, 7*(4), 417–421.

Herrick, M. (1973b). Disabled or disadvantaged: What's the difference? *The Journal of Special Education, 7*(4), 381–386.

Human Services Authorization Act of 1984, P. L. 98-558, 98 Stat. 28-78, October 30, 1984.

Karweit, N. (1985). Time scales, learning events, and productive instruction. In C. W. Fisher & D. C. Berliner (Eds.), *Perspectives on instructional time* (pp. 169–185). New York: Longman.

Lampert, M. (1986). Knowing, doing, and teaching multiplication. *Cognition and Instruction, 3*(4), 305–342.

Larry P. V. Riles, 343 F. Supp. 1306 (N.D. Cal. 1972).

Lazar, I., & Darlington, R. (1982). *Lasting effects of early education: A report from the consortium for Longitudinal Studies, Monographs of the Society for Research in Child Development, 47* (Serial #195).

Lazerson, M. (1983). The origins of special education. In J. G. Chambers & W. J. Hartman (Eds.), *Special Education Policies* (pp. 15–47). Philadelphia: Temple University Press.

Leinhardt, G. (1976). Observation as a tool for evaluation of implementation. *Instructional Science, 5,* 343–364.

Leinhardt, G. (1977). Program evaluation: An empirical study of individualized instruction. *American Educational Research Journal, 14*(3), 277–293.

Leinhardt, G. (1980a). Modeling and measuring educational treatment in evaluation. *Review of Educational Research, 50*(3), 393–420.

Leinhardt, G. (1980b). Transition rooms: Promoting maturation or reducing education? *Journal of Educational Psychology, 72*(1), 55–61.

Leinhardt, G. (1982, March). *Case studies of academic mainstreaming.* Paper presented at the annual meeting of the American Educational Research Association, New York.

Leinhardt, G. (1985). Instructional time: A winged chariot? In C. W. Fisher & D. C. Berliner (Eds.), *Perspectives on instructional time.* New York: Longman.

Leinhardt, G., Bickel, W., & Pallay, A. (1982). Unlabeled but still entitled: Toward more effective remediation. *Teachers College Record, 84*(2), 391–422.

Leinhardt, G., & Greeno, J. (1986). The cognitive skill of teaching. *Journal of Educational Psychology, 78*(2), 75–95.

Leinhardt, G., & Pallay, A. (1982). Restrictive Educational Settings: Exile or haven? *Review of Educational Research, 52*(4), 557–578.

Leinhardt, G., & Seewald, A. M. (1981). Overlap: What's tested, what's taught? *Journal of Education Measurement, 18*(3), 171–177.

Leinhardt, G., & Smith, D. (1985). Expertise in mathematics instruction: Subject matter knowledge. *Journal of Educational Psychology, 77*(3), 247–271.

Leinhardt, G., Zigmond, N., & Cooley, W. (1981). Reading instruction and its effects. *American Educational Research Journal, 18*(3), 343–361.

Levine, D. U., & Associates (1985). *Improving student achievement through mastery learning programs.* San Francisco, Ca: Jossey-Bass.

Lloyd, J. W. (in press). Direct academic interventions in learning disabilities. In M. C. Wang, M. C. Reynolds, & H. J. Walberg (Eds.), *Handbook of special education: Research and practice.* (Vol. 2). New York: Pergamon Press.

Machie, R. P. (1969). *Special education in the United States: Statistics, 1948–1966.* New York: Teachers College Press.

MacKenzie, D. E. (1983). School effectiveness research: A synthesis and assessment. In P. C. Duttweiler (Ed.), *Educational productivity and school effectiveness* (pp. 3–107). Austin, TX: The Southwest Educational Development Laboratory.

MacMillan, D. L. (1977). *Mental retardation in school and society.* Boston, MA: Little, Brown, & Co.

Marliave, R., & Filby, N. N. (1985). Success rate: A measure of task appropriateness. In C. W. Fisher & D. C. Berliner (Eds.), *Perspectives on instructional time* (pp. 217–262). New York: Longman.

McKey, R. H., Condelli, L., Ganson, H., Barrett, B., McConkey, C., & Plantz, M. (1985, June). *The impact of Head Start on children, families, and communities.* (A final report of the Head Start Evaluation, Synthesis and Utilization Project). Washington, DC: CSR, Inc.

Mercer, J. R. (1973). *Labeling the mentally retarded.* Berkeley, CA: University of California Press.

Myers, P., & Hammil, D. (1973). Deprivation or learning disability: Another dilemma for special education. *Journal of Special Education, 7*(4), 409–411.

Norman, C. A., Jr., & Zigmond, N. (1980). Characteristics of children labeled and served as learning disabled in school systems affiliated with child service demonstration centers. *Journal of Learning Disabilities, 13*(10), 542–547.

Olson, L. (1985, August 21). Chicago scuttles mastery-reading program plan after $7.5 million, 5 year commitment. *Education Week, 4,* (40 & 41), 1–17.

Palinscar, A. S., & Brown, A. L. (1984). Reciprocal teaching of comprehension fostering and comprehension monitoring activities. *Cognition and Instruction, 1*(2), 117–175.

Plisko, V. W., (Ed.). (1983). *The condition of education.* Washington, DC: U.S. Government Printing Office.

Resnick, L. B. (1987). *Education and learning to think.* Washington, DC: National Academy Press.

Reynolds, M. C. (1984). Classification of students with handicaps. *Review of Research in Education, 11,* 63–92.

Reynolds, M. C., & Lakin, K. C. (in press). Noncategorical special education: Models for research and practice. In M. C. Wang, M. C. Reynolds, & H. J. Walberg (Eds.), *Handbook of special education: Research and practice.* (Vol. 1). New York: Pergamon Press.

Richmond, J. B., Stipek, D. J., & Zigler, E. (1979). A decade of Head Start. In E. Zigler & J. Valentine (Eds.), *Project Head Start: A legacy of the war on poverty* (pp. 135–152). New York: The Free Press.

Riley, A., & Nachtigal, P. (1984). *Cotopaxi/Westcliffe Follow Through Project.* Kansas City, MO: Mid-continent Regional Educational Laboratory.

Rosenshine, B. V. (1978, March). *Academic engaged minutes, content covered and direct instruction.* Paper presented at the annual meeting of the American Educational Research Association, Toronto, Canada.

Scheutz, P. (1980). *The instructional effectiveness of classroom aides.* Unpublished manuscript, University of Pittsburgh.

Schoenfeld, A. H. (1983). Episodes and executive decisions in mathematical problem-solving. In R. Lesh & M. Landau (Eds.), *Acquisition of mathematics concepts and processes.* (pp. 345–395). New York: Academic Press.

Schweinhart, L. J., & Weikart, D. P. (1980). *Young children grow up: The effects of the Perry Preschool Program on youths through age 15.* Ypsilanti, MI: The High/Scope Press.

Schweinhart, L. J., & Weikart, D. P. (1985). Evidence that good early childhood programs work. *Phi Delta Kappan, 66*(8), 545–548.

Secretary's Committee on Mental Retardation (1970). Programs of the Bureau of Education for the Handicapped: U.S. Office of Education. *Programs for the Handicapped.* Washington, DC: U.S. Department of Health, Education and Welfare.

Shulman, L. S. (1986). Paradigms and research programs in the study of teaching. A contemporary perspective. In M. C. Wittrock (Ed.), *Handbook of research on teaching* (3rd ed.) (pp. 3–36). New York: Macmillan.

Slavin, R. E. (1983a). *Cooperative learning.* New York: Longman.

Slavin, R. E. (1983b). When does cooperative learning increase student achievement? *Psychological Bulletin, 94*(3), 429–445.

Slavin, R. E. (1984). Meta-analysis in education: How has it been used? *Educational Researcher, 13*(8), 6–15.

Slavin, R. E. (1985). Team-assisted individualization: A cooperative learning solution for adaptive instruction in mathematics. In M. C. Wang & H. T. Walberg (Eds.), *Adapting instruction to individual differences* (pp. 236–253). Berkeley, CA: McCutchan.

Slavin, R. E., & Karweit, N. L. (1985). Effects of whole class, ability grouped, and individualized instruction on mathematics achievement. *American Educational Research Journal, 22*(3), 351–367.

Smith, M. L., & Glass, G. V. (1979). *Relationship of class-size to classroom processes, teacher satisfaction and pupil affect: A meta-analysis.* San Francisco, CA: Far West Laboratory for Educational Research and Development.

Stainback, W., & Stainback, S. (1984). A rationale for the merger of special and regular education. *Exceptional Children, 51*(2), 102–111.

Stallings, J. A. (1980). Allocated academic learning time revisited, or beyond time on task. *Educational Researcher, 9*(11), 11–16.

Stallings, J., Coury, R., Fairweather, J., & Needles, M. (1977). *Early childhood education classroom evaluation.* Menlo Park, CA: SRI International.

Stallings, J. A., & Robbins, P. (1985). *Phase II evaluation report of the Nappa County Office of Education's Follow Through research project to increase learning time and achievement.* Technical Report submitted to National Institute of Education, Washington, DC.

Stallings, J. A., & Stipek, D. (1986). Research on early childhood and elementary school teaching programs. In M. C. Wittrock (Ed.), *Handbook of research on teaching* (3rd ed.) (pp. 727–753). New York: Macmillan.

Stebbins, L. B., St. Pierre, R. G., Proper, E. C., Anderson, R. B., & Cerva, T. R. (1977). *Education as experimentation: A planned variation model. An evaluation of Follow Through,* (Vol IV-A. Report No. 76-196A). Cambridge, MA: Abt Associates.

Stodolsky, S. S. (1983). *Classroom activity structures in the fifth grade.* (Final Report, NIE Contract #400-77-0094). Chicago: University of Chicago.

Strain, P. S., & Kerr, M. M. (1981). *Mainstreaming of children in schools: Research and programmatic issues.* New York: Academic Press.

U.S. Office of Education. (1971). *Estimated number of handicapped children in the United States, 1971–1972.* Washington, DC: U.S. Office of Education.

Walberg, H. J. (1984). Improving the productivity of America's schools. *Educational Leadership, 41*(8), 19–30.

Wang, M. C., & Birch, J. W. (1984). Effective special education in regular classes. *Exceptional Children, 50*(5), 391–398.

Wang, M. C., & Walberg, H. J. (Eds.). (1985). *Adapting instruction to individual differences.* Berkeley, CA: McCutchan Publishing Company.

Wolff, M., & Stein, A. (1966). *Study I: Six months later, a comparison of children who had Head Start, summer 1965 with their classmates in kindergarten.* Washington, DC: Research & Evaluation Office, OEO (EDO 15026).

Ysseldyke, J. E., Algozzine, B., Shinn, M., & McGue, M. (1979). *Similarities and differences between underachievers and students labeled learning disabled: Identical twins with different mothers.* (Research Rep. No. 13). Minneapolis, University of Minnesota, Institute for Research on Learning Disabilities.

Zigler, E., & Anderson, K. (1979). An idea whose time had come: The intellectual and political climate. In E. Zigler & J. Valentine (Eds.), *Project Head Start: A legacy of the war on poverty.* New York: The Free Press.

9 The Impact of Evaluation Processes on Students

Gary Natriello
Teachers College
Columbia University

The evaluation of student performance is a central task of schools and teachers. Indeed, evaluation activities permeate the educational process. Although this is particularly apparent during times such as the present, when schools are under increased pressure for greater accountability and improved performance, the pressure on and interest in evaluation processes is nothing new. Throughout the history of American education, evaluation of student performance has been an element of enduring concern to educators, to students, and to parents (Crooks, 1933). It is thus a fitting subject for the continuing interest of social scientists and educators who have amassed a considerable body of research and commentary related to the evaluation process.

This review summarizes the research on evaluation processes in schools and classrooms by: (a) briefly reviewing a conceptual framework for thinking about the evaluation process, (b) examining research on the impact of features of the evaluation process on students, with particular emphasis on alterable elements of the process, and (c) considering the limitations of previous research and directions for future research.

CONCEPTUAL FRAMEWORK FOR SCHOOL AND CLASSROOM EVALUATION PROCESSES

A variety of frameworks for thinking about the evaluation of performers has been proposed (Natriello, 1985). Figure 9.1 presents one model of the evaluation process that is relatively simple yet sufficiently robust to permit discussion of most of the major elements of evaluation processes for students in schools and

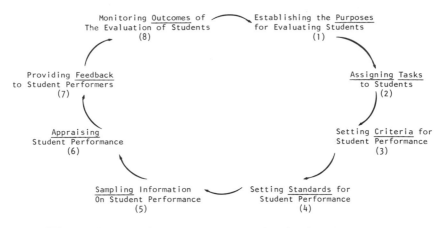

FIG.9.1.   A model of evaluation processes in schools and classrooms.

classrooms. Each of the stages of the model suggests features of the evaluation process that must be attended to by evaluators and that have an impact on students. Brief consideration of each of these stages suggests some emerging issues concerning evaluation processes that confront teachers, students, and researchers.

Establishing the Purposes for Evaluating Students   represents the first stage in the model and suggests that there are multiple purposes for the evaluation of student performance. Although there are a number of brief discussions of the purposes of evaluation at the outset of numerous texts on measurement and evaluation (e.g., Ahmann & Glock, 1967; Lien, 1967; Remmers, Gage, & Rummel, 1960), the purposes of evaluation receive scant attention in the literature overall.

Discussions of the purposes of evaluation of student performance suggest that there are four generic functions that evaluation processes are thought to serve: certification, selection, direction, and motivation. Certification refers to the assurance that a student has attained a certain level of accomplishment or mastery. Selection entails the identification of students or groups of students to be recommended or permitted to enter or continue along certain educational and occupational paths. Direction refers to the use of evaluation processes to communicate the specific desires of evaluators to those being evaluated and to allow evaluators to engage in diagnosis and further planning. Motivation entails engaging those being evaluated in the tasks at hand.

Assigning Tasks to Students   is the second stage of the evaluation process. It is only through the process of assignment that students are put on notice that they are expected to perform a certain task. Tasks consist of stimulus materials, instructions about operations, and instructions about goals (Hackman, 1969).

Certain characteristics of academic tasks are particularly likely to affect the operation of the evaluation system in a classroom. Academic tasks that are less predictable or that carry greater ambiguity or risk appear to place greater demands on evaluation processes. Such tasks often lead to evaluation processes that seem to be arbitrary, leaving students unable to relate their performances to the evaluations they receive and teachers unable to rationally justify the evaluation process (Thompson, 1967; Dornbusch & Scott, 1975). When the relationship between procedures or operations and results is not straightforward, teachers are not justified in basing evaluations only on the results of assignments; they must also consider procedures. However, assessing student performance of procedures is often problematic because academic tasks generally involve mental processes that are not readily visible to teachers in classrooms (Natriello & Dornbusch, 1984).

The strain placed on evaluation processes in schools and classrooms by less predictable tasks leads to two tendencies. First, there is a tendency to avoid ambiguous tasks, both on the part of students (Davis & McKnight, 1976; Doyle, 1983; Wilson, 1976) and on the part of teachers (Holmes, 1978; Natriello & Dornbusch, 1984). Second, there is a tendency to structure evaluation activities as if the tasks being evaluated are predictable and unambiguous. For example, in a study of three reading curricula, Armbruster, Stevens, and Rosenshine (1977) found that although the texts emphasized comprehension and interpretation skills, the tests solicited factual information from students based on the ability to locate information in the text. In the face of the considerable complexity of most school tasks (Doyle, 1983), avoiding less predictable tasks and treating all tasks as if they are predictable simplifies the evaluation process and makes life in classrooms more secure both for students who must attain acceptable evaluations and for teachers who must be able to justify their evaluation practices to students, parents, and adminstrators. Of course, this diminishes the likelihood that teachers and students will engage in creative or heuristic tasks.

Setting Criteria for Student Performance   moves beyond the general assignment of a task to provide information on the properties of the task that will be considered important in the evaluation of performance. Although there is little discussion of task-specific criteria for evaluation in the evaluation literature, attention has been devoted to the types of criteria employed in the evaluation process. It is generally accepted that the achievement of students in a subject is the one criterion common to all evaluation systems in schools and classrooms (Brown, 1971). There is little discussion as to the appropriateness of using achievement criteria, although in recent years there has been increased attention devoted to determining whether the evaluation process is actually linked to the instructional process (Linn, 1983; Rudman, Kelly, Wanous, Mehrens, Clark, & Porter, 1980) so that students are not placed in a position where they are evaluated on things not covered in the instructional program (Natriello, 1982). Although there is agreement that types of criteria other than achievement criteria enter into evaluation processes in schools and classrooms (Thorndike, 1969), there is less agreement as to which of these other types of criteria, such as participation, effort, and conduct (Natriello & McPartland, 1987; Salganik, 1982; Schunk, 1983; Weiner, 1979), may be appropriate.

Setting Standards for Student Performance, the fourth stage in the evaluation process, has received considerable attention amidst renewed calls for higher standards in U.S. schools (National Commission on Excellence in Education, 1983). Standards communicate the level of performance that students are supposed to achieve.

Research and commentary on appropriate standards for the evaluation of student performance in schools and classrooms can be seen as evidence of the struggle to accomodate both universalism and individualism in a single system (Bidwell, 1965; Varenne & Kelly, 1976; Waller, 1932). Out of this struggle have emerged three types of standards, those set in reference to the criterion level of a group, those set in reference to some absolute criterion level, and those set in reference to the previous criterion level of an individual (Rheinberg, 1983; Thorndike, 1969, Wise & Newman, 1975). Discussions of standards for the evaluation of students revolve around the advantages and disadvantages of employing each of these three types of standards (Bresee, 1976; Deutsch, 1979; Glaser, 1963; Glass, 1978; Levine, 1976; Michaels, 1977; Natriello & McPartland, 1987; Slavin, 1977; Terwilliger, 1977).

Sampling Information on Student Performance, the fifth stage in the evaluation process, involves the collection of partial information on student performance of assigned tasks and the outcomes of those performances. The collection of such information requires a sampling process because it would be impractical, if not impossible, to collect total information on student performance. Most of the important decisions about the collection of performance information thus involve sampling decisions to insure that the information collected provides a valid and reliable estimate of performance appropriate to the purposes, tasks, criteria, and standards that have already been determined.

By far the dominant technique for collecting information on student performance is some form of testing. A number of analysts have contributed important observations about the relationship between testing practices and the purposes, tasks, criteria, and standards for the evaluation of students. For example, Deutsch (1979) objects to the overwhelming use of tests employing norm-referenced standards for the purpose of selection at the expense of student motivation and individual development. Others have rejected norm-referenced tests in favor of criterion-referenced tests for the purpose of certification (Glaser, 1963; Hambleton, Swaminathan, Algina & Coulson, 1978; Popham and Husek, 1969).

The relationship between tests and assigned tasks and the biases that result when tests do not correspond to the curriculum have also been given serious attention (Leinhardt & Seewald, 1981; National Institute of Education, 1979; Rudman et al., 1980). Descriptive accounts of testing reveal a wide range of testing practices and the use of tests from various sources for multiple purposes together with evidence that the level of expertise for test construction among teachers may be quite low (Gullickson, 1982, 1984; Herman & Dorr-Bremme, 1984; Natriello, 1982).

Alternatives to traditional testing have also been examined, including routine class and homework assignments, classroom interaction during question and answer sessions, recitations, discussions, oral reading, problem solving at the chalkboard, special projects, presentations, and reports (Heller, 1978; Herman & Dorr-Bremme, 1984; Gaston, 1976). Although such practices appear to broaden the base of information on student performance, there are serious questions about the quality of the information they provide (Rudman et al., 1980).

Appraising Student Performance involves comparing the information collected on student performance on assigned tasks with the criteria and standards previously established for those tasks. Studies of teacher appraisals of student performance have typically focused on teacher bias related to student characteristics. These studies may be criticized on a number of grounds (Natriello & Dornbusch, 1984) and have not led to culmulative knowledge of the appraisal process. Egan and Archer (1985) have pointed out that the decision to examine teacher appraisal of students using experimental models of prejudice borrowed from social psychology (e.g., Rosenthal & Jacobson, 1968) is in contrast to the study of diagnosis in other professions where accuracy and rationality of the appraisal process are assumed and interest is directed to the strategy of the appraisal process. Egan and Archer conclude that there is little basis to claim that teachers' ratings are inaccurate because it has not been possible to produce a rational strategy of classification that gives substantially better results.

Providing Feedback on Student Performance, the seventh stage of the model, involves the communication of the results of the evaluation to relevant parties, including the student, parents, school officials, and potential employers (Ahmann & Glock, 1967). Designating feedback as a distinct stage serves to underline the point that a good deal of evaluative information is never communicated to performers or other relevant parties.

The nature and extent of communications regarding student performance have been the subjects of various investigations and commentaries. Some of these have focused on the various forms of feedback from traditional report cards (Chansky, 1975; Jarrett, 1963; Walling, 1975), to checklists (Rudman, 1978); to graded tests (Gullickson, 1982) to conferences (Ediger, 1975; Natriello, 1982). Other investigations have considered the relationship of feedback techniques to other dimensions of the evaluation process. The relationship between the type of feedback and the purpose of the evaluation process has received the attention of numerous authors (Cross & Cross, 1980; Hansen, 1977; Lissman & Paetzoid, 1983; Oren, 1983; Slavin, 1978). Several investigators have considered the relationship between task characteristics and the nature of feedback (Lintner & Ducette, 1974; Lissman & Paetzoid, 1983).

Monitoring the Outcomes of the Evaluation of Students involves consideration of the impact of the evaluation process in light of the original purposes of the process. The purposes of certification, selection, direction, and motivation might suggest an analysis of mastery, classification, progress, and continued engagement, respectively. This eighth stage of the evaluation process leads back to the first stage of establishing or re-establishing the purpose for evaluating students as the cycle continues.

Of course, the eight stages of the model are an oversimplification of reality. It might be argued that later stages of the model have an impact on earlier stages. For instance, some would argue that the criteria and standards set for a task really define the task assignment or that the constraints of the sampling process help to define the real criteria and standards. Moreover, although the first six stages of the model are portrayed as having an impact on outcomes only through the mediation of the feedback process designated as the seventh stage, in reality, each stage of the process may have direct effects on the outcomes of the evaluation process as is shown in the next section. Limitations such as these notwithstanding, the model does highlight some key elements of evaluation processes and provides a set of broad categories within which to consider the impact of various features of evaluation processes on students.

THE IMPACT OF THE EVALUATION PROCESS ON STUDENTS

The impact of various features of evaluation processes on students has been the focus of numerous studies. Considering these studies in terms of the stages of the conceptual model outlined previously places them in a broader context and indicates where additional research is needed.

Purposes of Evaluations

As noted earlier, the relationship between the purposes of evaluation systems and the impact or outcomes of evaluation processes has not received systematic attention. Indeed, most studies of the effects of evaluations pit two or more systems seemingly developed for different purposes against one another in an attempt to determine their impact in terms of a narrowly defined outcome (e.g.

Lissman & Paetzoid, 1983; Schunk, 1983; Williams, Pollack & Ferguson, 1975). As a result, little is known about the development and implementation of evaluation systems in school and classroom contexts where evaluation must serve multiple purposes.

Resolution of Tasks

Investigators are only beginning to recognize the importance of classroom tasks in understanding educational and evaluation processes (Doyle, 1983). Although there are few studies in this area, a particularly interesting line of research focuses on the impact of the task structure of classrooms on students' conceptions of the distribution of ability in the class. In a study of fifth and sixth graders, Rosenholtz and Wilson (1980) found that in classes characterized by what they called higher "resolution" (i.e., less task differentiation, more ability grouping, more evaluations comparing the work of one student with another, and less student autonomy to choose tasks) there was higher conconcurrence among classmates, between self and classmates, between teacher and classmates, and between self and teacher in ratings of reading ability. Rosenholtz and Rosenholtz (1981) found that these same high resolution classroom structures led to more dispersed evaluations of reading ability by students themselves, by classmates, and by teachers. In addition, they also found that low resolution classroom structures diminished the effect of teacher evaluation on peer evaluations of an individual's reading ability. In a study of third grade classrooms, Simpson (1981) found that low levels of curricular differentiation led to "a more nearly normal distribution of self-reports of ability by increasing the proportion of students reporting ability levels below average and far below average" (p. 127). Moreover, low curricular differentiation also appeared to lead to a more generalized view of academic ability, greater peer consensus about students' performance levels, and to greater influence for peers on an individual's self-reported ability.

Clarity of Criteria

Dornbusch and Scott (1975) make the point that criteria add to the definition of the assigned task and direct the attention of performers to the key elements of the task for which they will be held accountable. Schunk (1983) reports on a study in which some children were offered rewards for participating in a task, others were offered rewards for careful work on the task, and still others were not offered rewards until they had completed the task. The results indicated that the first group of children, those who had received both a task assignment and information on the criteria for performance, showed the highest levels of skill, self-efficacy, and rapid problem solving.

This should not be surprising. As Deutsch (1979) points out:

"students are in a bewildering position if a teacher marks them without telling them in sufficient detail the values, rules, and procedures employed in his or her grading. In such a situation, the mark-oriented students are necessarily anxiously dependent on the teacher's approval, since they have no other basis for guiding their behavior to achieve merit. . . Where the instructor is explicit in his or her style of grading, the student can be more independent of the teacher. (p. 396)

Natriello (1982) found that over 30% of the students in his study of four suburban high schools reported that they had received unsatisfactory evaluations because they had misunderstood the criteria by which they were to be evaluated. Smith (1984) observed that clarity has been demonstrated to be an important component of teaching in research on teaching effectiveness (Rosenshine & Furst, 1973). In his study of the impact of teacher "use of uncertainty phrases" on student achievement Smith (1984) found that such phrases negatively affected achievement.

However, explicitness may have undesirable effects as well. Deutsch (1979) notes that explicit evaluation systems may lead the mark-oriented student to limit his or her work to what is being assessed by the procedures employed in the grading or to attempt to outwit the procedures. He cites as an example managers in the Bell System who are graded or evaluated by "profit indices" and who often outwit the system by postponing routine maintenance costs, which results in equipment breakdowns several years later when successful managers have moved on to new positions. Thus, clarity seems to be a two-edged sword.

Demandingness of Standards

The effects of performance standards seem to be more complex than is typically thought. Early studies of the impact of school standards on student performance (Brookover & Schneider, 1975) seem to have survived the challenge that the correlation between teacher standards and student performance could result from the impact of the latter on the former (Crano & Mellon, 1978). Findings from the school effectiveness literature (Purkey & Smith, 1983), the teacher expectations literature (Brophy & Evertson, 1981) and the task goals literature (Locke, 1968; Rosswork, 1977) suggest that higher standards yield better student performance. In studies specifically focused on evaluation processes, Natriello and Dornbusch (1984) found that higher standards led to greater student effort on school tasks and to students being more likely to attend class, and Natriello and McDill (1986) found that when teachers had standards for homework, students were more likely to spend time on homework.

However, the effects of higher standards may not be uniformly positive under all conditions. Natriello (1982) found that students who perceived standards for their performance as unattainable were more likely to become disengaged from high school. McDill, Natriello, and Pallas (1985) suggested that higher standards may actually have detrimental effects for at-risk students in secondary schools. There seems to be a curvilinear relationship between the level of standards and student effort and performance. The goal would seem to be to challenge students without frustrating them (Atkinson, 1958).

Referents of Standards

The impact of different types of standards has also been investigated. Perhaps the most attention has been devoted to norm-referenced standards, or "grading on the curve". Michaels (1977) designates the reward structure associated with this practice as "individual competition, in which grades are assigned to students based on their performances relative to those of their classmates," and distinguishes it from "individual reward contingencies, in which grades are assigned to students on the basis of how much material each student apparently masters" (p. 87). He considers the effects of these two reward structures along with two other reward structures (group competition and group reward contingencies) on student academic performance. Reviewing the relevant literature, he concludes that individual competition consistently produces superior academic performance.

However, Michaels (1977) observes that the superior academic performance found to be associated with individual competition may be limited to the top third of the class, to those students who are most responsive to the reward structure. Deutsch (1979) presents a more critical analysis of individual competition or grading on the curve, a situation he describes as an artificially created shortage of good grades. He argues that the "Disappointing rewards, induced by an artificial scarcity, are likely to hamper the development of educational merit and the sense of one's own value" (p. 394). Moreover, under individual competition, "Students are more anxious, they think less well of themselves and of their work, they have less favorable attitudes toward their classmates and less friendly relations with them, and they feel less of a sense of responsibility toward them" (p. 399).

In considering the impact of individual competition and individual reward contingencies on actual student performance, Deutsch disagrees with the conclusions reached by Michaels. Examining the same studies examined by Michaels, Deutsch (1979) concludes that a number of these studies were flawed because they did not equate the objective probability of reward in the reward structures being compared. Deutsch's reanalysis of these studies shows "no systematic differences in performance on isolated work under several different reward systems" (p. 398). This position is confirmed by Williams, Pollack, and Ferguson (1975), who found no significant differences between the achievement and self-reported attitudes or school-related behavior of students exposed to norm-referenced and criterion-referenced standards. However, they also found that criterion-referenced standards provided assurance to students who performed poorly initially that enabled at least some of them to increase their performance on later tests and that criterion-referenced standards allowed students who did well initially to become confident and work less hard than students working under a norm referenced system.

Norm referenced standards have also been compared to individually referenced standards for their effects on student performance. Slavin (1980) found that students in classes in which evaluations were based on experimental individually referenced standards achieved more on a final standardized test than students in control classes evaluated by norm-referenced standards. However, Beady, Slavin, and Fennessey (1981) found no differences in the effects of norm-referenced standards and individually referenced standards among students participating in a program of focused instruction, a particular model of direct instruction. Under different task conditions, Rheinberg (1983) found that students working under individually referenced standards showed more realistic strategies of goal setting, more often attributed their successes to their own effort, and performed better than students working under norm-referenced standards.

In an interesting complication to the issue of the impact of different standards, Bolocofsky and Mescher (1984) considered the effects of different standards for students who differ in terms of self-esteem and locus of control. They found that students with different characteristics performed differently under different kinds of standards. Self-referenced standards worked best with students with low self-esteem and internal locus of control. Criterion-referenced or absolute standards worked best with students with low self-esteem and external locus of control. Norm-referenced standards worked best with students with high self-esteem, regardless of locus of control.

A great deal of attention has been devoted to the impact of different types of standards on student cooperation and competition. These studies typically examine the relationships between the evaluations made and rewards distributed and the tendency for students to perform tasks independently, cooperatively, or competitively. Slavin (1977), in a review of much of this research, uses the term "interpersonal reward structure" (p. 634) to refer to the dependence or lack of dependence of any given student on any other student. He distinguishes three types of interpersonal reward structures: competitive reward structures, where the probability of one student receiving a reward is negatively related to the probability of other students receiving a reward; independent reward structures, where the tendency of one student receiving a reward is unrelated to the tendency of other students receiving a reward; and cooperative reward structures, where the probability of one student receiving a reward is positively related to the probability of other students receiving a reward.

Slavin (1977) reviewed the research on the impact of these various reward structures on student social behavior and academic performance in the classroom. He concluded that cooperative structures enhance social behavior along a number of dimensions, including interpersonal attraction, friendliness, positive group evaluation, helpfulness, and cross-racial interaction. Although competitive and independent reward structures were found to be more effective in increasing performance when tasks required little cooperation or when there was little opportunity to share resources to facilitate performance, cooperative structures should be effective in promoting performance when such cooperation and sharing are necessary and permitted.

Frequency of Sampling

A number of investigations have focused on the frequency of the sampling process, more particularly, the frequency of testing. Reviewers of the research on the frequency of testing (Feldhusen, 1964; Peckham & Roe, 1977) have found that whereas early studies of testing frequency indicated uniformly positive effects on student learning and motivation of more frequent testing, more recent studies incorporating more variables have suggested that more frequent testing may not be beneficial for all students in all contexts. However, considering evaluation activities as contests, Deutsch (1979) concludes that "The existence of many diverse contests diffuses competition and reduces the negative implications of any particular contest: It is less harmful to one's self-esteem and social standing" (p. 396).

Studies of testing frequency have not typically viewed testing as part of a larger evaluation process. From the perspective of the model in Fig. 9.1, testing is merely one method of sampling student performance and outcomes. Thus, it is difficult to understand the impact of testing frequency in the classroom apart from information on the frequency with which teachers use other methods to collect information on student performance.

Soundness of Appraisals

Consideration of the appraisal process focuses attention on the connection between student performances and the evaluations made of those performances by teachers, often from the perspective of the teacher attempting carefully to relate performance information to predetermined tasks, criteria, and standards. The quality of the connection between student performance and evaluations appears to have important effects on students. Natriello and Dornbusch (1984) found that when students perceived the evaluations of their performance on school tasks to be unsound (i.e., not to accurately reflect their effort and performance), they were less likely to consider these evaluations important and less likely to devote effort to the associated tasks.

An interesting complication of these effects is found in work on the theory of learned helplessness, which suggests that experiencing uncontrollable outcomes should depress performance (Abramson, Seligman & Teasdale, 1978; Seligman, 1975), as well as in work that suggests that the experience of uncontrollable outcomes facilitates increased performance by producing an increased need for control (Roth & Bootzin, 1974; Thornton & Jacobs, 1972). An integrative model developed by Wortman and Brehm (1975) suggests that brief exposure to uncontrollable outcomes will lead to improved performance, whereas extended exposure will lead to decreased performance. Research involving high school students (Buys & Winfield, 1982) reveals only decreased student performance in reaction to the experience of uncontrollable outcomes, a pattern the authors link to the relatively less self-reliant and less self-confident nature of high school students compared to adults, and to the tendency of the school environment to foster helplessness.

Of course, students may differ in their perceptions of appraisal processes independent of the process itself. Taking a developmental approach, Evans and Engelberg (1985) found that older and higher-achieving students understood grading practices better than younger and lower-achieving students and that younger and lower-achieving students were more likely to attribute grades to external and uncontrollable factors, whereas high achievers and older students attributed grades to internal and controllable factors.

Differentiation of Feedback

A number of studies have examined the impact of the feedback presented as part of the evaluation process. Stewart and White (1976) present the results of their own study and review those of 12 others that attempted to replicate Page's (1958) classic study of the effects of grades alone versus the effect of grades and teacher comments as forms of feedback. Page found that "When the average secondary teacher takes the time and trouble to write comments (believed to be "encouraging") on student papers, these apparently have a measurable and potent effect upon student effort, or attention, or attitude, or whatever it is which causes learning to improve" (180–181). Stewart and White (1976) reach a slightly less confident conclusion, noting that the positive effect obtained by Page may depend on the particular learning conditions and the nature of the teacher comments. Cross and Cross (1980) find that personalized encouraging comments from the teacher used in addition to a grade on tests and assignments enhanced the "internality" of students in an inner-city junior high school.

Feedback may also have effects in schools and classrooms that extend beyond the individual students to whom the feedback pertains. Because feedback is often given publicly, it may have effects on other students as well. A study of third graders by Simpson (1981) illustrates how evaluative feedback decisions can have an effect on students' perceptions of the ability levels of their classmates. Simpson (1981) argues that "Grades are singular symbols taking on unidimensional comparative meaning from the abstract numerical system which defines them. Frequent grading is capable of reducing even relatively complex performances to a single dimension, because grades reduce information to numbers, because these numbers can be averaged, and because teachers and student peers can use these numbers to place students on a single global stratification scale'' (p. 124). Simpson finds that in classrooms where teachers report "always" or "usually" grading student work (as opposed to those in which they "never" or "seldom" grade such work) and where they report using few kinds of instructional materials and where they seldom use alternative media and seldom allow students to choose their tasks, there is a higher dispersion among students' reported ability levels, higher generalization of students' reported ability levels, higher peer consensus as to students' relative performance levels, and greater peer influence over student's reported ability levels. Thus, the use of less differentiated forms of feedback such as grades seems to lead to more pronounced and more powerful ability stratification processes in the classroom.

A similar effect on the distribution of attributional tendencies in classrooms was found by Oren (1983). Oren explored the effects of evaluation feedback on the attributional tendencies of students. Results indicated that in classrooms with differentiated, specific, and individualized feedback, the attributional tendencies of low achievers were more like those of high achievers. Specifically, low achievers in such classrooms scored higher on internal control than low achievers in classrooms with less differentiated feedback systems.

Affective Value of Feedback

The affective value of feedback has also been shown to influence attributions in classrooms. Meyer, Bachmann, Biermann, Hempelmann, Ploger, and Spiller (1979) report on a series of six experimental studies that investigated the extent to which praise and criticism in response to task performance provided information about others' perceptions of a focal actor's ability. In these studies, subjects were presented with descriptions of two students who had obtained identical results at a task. One of the students received neutral feedback; the other was praised for success or criticized for failure. Studies using adult subjects revealed that praise after success and neutral feedback after failure led to the perception that the focal actor's ability was low, and neutral feedback for success and criticism after failure led to the perception that the focal actor's ability was high. However, these findings varied by the age of the respondents. For example, third grade students believed that the student praised by the teacher was the brighter one; students in Grades 4 to 7 selected the praised student and the student receiving neutral feedback in approximately equal numbers; and students in grades 8 and above believed that the student receiving neutral feedback was brighter than the one receiving positive feedback following successful performance. Although the effects of feedback in the classroom appear to be powerful, they are multidimensional and complex. Simple injunctions to increase feedback for one purpose or another are likely to set in motion a range of processes that are in need of further examination.

Consistency Across Stages of the Evaluation Process

Although the studies of the effects of features of the evaluation process noted previously have suggested some possible consequences for certain individual features, little attention has been devoted to developing an understanding of entire evaluation systems composed of purposes, tasks, criteria, standards, samples, appraisals, and feedback. One of the key issues to be examined in thinking about systems of evaluation is the relationship between various aspects of the process and the extent to which there is consistency among them. For instance, evaluations and evaluation systems may differ in terms of the consistency between task assignments and criteria set for the task. Some teachers may take care that the performance criteria set for a task be appropriate to the nature of the task assignment, whereas others may not. In the latter case, a teacher may designate a task as a creative opportunity when an assignment is made but hold students accountable for a formulaic set of criteria. A second instance might be the consistency between the criteria and standards set for the task and the process of sampling student performances and outcomes. For example, a teacher may specify criteria related to the actual performance of the task (e.g., how to proceed to solve a math problem), but only sample the outcome of the performance (e.g., the correctness of the answer).

Although little research has been conducted to examine the actual extent to which teachers implement a consistent system of performance evaluation for students, interviews conducted by Natriello (1982) with secondary school teachers suggest that teachers vary widely in their ability to articulate a systematic approach to the evaluation of student performance. Examinations of teacher preparation curricula, which indicate that prospective teachers receive little or no training in the evaluation of student performance (Mayo, 1967; Roeder, 1973), suggest that this finding may be widely applicable. The effects of this lack of consistency could be quite negative. Natriello (1982) reported that high school students who experienced more inconsistencies in the evaluation system were also more likely to become disengaged from school.

RESEARCH ON EVALUATION PROCESSES: PAST PATTERNS AND FUTURE DIRECTIONS

Previous studies on evaluation processes in schools and classrooms have been characterized by three features that limit their utility to practitioners and researchers interested in the culmulation of knowledge about this key educational process. First, relatively little descriptive information on evaluation processes in schools and classrooms has been considered in designing effects studies even though many studies seek to create new knowledge as the basis for improved practice. For example, more than a few studies seek to develop alternatives to norm-referenced standards, but descriptive accounts suggest that such standards may not be used extensively by teachers at the present time (Natriello & McPartland, 1987).

Second, most of the effects studies concentrate on one or two aspects of the evaluation process. As a result, they fail to consider the impact of other key elements in determining the effects of evaluations. The conclusions drawn from such studies should be approached with caution. For example, few studies consider the nature of the assigned tasks on which students are being evaluated, yet it is clear that task differences condition the impact of evaluation processes (Doyle, 1983).

Third, few of the effects studies consider the multiple purposes for evaluations in schools and classrooms. As a result, they often compare different evaluation methods in terms of some outcome that has nothing to do with the purpose for which one of the methods was developed. For instance, a study demonstrating that differentiated feedback contributes more to directing future student performance than a single letter grade may be doing nothing more than showing that an evaluation system created for the purpose of providing direction to students does a better job of providing that direction than another evaluation system created for the purpose of selecting students.

The limitations of previous studies of the impact of evaluation processes on students suggest important directions for further research. Research is needed on the basic patterns of evaluation practices in schools and classrooms. Investigators have typically begun with some common assumptions about the current state of practice as they planned intervention studies of evaluation processes. However, additional research is needed to provide a better descriptive account of how students are currently evaluated in schools and classrooms.

Research on evaluation practices in schools and classrooms will need to consider explicitly which of the multiple purposes of evaluation processes can be served by which combinations of practices. For example, previous research suggests that the design of an evaluation system for the purpose of enhancing student motivation might involve a differentiated task structure in the classroom, a mix of more and less predictable tasks, clearly articulated criteria, challenging yet attainable, self-referenced standards, relatively frequent collection of information on student performance, appraisals that truly reflect student effort and performance, and differentiated and encouraging feedback. An evaluation system designed for purposes of certification would look quite different. Researchers should be sensitive to the purposes of evaluation systems when they examine existing evaluation arrangements, which typically involve compromises among the competing demands of multiple purposes. They should also be aware of the multiple purposes served by evaluation systems when they design interventions to achieve certain purposes at the expense of neglecting other purposes that must be attended to in operating schools and classrooms.

Research on evaluation practices might be improved considerably if investigators moved beyond the study of particular elements of the evaluation process, such as frequency of testing, and approached the evaluation process as a system involving, at a minimum, tasks, criteria, standards, samples of information on performance and outcomes, appraisals, and feedback. Studies based on programs of intervention (e.g., Rosenholtz & Wilson, 1980) have employed this kind of more comprehensive strategy, and teachers confronted with the demands of classrooms will always have to consider the full range of these issues in developing an approach to student evaluation. In this case, both research and practice will be improved by adopting a more comprehensive framework for studies of the evaluation process.

Finally, future research on evaluation processes should explicitly consider four basic types of evaluative situations that occur in schools. Many studies have been conducted that assume that a single student is being evaluated by a single teacher (e.g., Bolocofsky & Mescher, 1984). These studies typically examine the impact of various evaluation practices on students as individuals who happen to be in classrooms. Yet aside from tutorial situations, these conditions almost never occur in schools and classrooms. The findings of these studies would be difficult for most teachers to apply in their daily work. Fewer studies have focused on the conditions found in the typical self-contained elementary classroom, in which a single teacher evaluates multiple students (e.g., Rosenholtz & Wilson, 1980). These studies also examine the impact of evaluation processes on the student group. Fewer studies still have been concerned with the situation in which a single student is confronted with evaluations from multiple teachers (e.g., Natriello, 1982), the situation in which most secondary school students find themselves. These studies focus on the plight of the student in a complex authority system. Finally, almost no studies have examined the situation confronted by educators attempting to manage an evaluation system in which multiple teachers evaluate multiple students, the situation confronting educators attempting to design and manage evaluation processes in most secondary schools. If researchers expect educators to utilize the results of research on the evaluation of students, studies must be designed that grapple with the complexity presented by the multiple evaluator, multiple student situation. Very few of the findings gleaned from studies of single evaluators and single students can be applied in a straightforward way to the typical school and classroom setting.

REFERENCES

Abramson, L. Y., Seligman, M. E. P., & Teasdale, J. D. (1978). Learned helplessness in humans: Critique and reformulation. *Journal of Abnormal Psychology, 87,* 49–74.

Ahmann, J. S., & Glock, M. D. (1967). *Evaluating pupil growth: Principles of tests and measurements* (4th ed.). Boston: Allyn and Bacon.

Armbruster, B. B., Stevens, R. J., & Rosenshine, B. (1977). *Analyzing content coverage and emphasis: A study of three curricula and two tests.* (Tech. Rep. No. 26). Urbana: University of Illinois, Center for the Study of Reading.

Atkinson, J. W. (1958). Towards experimental analysis of human motivation in terms of motives, expectancies, and incentives. In J. W. Atkinson (Ed.), *Motives in fantasy, action and society.* Princeton, NJ: Van Nostrand.

Beady, C. J., Jr., Slavin, R. E., & Fennessey, G. M. (1981). Alternative student evaluation structures and a focused schedule of instruction in an inner-city junior high school. *Journal of Educational Psychology, 75,* 518–523.

Bidwell, C. E. (1965). The school as a formal organization. In J. G. March (Ed.), *Handbook of organizations* (pp. 972–1022). Chicago: Rand McNally.

Bolocofsky, D. N., & Mescher, S. (1984). Student characteristics: Using student characteristics to develop effective grading practices. *The Directive Teacher, 6,* 11–23.

Bresee, C. W. (1976). On "Grading on the Curve". *The Clearing House, 5,* 108–110.

Brookover, W. B., & Schneider, J. M. (1975). Academic environments and elementary school achievement. *Journal of Research and Development in Education, 9,* 82–91.

Brophy, J., & Evertson, C. (1981). *Student characteristics and teaching.* New York: Longman.

Brown, D. J. (1971). *Appraisal procedures in the secondary schools.* Englewood Cliffs, NJ: Prentice-Hall.

Buys, N., & Winfield, A. H. (1982). Learned helplessness in high school students following experience of noncontingent rewards. *Journal of Research in Personality, 6,* 6–9.

Chansky, N. M. (1975). A critical examination of school report cards from K through 12. *Reading Improvement, 12,* 184–192.

Crano, W. D., & Mellon, P. M. (1978). Causal influence of teachers' expectations on children's academic performance: A cross-lagged panel analysis. *Journal of Educational Psychology, 70,* 39–49.

Crooks, A. D. (1933). Marks and marking systems: A digest. *Journal of Educational Research, 27,* 259–272.

Cross, L. J., & Cross, C. M. (1980). Teachers' evaluative comments and pupil perception of control. *Journal of Experimental Education, 49,* 68–71.

Davis, R. B., & McKnight, C. (1976). Conceptual, heuristic, and S-algorithmic approaches in mathematics teaching. *Journal of Children's Mathematical Behavior, 1(Supplement 1),* 271–286.

Deutsch, M. (1979). Education and distributive justice: Some reflections on grading systems. *American Psychologist, 34,* 391–401.

Dornbusch, S. M., & Scott, W. R. (1975). *Evaluation and the exercise of authority.* San Francisco: Jossey-Bass.

Doyle, W. (1983). Academic work. *Review of Educational Research, 53,* 159–199.

Ediger, M. (1975). Reporting pupil progress: Alternatives to grading. *Educational Leadership, 32,* 265–267.

Egan, O., & Archer, P. (1985). The accuracy of teachers' ratings of ability: A regression model. *American Educational Research Journal, 22,* 25–34.

Evans, E. D., & Engelberg, R. A. (1985 April). *A developmental study of student perceptions of school grading.* Paper presented at the Biennial Meeting of the Society for Research on Child Development, Toronto.

Feldhusen, J. F. (1964). Student perceptions of frequent quizzes and post-mortem discussions of tests. *Journal of Educational Measurement, 1,* 51–54.

Gaston, N. (1976). Evaluation in the affective domain. *Journal of Business Education, 52,* 134–136.

Glaser, R. (1963). Instructional technology and the measurement of learning outcomes. *American Psychologist, 18,* 519–521.

Glass, G. V. (1978). Standards and criteria. *Journal of Educational Measurement, 15,* 237–261.

Gullickson, A. R. (1982). *The practice of testing in elementary and secondary schools.* Unpublished report. ERIC Document Reproduction Service No. ED229391, University of South Dakota.

Gullickson, A. R. (1984). Teacher perspectives of their instructional use of tests. *Journal of Educational Research, 77,* 244–248.

Hackman, J. R. (1969). Toward understanding the role of tasks in behavioral research. *Acta Psychologica, 31,* 97–128.

Hambleton, R. K., Swaminathan, H., Algina, J. & Coulson, D. B. (1978). Criterion-referenced testing and measurement: A review of technical issues and developments. *Review of Educational Research, 48,* 1–47.

Hansen, J. M. (1977). Personalized achievement reporting: Grades that are significant. *The High School Journal, 60,* 255–263.

Heller, L. (1978). Assessing the process and the product: An alternative to grading. *English Journal, 6,* 66–69.

Herman, J., & Dorr-Bremme, D. W. (1984). *Testing and assessment in American public schools: Current practices and directions for improvement.* Los Angeles: University of California at Los Angeles, Center for the Study of Evaluation.

Holmes, M. (1978). Evaluating students in the affective domain. *School Guidance Worker, 33,* 50–58.

Jarrett, C. D. (1963). Marking and reporting practices in the American secondary school. *Peabody Journal of Education, 41,* 36–48.

Leinhardt, G., & Seewald, A. M. (1981). Overlap: What's tested, what's taught? *Journal of Educational Measurement, 18,* 85–96.

Levine, M. (1976). The academic achievement test: Its historical context and social functions. *American Psychologist, 31,* 228–238.

Lien, A. J. (1967). *Measurement and evaluation of learning: A handbook for teachers.* Dubuque, IA: Wm. C. Brown.

Linn, R. L. (1983). Testing and instruction: Links and distinctions. *Journal of Educational Measurement, 20,* 179–189.

Lintner, A. C., & Ducette, J. (1974). The effects of locus of control, academic failure and task dimensions on a student's responsiveness to praise. *American Educational Research Journal, 11,* 231–239.

Lissman, U., & Paetzoid, B. (1983). Achievement feedback and its effects on pupils—a quasi-experimental and longitudinal study of two kinds of differential feedback, norm-referenced and criterion-referenced feedback. *Studies in Educational Evaluation, 9,* 209–222.

Locke, E. A. (1968). Toward a theory of task motivation and incentives. *Organizational Behavior and Human Performance, 3,* 157–189.

Mayo, S. T. (1967). *Pre-service preparation of teachers in educational measurement.* Chicago: Loyola University.

McDill, E. L., Natriello, G., & Pallas, A. M. (1985). Raising standards and retaining students. *Review of Educational Research, 55,* 415–434.

Meyer, W., Bachmann, M., Biermann, U., Hempelmann, M., Ploger, F., & Spiller, H. (1979). The informational value of evaluative behavior: Influences of praise and blame on perceptions of ability. *Journal of Educational Psychology, 71,* 259–268.

Michaels, J. W. (1977). Classroom reward structures and academic performance. *Review of Educational Research, 47,* 87–98.

National Commission on Excellence in Education. (1983). *A nation at risk: The imperative for educational reform.* Washington, D.C.: U.S. Government Printing Office.

National Institute of Education. (1979). *Testing, teaching, and learning.* Report of a Conference on Research on Testing. Washington, D.C.: National Institute of Education.

Natriello, G. (1982). *Organizational evaluation systems and student disengagement in secondary schools.* Final Report to the National Institute of Education, St. Louis, MO: Washington University.

Natriello, G. (1985). Merit pay for teachers: The implications of theory for practice. In H. C. Johnson, Jr., (Ed.), *Merit, money and teachers' careers.* Sanham, MD: University Press of America.

Natriello, G., & Dornbusch, S. M. (1984). *Teacher evaluative standards and student effort.* New York: Longman.

Natriello, G., & McDill, E. L. (1986). Performance standards, student effort on homework and academic achievement. *Sociology of Education, 59,* 18–31.

Natriello, G. & McPartland, J. (1987, April). *Adjustments in high school teachers' grading criteria: Accommodation or motivation?* Paper presented at the Annual Meeting of the American Educational Research Association, Washington, DC.

Oren, D. L. (1983). Evaluation systems and attributional tendencies in the classroom: A sociological approach. *Journal of Educational Research, 76,* 307–312.

Page, E. B. (1958). Teacher comments and student performance: A seventy-four classroom experiment in school motivation. *Journal of Educational Psychology, 49,* 173–181.

Peckham, P. D., & Roe, M. D. (1977). The effects of frequent testing. *Journal of Research and Development in Education, 10,* 40–50.

Popham, W. J., & Husek, T. R. (1969). Implications of criterion-referenced measurement. *Journal of Educational Measurement, 6,* 1–9.

Purkey, S. C., & Smith, M. S. (1983). Effective schools: A review. *The Elementary School Journal, 83,* 427–452.

Remmers, H. H., Gage, N. L., & Rummel, J. F. (1960). *A practical introduction to measurement and evaluation.* New York: Harper and Brothers.

Rheinberg, F. (1983). Achievement evaluation: A fundamental difference and its motivational consequences. *Studies in Educational Evaluation, 9,* 185–194.

Roeder, H. H. (1973). Teacher education curriculum—your final grade is F. *Journal of Educational Measurement, 10,* 141–143.

Rosenholtz, S. J., & Rosenholtz, S. H. (1981). Classroom organization and the perception of ability. *Sociology of Education, 54,* 132–140.

Rosenholtz, S. J., & Wilson, B. (1980). The effect of classroom structure on shared perceptions of ability. *American Educational Research Journal, 17,* 75–82.

Rosenshine, B., & Furst, N. (1973). The use of direct observation to study teaching. In R. M. W. Travers (Ed.), *Second handbook of research on teaching.* Chicago: Rand McNally.

Rosenthal, R., & Jacobson, L. (1968). *Pygmalion in the classroom.* New York: Holt, Rinehart, and Winston.

Rosswork, S. G. (1977). Goal setting: The effects on an academic task with varying magnitudes of incentive. *Journal of Educational Psychology, 69,* 710–715.

Roth, S., & Bootzin, R. R. (1974). The effects of experimentally induced expectancies of external control: An investigation of learned helplessness. *Journal of Personality and Social Psychology, 28,* 253–264.

Rudman, H. C., Kelly, J. L., Wanous, D. S., Mehrens, W. A., Clark, C. M., & Porter, A. C. (1980). *Integrating assessment with instruction: A review (1922–1980).* East Lansing, MI: Institute for Research on Teaching, Michigan State University, College of Education.

Rudman, M. K. (1978). Evaluating students: How to do it right. *Learning, 7,* 50–53.

Salganik, L. H. (1982 April). *The effects of effort marks on report card grades.* Paper presented at the Annual Meeting of the American Educational Research Association, Los Angeles.

Schunk, D. H. (1983). Reward contingencies and the development of children's skills and self-efficacy. *Journal of Educational Psychology, 75,* 511–518.

Seligman, M. E. P. (1975). *Helplessness: On depression, development, and death.* San Francisco: Freeman.

Simpson, C. (1981). Classroom structure and the organization of ability. *Sociology of Education, 54,* 120–132.

Slavin, R. E. (1977). Classroom reward structure: An analytical and practical review. *Review of Educational Research, 47,* 633–650.

Slavin, R. E. (1978). Separating incentives, feedback, and evaluation: Toward a more effective classroom system. *Educational Psychologist, 13,* 97–100.

Slavin, R. E. (1980). Effects of individual learning expectations on student achievement. *Journal of Educational Psychology, 72,* 520–524.

Smith, L. R. (1984). Effect of teacher vagueness and use of lecture notes on student performance. *Journal of Educational Research, 78,* 68–74.

Stewart, L. G., & White, M. A. (1976). Teacher comments, letter grades and student performance: What do we really know? *Journal of Educational Psychology, 68,* 488–500.

Terwilliger, J. G. (1977). Assigning grades—philosophical issues and practical recommendations. *Journal of Research and Development in Education, 10,* 21–39.

Thompson, J. D. (1967). *Organizations in action.* New York: McGraw-Hill.

Thorndike, R. L. (1969). Marks and marking systems. In R. L. Ebel (Ed.), *Encyclopedia of educational research* (pp. 759–766). New York: Macmillan.

Thornton, J. W., & Jacobs, P. D. (1972). The facilitating effects of prior inescapable unavoidable stress on intellectual performance. *Psychometric Science, 26,* 265–271.

Varenne, H., & Kelly, M. (1976). Friendship and fairness: Ideological tensions in an American high school. *Teachers College Record, 77,* 601–614.

Waller, W. (1932). *The sociology of teaching.* New York: Wiley.

Walling, D. R. (1975). Designing a "report card" that communicates. *Educational Leadership, 32,* 258–260.

Weiner, B. (1979). A theory of motivation for some classroom experiences. *Journal of Educational Psychology, 71,* 3–25.

Williams, R. G., Pollack, M. J., & Ferguson, N. A. (1975). Differential effects of two grading systems on student performance. *Journal of Educational Psychology, 67,* 253–258.

Wilson, S. (1976). You can talk to teachers: Student-teacher relations in an alternative high school. *Teachers College Record, 78,* 77–100.

Wise, R. I., & Newman, B. (1975). The responsibilities of grading. *Educational Leadership, 32,* 253–256.

Wortman, C. B., & Brehm, J. W. (1975). Responses to uncontrollable outcomes: An integration of reactance theory and the learned helplessness model. In L. Berkowitz (Ed.), *Advances in experimental social psychology, (volume 8).* New York: Academic Press.

10 Achievement Effects of Substantial Reductions in Class Size*

Robert E. Slavin
Center for Research on Elementary and Middle Schools
Johns Hopkins University

One of the most hotly debated issues of school organization for many years has been the achievement effects of reductions in class size. On one hand, it seems intuitively obvious that teachers can do a better job with a small group of children than with a larger group. On the other, many reviewers of research on this topic have concluded that the evidence relating to achievement effects of reducing class size shows few consistent effects. Recently, a meta-analysis by Glass, Cahen, Smith, and Filby (1982) questioned the conclusion that class size made little difference in achievement, and a review by Robinson and Wittebols (1986) held out the possibility that class size may make a difference in the early grades.

The question of achievement effects of class size has taken on particular importance in recent years as educators have proposed dramatic reductions in class size, particularly in the early elementary grades, as a means of accelerating the achievement of students who are at risk for school failure (e.g., Bain & Achilles, 1986). Changes in federal legislation are expected to make Chapter 1 funds available to help all students in high-poverty schools. Experience with earlier school-wide Chapter 1 projects suggests that many districts will use their Chapter 1 funds to reduce class size (e.g., Doss & Holley, 1982); also, remedial pull-out programs traditionally supported by Chapter 1 funds have been justified on the basis that they reduce class size for some portion of the school day (Cooper, in press).

What does the research say about achievement effects of substantial reductions in class size? This chapter critiques the two major reviews that have claim-

---

*This chapter is adapted from an earlier article by Slavin (in press).

ed positive effects of class size on student achievement and then discusses the primary research bearing on this question.

The Glass and Smith Meta-Analyses

In 1978, Glass and Smith issued a technical report which was one of the first applications of the then-new technique of meta-analysis. The final form of the meta analysis was published in a book by Glass, Cahen, Smith, and Filby (1982).

Glass et al. (1982) identified 77 studies comparing larger and smaller classes, which produced a total of 725 comparisons. They found essentially no effects of class size on achievement among the 63 "poorly controlled" (i.e., correlational) studies, so their claims concerning effects of class size on achievement depend entirely on comparisons from only 14 studies in which students were randomly assigned to larger or smaller classes.

Insisting on use of random assignment as the only criterion for study inclusion in a review or meta-analysis is helpful in ensuring the internal validity of the studies synthesized, but often runs the risk of focusing on studies that are very low in external validity. This is manifestly the case in the Glass et al. (1982) meta-analysis (see Slavin, 1984). One study with the highest effect sizes by far for class sizes more than three was a study by Verducci (1969) on *tennis*. This study, which produced effect sizes of 1.25, .65, and .40, used an "achievement" test that consisted of "rallying a tennis ball against the wall . . . as many times as possible in 30 sec." (p. 392). Two studies, by Moody, Bausell, and Jenkins (1973) and Bausell, Moody, and Walzl (1972), involved a total treatment duration of 30 minutes. In addition, three studies used post-secondary samples.

The eight remaining studies, those of non-trivial duration that took place in elementary or secondary schools and used achievement measures other than hitting a ball against a wall, are displayed in Table 10.1 according to the size of the smaller classes involved.

The figures for the individual studies in Table 10.1 are taken directly from Appendix A.1 in Glass et al. (1982, p. 141), which lists the entire body of evidence on which Glass and his colleagues base their claim that "large reductions in school class size promise learning benefits of a magnitude commonly believed not within the power of educators to achieve" (p. 50). As is apparent from Table 10.1, such learning benefits do not appear until class size is reduced to three. Even among the studies that nearly halved class size, from an average of 31 to an average of 16, the mean effect size was a trivial .04. Incidentally, including the college studies and the 30-minute studies does not change the overall picture at all; the only exclusion that affects the means is the exclusion of the Verducci (1969) tennis study. Even including all 14 of the Glass et al. (1982) studies would only raise the median effect size for comparisons involving smaller

TABLE 10.1
Effect Sizes for Randomized Studies of Class Size Achievement
in Elementary and Secondary Schools[a]

	Size of Smaller Classes			
	1	3	14-17	20-23
	.65 (1-32)	1.22 (3-25)	.17 (14-30)	.15 (20-28
	.78 (1-30)		.17 (15-30)	.04 (23-27)
	1.52 (1-25)		.08 (16-37)	.04 (23-30)
	.72 (1-14)		.04 (16-30)	.00 (30-37)
	.30 (1-8)		.05 (16-23)	
	.22 (1-3)		-.29 (17-35)	
mean	.69		.04	.06
median	.69		.06	.04

[a]Effect sizes are all from Glass, Cahen, Smith, and Filby (1982), Table A.1, p. 141.

classes in the range 14–17 from .06 to .08, although it considerably affects the means.

Thus, the results from randomized elementary and secondary studies of class size completely agree with those of the correlational studies; effects of class size on achievement are extremely small.

On the other hand, the effect sizes summarized in Table 10.1 do support the idea that dramatic achievement effects can be obtained from one-to-one tutoring. Only by considering tutoring as a "class size" of one is there a glimmer of truth to the conclusion that class size can significantly affect achievement. One study, by Shaver and Nuhn (1971), found that one-to-three tutoring could also be very effective for underachieving secondary students. Questions relating to very small class sizes are relevant to discussions of effective Chapter 1 services, and are discussed later in this chapter. At this point, however, it can be concluded that nothing in the Glass et al. (1982) meta-analyses challenges the idea that reducing class size, even halving it to approximately 16 students, has no substantial impact on student achievement.

The ERS Reviews

In 1978, the Educational Research Service published a review of research on the effects of class size on achievement in elementary and secondary schools. The review essentially concluded that research on class size and achievement was inconclusive; some of the studies cited found that small classes were better, some found that large classes were better, and most found no differences. However, the study authors made some *tentative* conclusions (the emphasis is theirs) which pointed to low achievers in the early grades as the group most likely to benefit from smaller classes.

The ERS (1978) review made no attempt to select studies on the basis of design or other indications of study quality. Most of the studies cited are correlational; researchers simply computed a correlation between class size and achievement, sometimes controlling for other variables and sometimes not. One problem inherent to this type of study is that in studying the natural range of variation, there are rarely many very large or very small classes. Few people familiar with the class size literature would expect much of a difference between class sizes of, say, 30 and 25, yet the correlational studies are usually focused on differences in this range. This could explain why the correlational literature almost without exception finds tiny, usually nonsignificant, positive or negative differences. The tentative conclusions advanced in the ERS (1978) studies are based on small trends observed in just a few of the many correlational studies, most of which found no differences.

More recently, the ERS conducted an updated review of the class size literature (Robinson & Wittebols, 1986). This review broke the literature down into "clusters" according to grade levels, subjects, and so on. It categorized studies as significantly favoring small classes, no significant differences, or significantly favoring large classes, and then counted the number of studies in each category, without regard to study characteristics or quality.

As in the earlier ERS (1978) review, Robinson & Wittebols (1986) conclude that effects of class size are relatively consistent in grades K–3, slight in grades 4–8, and essentially nonexistent in grades 9–12, and that they are stronger for disadvantaged than for advantaged students. However, it should be noted that even in the most "consistent" cluster, grades K–3, only 50% of the studies cited found significant differences favoring small classes (all but one of the rest found no differences). Also, counting significant differences gives no indication of the *size* of the class size effects.

ACHIEVEMENT EFFECTS OF SUBSTANTIAL REDUCTIONS IN CLASS SIZE

Neither the Glass et al. (1982) nor the two ERS reviews provide an adequate basis for policy relative to class size. Neither adequately considers the *quality* of the critical evidence. This section discusses the studies that speak most directly to the question of optimum class size in the elementary grades, using an abbreviated form of a review technique called best-evidence synthesis (Slavin, 1986), which combines elements of meta-analysis with narrative review, focusing on issues of study characteristics and quality.

Inclusion Criteria

The studies emphasized in this section met the following criteria:

1. The study had to compare the effects on standardized reading and/or mathematics tests of alternative class sizes in elementary schools (K–6) over a period of at least one year. This review is restricted to elementary schools for two reasons. First, ERS and others agree that if there are any effects of class size, they exist at the elementary level. Second, most Chapter 1 funds are applied at the elementary level, so the relevance of class size to Chapter 1 policy is greatest there.

2. The study had to compare larger classes to classes which are at least 30% smaller *and* no more than 20 students. This restriction focuses the review on substantial reductions in class size (e.g., 30 to 20); few researchers have ever suggested that smaller differences in class size will make meaningful differences in achievement.

3. The study had to use random assignment to alternative class sizes, or matching with evidence of initial equality. This restriction eliminates correlational studies lacking evidence that the groups studied were initially equivalent.

For each study that met the inclusion criteria, effect sizes were computed (if possible) as the difference between experimental and control means (or gains, if pre-tests were not equivalent) divided by the control group's post-test standard deviation. If effect sizes could not be computed, effects were characterized as positive (+), negative(−), or no difference (0), with "positive" implying that smaller class sizes produced higher achievement.

The characteristics and findings of eight studies that met the inclusion criteria are summarized in Table 10.2. The one study that used random assignment (Shapson, Wright, Eason, & Fitzgerald, 1980) is listed first, and then the matched studies are listed in order of sample size. The table shows that substantial reductions in class size do generally have a positive effect on student achievement, but that the effects tend to be small. Across the eight studies, the median effect size is only +.13. Multi-year studies found no cumulative effect of class size; in fact, significantly positive effects in the first year of the widely publicized Nashville first grade experiment (Bain & Achilles, 1986; Whittington, Bain & Achilles, 1985) had disappeared by the second grade, when students had been in small classes for 2 years (Dennis, 1987). Similarly, positive results in the first year of the Austin, Texas class size experiment (Doss & Holley, 1982) were no longer apparent in years 2 through 6 (Christner, 1987). In a study of staggered scheduling, in which half of all students came to school an hour early and half stayed an hour late (to reduce class size in reading by half), Balow (1969) found statistically significant but very small positive effects after three years; experimental students scored only 3 points more than control students (248 to 245) on the Sequential Tests of Educational Progress.

Considering that the studies listed in Table 10.2 reduced class size from an average of approximately 27 to approximately 16, a 40% reduction, these effects

TABLE 10.2
Elementary Studies of Class Size and Achievement

Article	Grades	Location	Sample Size	Class Sizes	Design	Effect Sizes by Subject, Grade Level		Total
Shapson, Wright, Eason, & Fitz-Gerald (1980)	4-5	Toronto	62 cl.	L = 37 30 23 S = 16	Teachers and students were randomly assign-ed to classes of 16, 23, 30, or 37.	16 vs. 37 16 vs. 30 16 vs. 23	Rdg. Math -.03 +.36 +.01 +.51 -.05 +.22	+.17
Jarvis, White-hurst, Gampert, & Schulman (1987)	1	New York City Low SES	99 Sch., exp. 22 Sch., ctrl.	L = 26 S = 16	Compared stu-dents in small classes	Reading		+.09
Mazareas (1981)	1	City near Boston, MA	146 cl.	L = 30 S = 20	Compared stu-dents in large and small clas-ses, controlling for IQ.	Rdg. -.12* Math +.09*		-.02*
Wilsberg & Castiglione (1968)	1-2	New York City Los SES	25 sch.	L = 25 S = 15	Compared stu-dents in small classes to matched regular classes	Rdg. Voc. +.29 Rdg. Comp. +.20		+.25
Balow (1969)	1-4	Riverside, CA	996 students	L = 30 S = 15	Experimental classes used staggered sched-uie, half came 1 hr early, half stayed 1 hr late for reading. Com-pared to matched schools. Same students followed for 3 years.	Reading		+.05 (first yr) +.16* (by end of 3 yrs)

(continued...)

(Table 10.2 continued)

Article	Grades	Location	Sample Size	Class Sizes	Design	Effect Sizes by Subject, Grade Level		Total
Doss & Holley (1982) Christner (1987)	K-6	Austin, TX Chapter 1 schools	2 exp.	L = 22 S = 15	Compared students in Chapter 1 school-wide projects to all other Chapter 1 students. Classes compared for 6 years.	Yr. 1: Gr.2 Gr.3 Gr.4 Gr.5 Gr.6 Years 2-6:	Rdg. +.26 +.16 +.10 +.21 +.08 (0) Math +.12 +.24 +.12 +.27 +.18 (0)	+.17 (first yr) (0) (by end of yrs 2-6)
Whittington, Bain, & Achilles (1985) Dennis (1987)	1-2	Nashville,TN	14 cl.	L = 25 S = 15	Compared students in small classes to matched regular classes. Same students followed for 2 years.	Gr.1: Rdg. +.57 Math +.49 Gr.2: Rdg. (0) Math (0)		+.53 (first yr) (0) (by end of 2 yrs)
Wagner (1981)	2	Toledo, OH	2 sch.	L = 25 S = 15	Students in one school assigned to small classes, compared with matched school.	Reading		+.55

Key: (+) Results favored small classes
(C) No differences
(-) Results favored large classes
* Effect sizes approximate, estimated from ANCOVA's

are certainly disappointing. Of course, it is important to note that reductions in class size do have significant effects on other variables, such as teacher and student morale (Glass et al., 1982; Robinson & Wittebols, 1986). Reducing class size may be justified on these and other quality-of-life grounds. However, as a means of increasing student achievement, even substantial reductions in class size have little apparent impact.

Why Are Effects of Class Size So Small?

Discussions of the small achievement effects of reductions in class size usually point to one critical factor: teachers do not vary their behaviors very much in large and small classes (Cahen, Filby, McCutcheon, & Kyle, 1983; Robinson & Wittebols, 1986; Shapson et al., 1980). More accurately, teachers do change their behavior in small classes, but the changes are relatively subtle and unlikely to make important differences to student achievement. Class size could have a substantial effect on achievement indirectly, in that there may be highly effective instructional programs that could not be successfully implemented in large classes. However, although this possibility seems logical, at present there is no hard evidence of it.

Implications for Chapter 1

The research on the achievement effects of class size has important implications for two separate questions relating to the design of Chapter 1 programs. First, should Chapter 1 funds be used in schoolwide projects to reduce class size? Second, what is the optimum class size for Chapter 1 pull-out programs?

The first question has taken on greater importance because the U. S. Congress has recently passed legislation making it much easier for Chapter 1 schools with at least 75% of their students in poverty to implement schoolwide projects. In schoolwide projects, Chapter 1 funds need not be used only for Chapter 1-identified students, but can be used to improve the school as a whole. Because high-poverty schools are usually located in underfunded school districts with large class sizes, there will almost certainly be pressure to use Chapter 1 funds to reduce class size.

The evidence summarized in Table 10.2 suggests that using Chapter 1 funds to reduce class size will not in itself make a substantial difference in student achievement. For example, the Austin schools that reduced class size as part of a schoolwide Title I/Chapter 1 project produced gains of only about 17% of a standard deviation in the first year (Doss & Holley, 1982), which were not maintained in five subsequent years (Christner, 1987). Most of the studies listed in Table 10.2 were conducted in low-SES schools; if reductions in class size made any meaningful difference in achievement, the huge Jarvis, Whitehurst,

Gampert, & Schulman, (1987) study in low-SES New York City schools would have detected it. Again, it may be that reductions in class size could be *part* of an effective school-wide approach, but research would not justify reliance on class size reduction alone as a means of improving the achievement of low achievers.

On the second question, the optimum size of Chapter 1 pullout groups, the evidence is less clear. We have very consistent evidence that one-to-one tutoring can be extremely effective (see Madden & Slavin, in press). Leaving aside the question of cost-effectiveness, providing low achievers with one-to-one tutors for some portion of their school day is probably the most effective instructional strategy we have. As noted earlier, one study, by Shaver & Nuhn (1971), also found very positive effects of tutoring seventh and tenth grade students in groups of three for 1 hour per day, but this was still less effective than one-to-one tutoring.

Unfortunately, there is very little evidence concerning achievement effects of class sizes in the range of 2–12. However, it is unlikely that tutoring could be successful in groups of more than two or three. Studies of remedial reading programs find that even with groups of 3–6, teachers tend to revert to use of large numbers of worksheets and whole-group instruction (see Allington, Stuetzel, Shake, & Lamarche, 1986). The tutoring paradigm is quite different; in tutoring, the teacher is in constant interaction with one student and is able to completely adapt the level, pace, and content of the lesson to that student's individual needs. A 30-minute tutoring session with three students could probably be seen as three 10-minute sessions, one for each student; the effectiveness of *tutoring*, as opposed to whole-class teaching, is probably a monotonic function of group size.

Following this line of reasoning, it is probably more effective to provide at-risk students with one-to-one tutoring than either to use the same resources to reduce overall class size or to pull out small groups of students for remedial instruction, as is usually done in Chapter 1 programs at present. In particular, there is some evidence that tutoring interventions in the first grade can prevent the development of reading deficits in at-risk students (Madden & Slavin, in press; Pinnell, 1987; Young & Pinnell, 1987).

At the same time, it is important to improve instruction in the regular classroom by implementing effective instructional strategies. For example, Slavin & Madden (in press; Slavin, 1987) have identified several classroom programs that typically produce gains on standardized reading and mathematics tests of .30 to nearly 1.00, far more than the gains typical of even large reductions in class size (also see Slavin, Karweit, & Madden, in press).

It is distressing that after 20 years of Title I/Chapter 1 and expenditure of more than $45 billion, we have not invested enough in research on effective uses of Chapter 1 funds to have firm answers to questions about how to address the needs of students at risk of school failure (Slavin, 1987). However, we do know enough at this point to say that simply reducing class size is not going to solve the achievement problems of at-risk students, at least not until class size is reduced to one for some portion of students' school days.

REFERENCES

Allington, R., Stuetzel, H., Shake, M., & Lamarche, S. (1986). What is remedial reading: A descriptive study. *Reading Research Quarterly, 26,* 15–30.

Bain, H. P., & Achilles, C. M. (1986). Interesting developments on class size. *Phi Delta Kappan, 67,* 662–665.

Balow, I. H. (1969). A longitudinal evaluation of reading achievement in small classes. *Elementary English, 46,* 184–187.

Bausell, R. B., Moody, W. B., & Walzl, F. N. (1972). A factorial study of tutoring versus classroom instruction. *American Educational Research Journal, 9,* 591–597.

Cahen, L. S., Filby, N., McCutcheon, G., & Kyle, D. (1983). *Class size and instruction.* New York: Longman.

Christner, C. A. (1987, April). *Schoolwide projects: The almost revolution (?) six years later.* Paper presented at the annual convention of the American Educational Research Association, Washington, DC.

Cooper, H. M. (in press). Chapter 1 programs reduce student-to-instructor ratios but do reduced ratios affect achievement? *Educational Psychologist.*

Dennis, B. D. (1987). *Effects of small class size (1 : 15) on the teaching/learning process in grade two.* Unpublished doctoral dissertation, Tennessee State University.

Doss, D., & Holley, F. (1982). *A cause for national pause: Title I school-wide projects.* Austin, TX: Office of Research and Evaluation, Austin Independent School District. (ERIC Document Reproduction Service No. ED 214 996).

Educational Research Service. (1978). *Class size: A summary of research.* Arlington, VA: ERS.

Glass, G., Cahen, L., Smith, M. L., & Filby, N. (1982). *School class size.* Beverly Hills, CA: Sage.

Glass, G. V., & Smith, M. L. (1978). *Meta-analysis of research on the relationship of class size and achievement.* San Francisco: Far West Laboratory for Educational Research and Development.

Jarvis, C. H., Whitehurst, B., Gampert, R. D., & Schulman, R. (1987, April). *The relation between class size and reading achievement in first-grade classrooms.* Paper presented at the annual convention of the American Educational Research Association, Washington, DC.

Madden, N. A., & Slavin, R. E. (In Press). *Effective pull-out programs for students at risk.* In R. E. Slavin, N. L. Karweit, and N. A. Madden (Eds.), *Effective programs for students at risk.* Needham Heights, MA: Allyn and Bacon.

Mazareas, J. (1981). *Effects of class size on the achievement of first grade pupils.* Unpublished doctoral dissertation, Boston University.

Moody, W. B., Bausell, R. B., & Jenkins, J. R. (1973). The effect of class size on the learning of mathematics: A parametric study with fourth grade students. *Journal for Research in Mathematics Education, 4,* 170–176.

Pinnell, G. S. (1987, April). *Reading Recovery: A pilot study and follow up of the effects of an early intervention program in reading.* Paper presented at the annual convention of the American Educational Research Association, Washington, DC.

Robinson, G. E., & Wittebols, J. H. (1986). *Class size research: A related cluster analysis for decision making.* Arlington, VA: Educational Research Service.

Shapson, S. M., Wright, E. N., Eason, G., & Fitzgerald, J. (1980). An experimental study of the effects of class size. *American Educational Research Journal, 17,* 144–152.

Shaver, J. P., & Nuhn, D. (1971). The effectiveness of tutoring underachievers in reading and writing. *Journal of Educational Research, 65,* 107–112.

Slavin, R. E. (1984). Meta-analysis in education: How has it been used? *Educational Researcher, 13(8),* 6–15, 24–27.

Slavin, R. E. (1986). Best-evidence synthesis: An alternative to meta-analytic and traditional reviews. *Educational Researcher, 15,* (9), 5–11.

Slavin, R. E. (1987). Making Chapter 1 make a difference. *Phi Delta Kappan, 69,* 110–119.

Slavin, R. E. (in press). Class size and student achievement: Small effects of small classes. *Educational Psychologist.*

Slavin, R. E., Karweit, N. L., & Madden, N. A. (in press). *Effective programs for students at risk.* Needham Heights, MA: Allyn and Bacon.

Slavin, R. E., & Madden, N. A. (in press). *Effective classroom programs for students at risk.* In R. E. Slavin, N. L. Karweit, & N. A. Madden (Eds.), *Effective programs for students at risk,* Needham Heights, MA: Allyn and Bacon.

Verducci, F. (1969). Effects of class size on the learning of a motor skill. *Research Quarterly, 40,* 391–395.

Wagner, E. D. (1981). *The effects of reduced class size upon the acquisition of reading skills in grade two.* Unpublished doctoral dissertation, University of Toledo.

Whittington, E. H., Bain, H. P., & Achilles, C. M. (1985). Effects of class size on first-grade students. *ERS Spectrum, 3,* 33–39.

Wilsberg, M., & Castiglione, L. V. (1968). *The reduction of pupil–teacher ratios in grades 1 and 2 and the provision of additional materials: A program to strengthen early childhood education in poverty schools.* New York, NY: Center for Urban Education, New York City Board of Education. ERIC Document Reproduction Service No. ED 034 003).

Young, I. P., & Pinnell, G. S. (1987, April). *Children at risk: Reading recovery.* Paper presented at the annual convention of the American Educational Research Association.

Author Index

Subject Index

269